IN THE TAIL OF THE PEACOCK
Travel and adventures
of an English woman in Morocco

by

Isabel Savory

TROTAMUNDAS PRESS

Trotamundas Press Ltd.
The Meridian, 4 Copthall House, Station Square, Coventry
CV1 2FL, UK

"In the Tail of the Peacock" by Isabel Savory

published in 1903 by James Pott & Co., New York

copyright © 2007 of this edition, Trotamundas Press Ltd.

ISBN: 978-1-906393-04-5

Trotamundas Press is an international publisher specializing in travel literature written by women travellers from different countries and cultures.

Our mission is to bring back into print great travel books written by women around the world which have been forgotten. We publish in several languages.

It is our privilege to rescue those travel stories which were widely acclaimed in the past and that are still relevant nowadays to help us understand better the diversity of the countries and the world.

The travel stories also make an enjoyable reading, full of adventure and the excitement of discovery.

We are proud to help preserving the memory of all those amazing women travellers which were unjustly forgotten and hope that you will enjoy reading about their interesting experiences as much as we have enjoyed researching them.

www.trotamundaspress.com

Isabel Savory

Isabel Savory's first book, published in 1900, was a best seller sensation about a game hunting expedition she made with friends from Bombay up to Peshawar, to the Khyber Pass into Kashmir and then down to the Nigiri Hills. She spent many months in the Himalayas hunting and shooting. Her book "A sportswoman in India" became a bestseller and made her famous. In less than a year she was trekking in Morocco and then published the book about her journeys there in 1903.

Isabel Savory travelled to Morocco in 1901 with a friend, Rose Bainbridge, who took the pictures for her book "In the tail of the Peacock". She described the different places she visited enabling us to learn about the culture, the colours, the people, the souks, the beautiful skies and all the things that made Morocco a favorite exotic destination for travellers around the world. Her vivid descriptions of the country can still bring us the flavours of Morocco as it used to be. She gave the title of her book after a moorish proverb : "The Earth is a peacock: Morocco is the tail of it"

IN THE TAIL OF THE PEACOCK
Travel and adventures
of an English woman in Morocco

CONTENTS

CHAPTER I

TANGIER—COUNTRY PEOPLE—THE PILGRIMAGE TO MECCA—MOORISH PRISONS—WE RIDE TO CAPE SPARTEL—DECIDE TO LEAVE TANGIER AND PUSH INLAND 1

CHAPTER II

CAMP OUTFIT—A NIGHT AT A CARAVANSERAI—TETUAN—THE BRITISH VICE-CONSUL—MOORISH SHOPS—WE VISIT A MOORISH HOUSE AND FAMILY 27

CHAPTER III

DIFFICULTIES OF "LODGINGS" IN MOROCCO—A SPANISH FONDA—A MOORISH TEA PARTY—POISON IN THE CUP—SLAVES IN MOROCCO—EL DOOLLAH—MOORISH CEMETERY—RIDE TO SEMSAR—SHOPPING IN TETUAN—PROVISIONS IN THE CITY . . 63

CHAPTER IV

THE FAST OF RÁMADHAN—MOHAMMED—HIS LIFE AND INFLUENCE—THE FLOOD AT SAFFI—A WALK OUTSIDE TETUAN—THE FRENCH CONSUL'S GARDEN-HOUSE—JEWS IN MOROCCO—EUROPEAN PROTECTION 97

CHAPTER V

PLANS FOR CHRISTMAS AT GIBRALTAR—A ROUGH NIGHT—THE STEAMER WHICH WOULD NOT WAIT—AN IGNOMINIOUS RETURN TO TETUAN—A RASCALLY JEW—THE ABORIGINES AND THE PRESENT OCCUPANTS OF MOROCCO—THE SULTAN, COURT, GOVERNMENT, AND MOORISH ARMY 121

CHAPTER VI

WE LOOK OVER A MOORISH COURTYARD HOUSE WITH A VIEW TO TAKING IT—WE RENT JINAN DOLERO IN SPITE OF OPPOSITION—AN ENGLISHMAN MURDERED—OUR GARDEN-HOUSE—THE IDIOSYNCRASIES OF MOORISH SERVANTS—A NATIVE GUARD—THE RIFF COUNTRY 153

CHAPTER VII

COUNTRY PEOPLE FORDING THE RIVER—WE CALL ON CI HAMED GHRALMIA—AN EXPEDITION ACROSS THE RIVER IN SEARCH OF THE BLUE POOL—MOORISH BELIEF IN GINNS—THE BASHA—POWDER PLAY—TETUAN PRISON 181

CHAPTER VIII

MISSIONARIES AT TETUAN—POISONING IN MOROCCO—FATIMA'S RECEPTION—DIVORCE—AN EXPEDITION INTO THE ANJERAS—AN EMERALD OASIS 217

CHAPTER IX

WE LEAVE TETUAN—A WET NIGHT UNDER THE STARS—S'LAM DESERTS US—WE SAIL FOR MOGADOR—THE PALM-TREE HOUSE—SUS AND WADNOON COUNTRIES—THE SAHARA—THE ATLAS MOUNTAINS 249

Contents

CHAPTER X

ON THE MARCH ONCE MORE—BUYING MULES—A BAD ROAD—FIRST CAMP—ARGAN-TREES—COOS-COOSOO—A TERRIBLE NIGHT—DOCTORING THE KHAYLIFA—ROUGHING IT UNDER CANVAS . 281

CHAPTER XI

A PARTING MONA—FORDING SHESHAOUA RIVER—JARS OF FOOD—FIRST SIGHT OF MARRAKESH—A PERILOUS CROSSING—RIDE INTO MARRAKESH—THE SLAVE MARKET 311

CHAPTER XII

THE THURSDAY MARKET—WE MIGHT HAVE GONE TO GLAOUIA—LEAVE MARRAKESH AND SET OUT ON OUR LAST MARCH FOR THE COAST—FLOWERS IN MOROCCO—ON THE WRONG TRAIL—ARAB TENTS—GOOD-BYE TO EL MOGHREB 339

LIST OF ILLUSTRATIONS

Except where otherwise stated, the Illustrations are from photographs by ROSE A. BAINBRIDGE.

	FACING PAGE
PHOTOGRAVURE PORTRAIT	*Frontispiece*
THE ROAD TO FEZ	6
R. ON A PACK	12
TWO SHEIKHS	18
TANGIER	24
TETUAN	30
Photo by A. Cavilla, Tangier.	
OURSELVES AND BAGGAGE	34
CLOUDS OVER TETUAN	44
ALARBI ABRESHA'S HOUSE	54
Photo by A. Cavilla, Tangier.	
OUR CAMP OUTSIDE TETUAN	60
A VEILED FIGURE OUTSIDE THE GATE	66
A MOHAMMEDAN CEMETERY	80
OUT SHOPPING	90
SHOPS IN TETUAN	94
A CLUSTER OF COUNTRY WOMEN	100
A TYPICAL MOORISH STREET	108
Photo by A. Cavilla, Tangier.	
A STREET IN THE JEWS' QUARTER, TETUAN	116
Photo by A. Cavilla, Tangier.	
REFUSE GOING OUT OF TETUAN	124
A MOORISH PRISON GATE	130
A PEEP OF TETUAN	138
Photo by A. Cavilla, Tangier.	

xii List of Illustrations

	FACING PAGE
A SAINT-HOUSE, TETUAN	148
JINAN DOLERO	158
OUR SERVANTS, S'LAM AND TAHARA	164
TWO WOMEN FROM THE RIFF COUNTRY	172
SELLING EARTHENWARE POTS	178
A FERRY-BOAT ON MARKET DAY	184
THE AUTHOR FORDING THE WAD-EL-MARTINE	188
THE BASHA GOING TO PRAY	198
THE FEDDAN, TETUAN	208
CHARMING SNAKES	214
MOORS AT HOME	222
STRAW FOR SALE	230
A GROUP IN THE FEDDAN, TETUAN	236
A BREEZY CAMPING-GROUND ON A ROOF-TOP	254
ILLUSTRATIVE OF THE WAY WE RODE IN MOROCCO	262
LIGHTERS LOADING	268
AFTER RAIN IN MOGADOR	274
WHERE MANCHESTER GOODS ARE SOLD, MOGADOR	284
OUR CAMP AT AIN-EL-HADGER	290
A BLINDFOLDED CAMEL WORKING A WATER-WHEEL	298
SHIPS OF THE DESERT WE PASS ON THE MARCH	308
TRANSPORTING OUR BAGGAGE	314
MARRAKESH	318
THE OPEN GATE	324
THE KUTOBEA, MARRAKESH *Photo by A. Cavilla, Tangier.*	328
THE WAD-EL-AZELL *Photo by A. Cavilla, Tangier.*	334
THE SULTAN'S GARDEN *Photo by A. Cavilla, Tangier.*	344
THE RIVER TENSIF OUTSIDE MARRAKESH *Photo by A. Cavilla, Tangier.*	346
ONE OF OUR LAST CAMPS. LOADING THE CAMEL	350

CHAPTER I

TANGIER—COUNTRY PEOPLE—THE PILGRIMAGE TO MECCA—MOORISH PRISONS—WE RIDE TO CAPE SPARTEL—DECIDE TO LEAVE TANGIER AND PUSH INLAND.

CHAPTER I

> The vague and hazy ideals which the white light of an English upbringing relegates to dreamland and dismisses as idle fancies, rise up in the glare of African sunlight, alive, tangible, unashamed; the things that are, not the things that might be:—the vivid colouring, the hot crowding, the stately men and veiled women, the despotism and stoicism, the unchanging picturesqueness of the Thousand and One Nights, the dramatic inevitability of the Old Testament.—A. J. D.

THERE was no desert in Morocco.
If a country has not been "read up" beforehand, the imagination has free play and forms many false conclusions: yet though it suffer on the one hand rude awakenings, it is on the other compensated by certain new lights—indelible and unique impressions—which come only in the train of things *inconnu*. So though we found no desert, there are other things in Morocco.

It is one of the few countries in the world, and they grow fewer each year, which is still unexplored—unknown. Thousands of square miles in Morocco have never been crossed by a European, or at any rate none have returned to tell the tale: maps mark only blank spaces, and have no names for villages, no records of mountains or rivers: there are no roads, still less railways, in the country: the only means of transport along the wild, worn tracks is by camels, mules, and donkeys: he who will not ride perforce walks.

The bare fringe alone of Morocco, its coast towns, and the choice, let us say, of two roads connecting them with its capitals, Fez and Morocco City, are open to travellers: beyond these limits it is difficult and dangerous for Europeans to venture. Of even its coasts towns England knows little enough: a daily paper printed in 1902 describes one flourishing seaport of thirty thousand inhabitants as "a village." There is more vagueness, in fact, about a country three times the size of Great Britain and four days' journey from London than of many a remote corner in the heart of Asia.

The reason is at hand. An old Arabic proverb, "The earth is a peacock: Morocco is the tail of it," typifies the entire satisfaction of its inhabitants with their native land. What is, is good; why "civilize" and "progress"? As far as possible there shall no European enter therein. Realizing that, were new blood allowed to come into Morocco, its own effete and uneducated people would have no chance in the race of life, and end by hopelessly knuckling under to the European, the country isolates itself; nor is it likely that the jealous Powers of Europe will allow any one of their number to disturb that isolation and pluck the tempting fruit.

And so to-day Morocco drowses in an atmosphere of *laissez faire*, a decadent nation, a collection of lawless tribes, who have changed little for the last two thousand years, living still much after the manner of Old Testament days. They are devout Mussulmans. They believe the world to be flat, and to come to an end with the west coast of Morocco. Their country they call *El Moghreb el Aksa*, which means, "The Extreme West," or "The Land of the Setting Sun": "Morocco" and "Moors" are entirely European words, and never used by the Moors themselves—the one being a corruption of the name of their capital city, the other having been given them by the Spaniards.

Morocco should be fascinating on the face of it: a great country running into hundreds of thousands of square miles, the only independent Mussulman state of North Africa, with six million followers of the great Prophet, and a perfect climate, soil, and water-supply to boot, needs no extolling. And yet its chiefest fascination lies in things which, from some points of view, ought not to be.

Its remote removal from all appertaining to the twentieth century, its strangely simple, untaught life, the solemn, stately men, the veiled women and their eyes, the steely blue cactus, the white cities and the glaring light, the mystery and the fatalism which intensify the air, are alike oddly inevitable and incomprehensible to a European. The other side of the closed door has always constituted, for the wandering vagrants among mankind, their hearts' desire. For them there is still Morocco; and the door will be shut in their faces again and again by a people and a faith and customs which they can never understand. And though it be useless they will still go on, because it seems the best thing.

About six weeks before 1902 was due, Rose A. Bainbridge and myself left behind us the last outpost of England—Gibraltar—with its cluster of civilization round the bottom of the great Rock. Four hours brought us across the Straits; and seen from the deck of the dirty little *Gibel Musa*, on to which we had changed from a P. & O. at Gibraltar, Morocco shaped itself into a rugged country, ridge behind ridge of low hills and jagged mountains cutting the sky-line. A long white sand-bank lying back in a bay on the African shore, broken at one end by irregular vegetation, gradually developed upon its slopes a yellowish-white, fantastic city, which resolved itself into Tangier.

Landing at Tangier among vociferating Moors has been described often enough, and needs no further enlargement.

The next morning, November 13, 1901, found us sitting over coffee and an omelette out of doors, on a little balcony opening off the hotel Villa Valentina, overlooking the road to Fez, and facing the broad, blue Straits which divided us from Europe.

It was like a June morning at home, soft and balmy: the city dropped from us down to the beach, and the sun poured upon the flat-roofed houses, coloured yellow to pale cream or washed-out blue, alternating with a lavish coat of glaring whitewash.

Tangier is an example of structure without architecture; at the same time there is a certain fitness in the crude Moorish buildings, whose flat expanse of wall is unbroken either by windows or ornament: they are simple and "reserved." Gleaming in high light under an equally light sky, they huddle almost one on top of the other, built upon every available square yard inside the "papery" old city wall, which looks as if cannon would blow it away. Patches of blue sea break the white city outline, and the towers of the mosques rise above it all: their tesselated surfaces, tiled in shades of green and polished by the years, shimmer in the sunshine like peacocks' tails.

Two or three gateways pierce the drab-coloured city wall, their horseshoe-shaped arches washed over with salmon-pink. The same plaster-work arch repeats itself occasionally in the rough stone- and mortar-work of the houses, all of an inferior quality, short-lived and rebuilt again and again on the *débris* of successive years, until they

THE ROAD TO FEZ.

[*To face p.* 6.

stand in time right above the cobble-stones of the narrow streets.

Outside the city wall a few private houses and two hotels lie back among eucalyptus, palms, and bushy stone-pines: several of the legations which represent the European Powers have modern houses, lost in greenery of sorts. Behind these, again, a suburb of jerry-built Spanish houses, with the scum of Spain, is inclined to grow, which offshoot of fifth-rate Europe gives at last upon the rolling pastures and windswept hills of the open country.

Our breakfast-table brought us face to face with every traveller who passed along the great sandy track leading eventually to Fez, which people in Morocco call a road, beaten to-day and for the last two thousand years by the feet of generations of camels, mules, donkeys, horses, cattle, and mankind.

Though the wayfarers, plodding through the dusty hoof-marks, were desultory, it was quiet for few hours even at night, and under our windows we waked to an eternal shuffling in the soft sand, the champing of bits, and guttural Arabic tones.

R. and I leaned over the balcony. Women passed us wrapped in voluminous whity-yellow garments—*haiks*—black eyes and red slippers alone showing. Date-coloured boys passed us, wearing red fezes and dirty-white turbans. Countrymen passed us in great, coarse, brown woollen cloaks—*jellabs*—the hood pulled right on over the head, short wide sleeves, the front joined all down, and having scarred bare legs and feet coming out from underneath. These drove strings of diminutive donkeys, a couple of water-barrels balanced across the back of each—supplies of water for Tangier when the rain-water tanks are giving out: there are few wells in the city.

More women, veiled to the eyes, passed us, in delightful

shoes—milk-coloured leather, embroidered with green: an African woman, black as a boot, with thick negro lips and yellow metal bracelets on her charcoal-sticks of arms. More donkeys passed us, carrying vegetables to market, driven by countrywomen in yellowish-white haiks, vast straw hats, and the inevitable veil. Two men passed us with an immense open box containing thousands of eggs, hung between them by a pole on the shoulder of each—export for England: forty-eight millions were sent off in 1902, and this morning's omelette might not be our first Morocco egg. A Moor of some means came by, riding at a hard-held ambling walk his star-gazing white mule: the high-peaked saddle and bridle were of scarlet cloth, the stirrup-leathers of scarlet twisted wool; he wore a creamy woollen haik, falling in soft folds down to his yellow slippers, a turban whose snowy disc of enormous size framed his cinnamon-coloured face in symmetrical folds of spotless white, and the top of a scarlet fez showed in the centre of it.

Almost opposite us a beggar had sat himself down at the edge of the road, under the shelter of the high cane fence—a grimy old greybeard, tanned and worn like a walnut, in a tattered jellab and shady turban. "For the love of God; for the love of God," he rolled out incessantly in Arabic, ending in a throaty gobble like a turkey; and the country people threw him, as they passed, of their bundles—here an orange, there a lump of charcoal—whatever it might be it was crammed into the hood of the jellab; and the sing-song and the gobble began again. In a Mohammedan country it is counted a duty as well as a holy deed to encourage beggars: almsgiving represents to the faithful Mussulman equivalent gain in Paradise; and no one starves in Morocco, though occasionally dismissed with a wave of the hand and "God provide for you." Mad people are regarded as saints, and credited with the gift of prophecy. It is an exceedingly holy thing to walk about naked. A holy man in Fez was in the habit of sitting at a missionary's gate stark naked; eventually this proceeding had to be put a stop to, because the holy man would insist upon holding the horses of the missionary's afternoon callers.

Our beggar sat in the same spot day after day, hour after hour, fatuitously happy, blissfully content. "God is great, and what is written is written": remorse, regrets, are alike unknown to Mussulmen; and it is this which dignifies their religion and themselves. Life passes lightly over them, and chisels few lines and puckers in the serene patriarchal faces—they may be scamps of the first water, for all one can tell; it sits lightly upon them.

A small boy in a white tunic and red fez, who called himself Larbi, was playing about near the beggar: being able to speak a little English, he made himself useful to visitors, and was rapidly exchanging his good qualities for the drawbacks of the hanger-on: he came out with us for a day or two, smoked several cigarettes in the course of the afternoon, and picked us useless bunches of ordinary flowers. Remonstrance was futile, but when no more little silver coins were forthcoming he left off shadowing us.

We found our own way down to the great *sok*, or market-place, in the wake of some donkeys carrying live cackling fowls, fastened by a bit of string and their feet to any part of the donkey and its baskets which came handy. On each side of the road and everywhere in Tangier the obstinate steely-grey cactus, or prickly pear, dominates the landscape: its fat fleshy leaves make as good a protection as the sharp-pointed aloe round the irregular plots of cultivated ground. Alternating with them, tall bound cane fences swish and rattle in the wind.

Steely-grey and a yellow-bleached white describe the vegetation of Tangier, set in its white sand-dunes. Morocco is far from having lot or part in the gorgeous East, as tradition says. To begin with, from the end of August to the end of April hazy days greatly predominate, and thirty inches of rain are put in: naturally the country and people take their cue from the general colour of the sky, from its white-yellow light, in which a wan sun is yet able to produce a glare. Morocco is yellow-white, and the Moors themselves run from the colour of cinnamon, through shades of coffee and old gold, to biscuit and skim-milk. Their houses and their clothes take on the same whites and greys, yellows and browns, and the sand and the scrub again and again repeat the tale. Perhaps it has a saddening effect, borne out in the colourless monotone of the lives of its countrywomen.

Presently we passed a skin-yard, salted goat-skins, drying by the hundred under the sun, spread upon the ground, upon the flat roofs, wherever a skin could lie, curling with dryness, the empty legs of the late owners standing stiff and upright, like petrified stockings, pointing dismally to heaven.

We overtook a string of camels as we neared the sok, strolling along and regarding the skies, R. and myself with an exaggerated superciliousness. They were laden with dates, carpets, and slippers from Fez, and, together with mules and donkeys, constitute the vans and railway-trucks of Morocco, substituting over the face of the land a dilatory calm in the place of speed and bustle.

But at first it was a real effort to take in a tenth part of surroundings so different from those of England; and when we found ourselves in the sok—the *hub* of Moorish

The Sok at Tangier

life—it was to be jostled by donkey-drivers shouting "Baarak! Baarak!" by black water-carriers from the Sus country, by veiled women, by negroes from Timbuctoo, by mules and camels, by men walking, men riding, without one sight or sound familiar, in a dream-world of intense life, recalling nothing so much as the Old Testament. It was worth the journey out from home to see this sok—an open space crawling with brown-and-white, cloaked and hooded humanity, mixed up with four-legged beasts, also brown, and the whole more like a magnified ant-hill on the flat than anything human. In front of the squatted country people their stock-in-trade lay in piles, gorgeous in tone: oranges and oranges and more oranges, selling at one thousand seven hundred for a shilling; scarlet chillies—hot blots of colour; pink onions; red carrots; white salt, collected down on the beach; green pumpkins blotched with yellow; besides grain of all sorts, basketsful of charcoal, bundles of wood, dried fruit, flat round loaves of bread, cabbages, and what not. The sound of a perpetual muffin-bell was ringing backwards and forwards—the *bhisti* of Tangier, with his hairy goatskinful of water across his back, and two bright brass bowls hung by a chain round his neck, a bell in one hand, with the other dealing out drinks of water for a Moorish copper coin of which a penny contains fifteen.

We elbowed our way through the *Báb-el-Sok*, or Gate of the Market-place, into the city, and found ourselves in a long, narrow, straight street, dropping down to the *marsa*, or harbour. The irregular, light colour-washed houses jut out promiscuously over the minute cupboard-like shops crammed with oddments of every sort and hue, and leaving scanty room for the owner to squat on some carpet or mattress, until it strikes him that it is time to eat or go to prayers, and he locks up the double doors of his "store cupboard" and strolls away.

Looking down this attenuated Piccadilly of Tangier, over the white turbans and red fezes of the multitude, right away at the far end a field of blue sea was to be seen: half-way between, the faithful were beginning to pass into the big mosque one by one for midday prayers, each leaving his shoes behind him and stepping over the high doorstep barefoot on to the marble floor beyond, thence disappearing behind the ponderous green iron doors, where the great line is drawn between Europeans and Asiatics, debarring from entry any except Mussulmen.

The Villa Valentina breakfasted at 12.45, and cut the morning short. We were out again later with a guide—Hadj Riffi he called himself—bent on a visit to the *Kasbah*, or fortress of the city.

Hadj Riffi provided a donkey and pack, which of all substitutes for saddles is most foolish, intended only for loads of all sorts to be slung across them; but packs are easy to slip off and on, and have answered their purpose in Morocco since the days when in Judæa Mary rode on one to Bethlehem.

Conducted through the queer, intricate city, we wound along maze-like alleys three or four feet wide, ever the old aromatic smell of the East, almost impossible to recall, yet recognized again in an instant's flash, and born of the Oriental world we jostled against—of Berbers, Arabs, negroes, men from the Sahara, men from the mountains of the Riff, Turks, Greeks, Levantines, Syrians, even an occasional Hindoo, all wanderers up and down the earth, unable to resist the call of the open road, engendered by nomadic habits of old.

One word on the inhabitants of the country. The Berbers are the aborigines of Morocco, and live more

R. ON A PACK.

[*To face p.* 12.

Pilgrimage to Mecca

or less in the hills and mountains, into which they were driven by the Arabs in the seventh century, when they overran Morocco. The Arabs, on the other hand, live in the plains; and Arabs and Berbers practically halve the country between them. Both peoples divide into numerous tribes, of which the men from the Riff are a Berber tribe. The negroes in Morocco are merely slaves imported from the south. One and all the Arab and Berber tribes are called indiscriminately by Europeans "Moors." The other wanderers in Tangier filter through the land from their own countries: who can tell why or wherefore? Hadj Riffi himself had obeyed his Prophet Mohammed in so far as to make the pilgrimage to Mecca. A journey the prospect of which would horrify a tradesman at home is undertaken by an earnest-minded shop-keeping Moor as a matter of course. What are the twelve uncomfortable days by sea to Jeddah? Or the journey thence to Mecca, lying stretched in a long pannier on one side of a camel, balanced by a second pilgrim in a pannier on the other side, and over the whole an awning spread? But this luxurious travelling is for the rich pilgrim, who swings silently along day after day, under the burning sun or the cold stars, across the tideless sea of sand, towards an illimitable horizon. Hadj Riffi "footed it," spent three days at Mecca, at this time transformed into a city of a myriad tents, among which it is easy enough to be lost, teeming with pilgrims—Chinese, Hindoos, Circassians, Georgians, Bosnians—most of them unable to understand each other, beyond a verse or two from the Korān and a few pious ejaculations.

Hadj Riffi and his fellow-Moors prayed three days at Mecca, and performed the ceremonies round the celebrated *Kāaba*, the chief shrine and holiest of all holy places, built by Adam and Eve after the pattern of their own Sanctum Sanctorum in the Garden of Eden.

The far-famed Black Stone, presented to the masons by the Angel Gabriel, built into the east corner of the outer wall of the Kāaba, is a semicircular fragment of volcanic basalt, sprinkled with coloured crystals, about six by eight inches large, bordered with silver, and the surface of it reddish brown, undulating, and polished.

Having kissed the Black Stone and performed other rites, the Moors went three days' journey to the Prophet's Mountain to pray; then they took themselves back to Morocco, but on their way, missing a steamer, were obliged to travel by land through Tunis, which took them five months, and, running short of money, lived, Hadj Riffi said, largely on roots.

In the meantime he urged our donkey along, breaking his discourse with "Arrah! Arrah!" until at last it was cajoled under the gateway and into the Kasbah. This fortress, reported a good specimen of Moorish architecture, could impress nobody: it has no regular garrison; the batteries are antiquated, the artillery hopelessly inefficient. The crumbling battlements are overgrown with rank grass and fig-trees, though tradition has it they were once brass, when the city was built of gold and silver.

Tangier is immensely old, and has seen many conquerors, many demolitions. Arabs, Greeks, Carthaginians, Romans, Goths, Spaniards, and Portuguese have all in their turn besieged and taken, ruled and deserted, the white city. England has had her turn too. When Charles II. married Catherine of Braganza, Tangier and Bombay formed part of her dowry and passed into British hands. The Portuguese, to whom Tangier then belonged, withdrew; the English entered, repaired the city wall, built forts, and in the course of three years a great mole across the harbour at a cost of £31,000. Trade increased rapidly under the protection of the plucky Tangier Regiment (now the Queen's Royal West Surrey). An English mayor and corporation—six aldermen and twelve Common Council men—were established in the little colony, and attended church in scarlet and purple.

And then the Home Government made a mistake. The slovenly Tangier board in London wasted money, sent adventurers out to Tangier as governors. An exposure of their mismanagement followed, which induced the Home Government to throw up a troublesome charge, and to evacuate as valuable a port as England ever possessed, in a country which, unlike India, is admirably adapted for European colonization, and blessed with every natural advantage Creation can offer.

The mole and fortifications were blown up, Lord Dartmouth and his garrison marched out of Tangier on February 6, 1684, and the Moors took possession of a heap of fragmentary ruins. With Tangier in our hands we could have confidently commanded the passage of the Straits for seventy miles, nor would there have been a risk to Gibraltar of having all her supplies cut off in the event of Spain and Morocco being hostile to us. Fresh-comers to Morocco regret these things: in a few weeks the spirit of the country induces a lazy tolerance and a general apathy towards the past as well as towards the present state of affairs.

We found inside the Kasbah an entirely Moorish element —one sacred spot where no "Christians" may live. A children's school was making a deafening noise on our right, and we looked in to see a group of small boys sitting round an ancient, turbaned Moor, who was sewing at a jellab and paying small attention to his pupils: one and all were on their heels, lighted by the open door, there being of course no windows ; and each held in his two hands a board inscribed with Arabic characters, which he swayed backwards and forwards as he swayed his body in time with sentences from the Korān, learnt thus by heart and chanted in a high sing-song key. There were no girls. Boys alone are taught anything ; and in general their education begins and ends, as above, with the Korān. Few Moors can write or read : there are no books in Morocco, except the Korān and a religious treatise or two, to tempt them to learn. As for geography, an intelligent Moor will know by name England, France, and Germany, not Russia, and that his own country is the biggest, the best, and the most powerful.

Leaving the noisy little school, which did not approve of being stared at, we came to the empty palace, with its great horse-shoe doorway, painted blue-white and carved in a rudimentary way, called in Arabic " The little garden," descriptive of its inside courtyard, planted with oranges, figs, and palms.

Farther on stands the forge of the fortress : " for the slippers for the horses," Hadj Riffi explained. The blacksmith wore an apron of a whole goat-skin ; he pared down the hoof with an instrument like a shovel, helped by the horse's owner or any chance onlooker, for Moors " hunt in packs," and only a mere Christian does anything by himself. The shoe is a complete circle of iron, has three nails on each side, and in some places a bar across the centre.

At last we reached the prison, the principal feature of the Kasbah. Much has been written about Moorish prisons, to be put down by ignorant critics as exaggerated. English visitors have shown up their horrors, only to be forbidden now by a stringent order to go inside.

Prisons in Morocco

It is hard to say what happens behind the scenes, but torture is lightly thought of in Morocco; "cruelty," as Europeans understand it, has no place nor meaning in ignorant, fanatical minds; and an unpleasant inference is therefore to be drawn.

Of course many of the prisoners are confined, in all good faith, for offences, and will be released in time; but there are also Moors, in high positions socially, or possessed formerly of means, who "wither and agonize" year after year in captivity, their only fault that they were rich or influential in bygone days, thus tempting a jealous rival to remove them out of his path, or a greedy Government to confine them and feed upon their money. If they ever come out, it will be because a wealthy friend has chosen to pay the Government for their release, or because it has happened to occur to the ministers at Court to send for them; and half of them will reappear but scarred remnants of the men who went in. Descriptions of tortures which were unknown even in the Middle Ages in England may well be omitted: tortures which result in blind and tongueless creatures, without hands; bled of every penny they once possessed, and maimed in order to induce them to reveal the spot where their money was hidden, or the friends' names with whom they traded.

We looked in through a small iron grating in the door about two feet square, revealing a space open to the skies, with roofed recesses in the walls round the four sides, where the prisoners had huddled themselves in their rags. At night they are chained by the leg. An Oriental does not require "a bed," but he is provided with no substitute in prison, still less with food and drink, for which he is dependent on friends or relations willing to supply him. Of late years, in certain prisons, a small loaf of bread per day is given to each man. He has the great advantage of being able to talk all day to his fellow-prisoners; but in the case of a refined man such close intercourse has its drawbacks, more especially when a raving lunatic happens to be chained by an iron collar round his neck to one of the pillars. Madmen and all alike, without respect of persons, veritably rot to death, cheek by jowl, in a Moorish prison. Disease, starvation, and injuries tend to shorten their captivity. Whoever has smelt the smell within those walls will endorse the adjective " kindly " Death, than which there surely can be no more welcome visitor.

A few of the sound prisoners, sitting on the ground, were weaving baskets, some of which we bought through the keeper of the prison; then turned away, struck by the stoicism among the prisoners themselves in a situation of such uncertainty. Was it to end in death or release? Who knows? They merely shrug their shoulders, and ejaculate, " Ift shallah " (God will show).

Passing the soldiers guarding the outside of the prison, and out under a second gateway of the Kasbah, we stumbled down what is called one of the Sultan's "highways," something very rocky and not far off the perpendicular. R. chose her own feet, much to Hadj Riffi's annoyance. Though the ways are such that no donkey can be ridden without stumbling among cobble-stones and pitfalls, and thereby running a risk of pitching the rider off the insecure pack into a refuse-heap, it was impossible for a European, in his eyes, to walk and to maintain his dignity at the same time.

That no Moor runs when he can walk, or walks when he can ride, or stands when he can sit, or sits when he can lie down, is a saying fulfilled to the letter. And what poor man, however heavily he loads his small donkey

TWO SHEIKHS.

[To face p. 18.

with garden produce, forgoes mounting himself on top
of all, and making the little beast stagger along, at a
fair pace too, to market? The life of such a man is
not eventful, but what there is of it is good: he sings
as he jogs along in a monotonous tone, and has a word
for every soul he meets, and a laugh too, curses his donkey
—he is never quiet—and lands the produce of his little
melon-patch in the market. The melons are sold by
degrees, much gossip is interspersed, possibly he washes
and prays, then eats, and sleeps a little; more gossip,
until the sun tells him it is time to get outside the city
gates; and then off he jogs again, singing, talking, back
to the little reed-thatched hut, fenced in by its hedge
of cactus. Life is too full of—call it resignation or
content—to leave room for disturbing speculations, and
he is born of a race which never repines: there is Allah
and the One Faith, and the sun to lie down beneath
and meditate and sleep. Not that the typical countryman is idle—far from it: he is hard-working, without any
beer to do it upon.

It is a matter of more speculation as to what the
courteous, solemn men, in turbans like carved snow, whom
one meets walking along the beach telling their beads,
or sees sitting in sunshine reading aloud in a low voice,
steadily praising Allah, occupy themselves with from
month to month; or the sleek sheikh—a countryman
of some means, with smooth coffee-coloured face and a
haik whiter than an iced birthday cake—perched between
the peaks of his red cloth saddle, under which his hard,
hammer-headed mule paces at an intermittent amble.

Probably the sheikh has ridden out of the city to
inspect his crops. His house, with his wife, he has locked
up: the keys are in his pocket. He swings along a
sandy track bordered with cactus, reaches his garden door,

which is painted Reckitt's blue, unlocks it, and, tying his mule up inside to a fruit-tree, proceeds to inspect his vines and prune casually some of the ashy-white branches of his fig-trees. Then he sets two ragged country-women to work to cut his vines and hoe his beans. He may read a few verses of the Korān later on. He may sleep. Eventually he ambles home. Other days he spends among his friends in the city, sitting in their little shops and gossiping consumedly. He may hire an empty shop of his own for the same purpose, and turn it into what might be called "a club." He will pray regularly; will play chess and draughts sitting in the front of a shop; will drink green tea. Whatever he does is done without haste, and towards evening he strolls serenely, with many interruptions, in the direction of his own house.

The climate of Morocco has never any of the brisk, freezing "grip" of a hard English winter, but rather tends towards encouraging indolence. In Tangier itself energetic English visitors find little superabundant scope for action: naturally enough, the residents, whom an enervating summer or two shears of much of the vitality with which they first landed, end in settling down into an enjoyable, mild routine. There is, however, shooting and a little pig-sticking for who will; but guns may not be brought into the country, and no European would be allowed to exploit its *nullahs*: if not killed, he would be turned back and escorted into trodden ways.

The principal day's excursion from Tangier is out to Cape Spartel and back again: before we left the place we started early one morning with this end in view, taking a donkey and boy carrying a camera, lunch, etc.— first along a cobbled roadway of which Tangier is immensely proud, across the river by a new bridge, and up the Mountain. The Mountain is the summer abode of Tangier, and shady houses and gardens civilize what was once a wild hill, in the days when our great British minister, Sir John Hay, did an unprecedented thing, and built himself a house there.

Forty years ago no Christian was safe outside Tangier without a guard, and it is largely to Sir John Hay's fearless trust in the honour of the Moor that the change is due. It may still be unwise to walk in lonely places after dark, or to become involved in a street row; for if one ruffian is excited to throw a stone, thirty will follow suit, and Europeans have thus been stoned to death. But those who live out in the Mountain and visitors to Spartel have nothing to fear in these days in the shape of attack and robbery.

It was about ten o'clock when we left behind us the leggy remains of a Roman aqueduct over the river, and, having climbed the Mountain, broke into open ground, stretching far away at the top. The cobbled road resolved itself into an unsophisticated path; the stiff cane fences, shutting out all but the tree-tops in the gardens from view, came to an end; and we were in a breeze off the Atlantic, on undulating hills covered with short scrub, gum-cistus, arbutus, tall white heather, oleander, and pink-and-white convolvulus.

The track led us up and down, and grew more stony as we went on, gradually rising, till we were about a thousand feet above the sea. Looking back, Tangier lay far below, and beyond it in the distance white cragged mountains glinted in the sun.

It was a glorious day, November 24: a fresh breeze, tempered as it so seldom is in England at that time of year. Our path wound round the hills and dipped towards the sea. From the stretches of heather through which we brushed we could hear below us the surf breaking on the rocks: it might have been a corner of the west coast of Scotland.

After eight miles' up-and-down tramp, the lighthouse at the end of the great cape, Spartel, the north-west corner of the African Continent, came into sight. This lighthouse was built at the instigation of the eleven Powers, but actually by the Sultan. The Powers—Great Britain, France, Germany, Spain, Austria, Belgium, Portugal, Italy, Russia, America, and Brazil—share the cost of its maintenance, and that of the whole road from Tangier to the lighthouse, which follows the line of telegraph-posts, the cable being laid to Spartel. The lighthouse is French built; its fixed intermittent white light can be seen thirty-six miles away, and it stands 312 feet above sea-level.

Sitting down at its base, looking out to sea, we watched the black spines of rock underneath us, set in whirlpools of foam—the Dark Continent showing the last of its teeth. On our left the coast trended away into the hazy distance: to our right across the blue Straits lay the yellow sands of the bay where Trafalgar was fought, and the irregular little town of Tarifa, backed by purple Spanish hills.

The evenings were short, and we were soon on our homeward way. The stunted bushes on each side of the path, disturbed by the devastating woodcutters, could hardly hold a lion in the present day. Yet in the course of Sir John Hay's forty odd years of administration in Morocco two were seen in these same woods, and he shot there himself a striped *Hyæna rufus*, a great shaggy animal with a bristling mane. One of the two lions ought to have been shot, but he doubled back, and was heard of afterwards travelling at a swinging trot between Tangier and Tetuan. He killed an ox in the valley the next day, and disappeared in the direction of the snow-topped mountains.

Sport

In this twentieth century lions in the north of Morocco would be a rare sight: towards the south the mountain-fastnesses hold them still, together with leopards, wild cats, etc.; but, like everywhere else, big game moves off as civilization moves on.

There remains the wild boar. The Moors hunt him with greyhounds, Europeans shoot him, and Englishmen have introduced pig-sticking. The largest pig Sir John Hay speared scaled twenty stone clean, and measured six foot four from snout to tail. But even pig are getting scarce. The Tent Club in Tangier organizes expeditions, and parties go out under canvas for a few days at a time: the result is nothing very great.

When it is a question of shooting pig, the Moors, born sportsmen, join one and all—small farmers and peasants—purely from the love of sport. Some act as beaters, wearing leathern aprons and greaves—such as the Greek peasantry wore—to protect their legs. They carry bill-hooks to cut their way through the thickets, and bring along a tribe of native dogs, which do good service—a cross between a collie and a jackal, veteran poachers, which prowl through the scrub, winding a boar at any distance. The thickets where pig lie are for the most part backed by the sea, and bordered by lake and marsh or plain, in which case it is not difficult to inveigle the driven boar to break where the guns are posted. A haunch of wild pig judiciously roasted, with a *soupçon* of wine in the gravy, is one of the delicacies of Morocco. As many as fifteen boars have been accounted for in a couple of days' shooting.

The sun went down; the soft air grew colder: we walked quickly back through the outskirts of Tangier, between gardens full of plumbago, dituria, geraniums, hibiscus, pointsettias, narcissus, frescia, and roses of all sorts, besides other flowers. Anything would grow in a soil which has been known to bear three crops of potatoes in one year, and where corn is sometimes sown and reaped all within the space of forty days.

An enterprising English market-gardener is this year growing vegetables and fruit for the London market, expecting to have green peas in Covent Garden in December, the duty on peas and tomatoes having been lowered to 5 per cent. This man acts as agent to a land-owner. Fortunes, indeed, might be made, if it were not a question of FIND THE LAND; for while land cannot now be bought in Morocco by Europeans, the few fortunates who own inherited acres price them high, and, hoping for a boom in the course of the next fifteen years, demand £400 an acre.

As we turned into the Villa Valentina a wonderful opal light warmed the white city and the sand-hills—they were no longer cold nor colourness; while banks of "rose" sunset-clouds were reflected "rose" in a grey-green sea.

Tangier has two sides to it—one native, the other European. The European side is all which appears on the surface, and it swamps the other. Given each of the eleven Powers, with its minister, its minister's family, its secretary, its attaché, its interpreter, its student; add to these a handful of English residents, a handful of English and American visitors, and a handful of varied nationalities thrown in; back them up with the necessary foundation of purveyors, and lower down still a substratum of leeches and black-sheep, greedy Jews, needy Spaniards, introducing drink and tobacco and gambling,—and there you have before you all the elements of a highly civilized town on the Mediterranean shore. It may be Tangier: it is not Morocco.

The Moorish aristocracy themselves speak of the place

TANGIER.

as "Christian-ridden Tangier," and will have none of it: the Sultan says it "no longer belongs to him." Its trade is *nil*, and what there is of it is in the hands of the Jews, who boast eleven synagogues, schools, and a Grand Rabbi at the head of all.

We brought introductions with us to various people, and met with every hospitality in Tangier. Sir Arthur and Lady Nicolson, representing Great Britain, do all in their power for visitors; and the colony of mixed nationalities fills its off hours together, most successfully, with a round of picnics, afternoon rides, tea parties, and other amusements, implied by "wintering at Tangier"; from all of which any knowledge of Morocco, or association with Moors, is far removed indeed.

A seaport which has neither roads nor railways to connect it with the surrounding country, is isolated a week's journey from the nearest capital town, and whose links with the outer world all tend seawards through steamers to foreign countries, can never constitute a study of the land to which it belongs only by right of position.

But Morocco itself had brought us to the north of Africa. Tangier could only be a base for future operations, and consequently a fortnight of Tangier sufficed, finding us bent upon moving on, before the heavy rains broke, and the swollen rivers made travelling impossible. Travelling in Morocco is never at the best of times luxurious. "Say explore, rather than travel," somebody writes, speaking of Morocco; and many were the injunctions and warnings which the post brought us from friends at home—above all, to expect no ransoms, in the event of capture by lawless tribes.

It is true that a *Wanderjahr* in Morocco has not the luxuries of travel in India; and Englishmen who would break new ground must wear Moorish dress, talk Arabic, and prepare to face considerable risks, with the off-chance of writing in some such strain as Davidson : " To-day I have parted with all my hair except one long tuft over my right ear. I never expect to become white again. My beard is very long. My legs covered with bites of vermin. My cheek-bones prominent, and my teeth sharp from having very little to do."

Not that R. and myself had such adventures in view ; but we believed that even as humble followers in the tracks of others we should find no lack of interest in a country so little known, among a people of " The Arabian Nights," under conditions which tempt the Unexpected to stalk out from behind every corner.

CHAPTER II

CAMP OUTFIT—A NIGHT AT A CARAVANSERAI—TETUAN—THE BRITISH VICE-CONSUL—MOORISH SHOPS—WE VISIT A MOORISH HOUSE AND FAMILY.

CHAPTER II

Tetuan—the tiger-cat! so curiously beautiful. Recollections of it hang in the gallery of one's memory, not so much as pictures, but as Correggio-like masses of vivid colouring and intangible spirals of perfume.

THE place we had set our hearts upon visiting, to begin with, was the northern capital, Fez—only to find, on going into particulars, that insurmountable barriers blocked the way. Even if we escaped the December rains on the ride there, they would break sooner or later, making sleeping out under canvas impossible: the flooded rivers might mean a long delay—probably a week or more—on the banks; bridges in Morocco are harder to find than diamonds on the seashore, and when a river is in flood there remains only to sit down in front of it until the waters abate.

The "road" to Fez, after the tropical rains, soon becomes a slough of clay and water, ploughed up by mules and donkeys, and so slippery that nothing can keep its legs. We decided, therefore, to leave Fez till the spring, when the rains would be over, and to visit for the present a city called Tetuan, only two days' journey from Tangier, camping out as long as we felt inclined, and returning to the Villa Valentina in a week, or when the weather should drive us back. But the gods thought otherwise.

Tetuan was, by report, in the most beautiful part of

Morocco: its situation reminded travellers of Jerusalem; it was among the Anjera and Riff Mountains; and though, of course, travel was impossible within the forbidden land of the Riff, it was likely we should gather some interesting crumbs of information, and come across a few of the famous tribesmen, while we were staying on the borders. Above all, it was a Moorish city, and counted an aristocratic one at that: no European element spoilt its originality. On the face of it Tetuan had attractions.

Accordingly we made preparations to be off.

The first thing to be done was to get hold of a man who could cook, act as guide, interpreter, and muleteer: plenty of them presented themselves, and we closed with a certain Mohammed, who had been with Colonel H——. Every third Moor is named Mohammed, or some corruption of it—eldest sons invariably.

Next we ransacked Tangier for commissariat and camp outfit. Out of a dirty little Spanish shop two men's saddles of antiquated English make, with rolls, were unearthed, and hired in preference to some prehistoric sidesaddles, with moth-eaten doe-skin seats and horned third pommels.

Then we obtained a permit from the English Consul, for the sum of seven-and-sixpence, authorizing us to apply to the governor of the Kasbah for one of the Moorish soldiers quartered in Tangier, who should act as our escort to Tetuan. The Sultan of Morocco undertakes to protect British subjects travelling in his dominions as far as possible, provided they supply themselves with an adequate escort and avoid roads through unsafe territory. The various tribes from among themselves sometimes provide an armed guard to see travellers safely across their own country, handing them on at the borders to the next tribe, who sends its mounted escort to meet them.

TETUAN.

Photo by A. Cavilla, Tangier.

Commissariat

The headman arranges for the safety of Europeans, and his tribe answers for their lives. But this plan involves prearrangement, publicity, and fuss. Now from Tangier to Tetuan the road by daylight is perfectly safe—though it happens that, at the time of writing, the body of a peasant, presumably out after sunset, has been found robbed and murdered close to it. Therefore one soldier was all we should want; and at last this bodyguard was supplied, a ragged Moor, with a lean mule and a French rifle—all for five shillings per day.

We next visited a general "stores," lined with the familiar Cadbury, Keiller, and Huntley & Palmer tins: there we invested in corned beef, tinned soup, potted meats, cheese, salt, macaroni, marmalade, tea, coffee, sugar, candles, soap, matches, etc. Things not to be forgotten were nails, hammer, rope, methylated spirit and etna. A revolver for its moral effect is necessary, and may be invaluable in a tight corner. We provided ourselves with two tents, one for the servants and a larger one for ourselves; a set of camp furniture, including kitchen pots and pans; and an enamel breakfast and dining service, which, if time had mattered little, would have been well exchanged for an aluminium set out from England, as lighter and more convenient.

Mohammed hired four mules and another man—Ali—himself taking charge of the cooking department, providing meat, bread, vegetables, fruit, etc.: then with our *bundobust* complete, and a letter of introduction from Sir Arthur Nicolson to the British Vice-Consul at Tetuan, we started on November 28.

It was one of the hottest mornings we had had, not a fleck of cloud in the sky, and what air there was due east: the sea lay flat as a blue pool, and five or six white sails might have been swans on its glassy surface.

Mohammed appeared early in the sandy road underneath our windows. To avoid waking people in the hotel, we handed our diminutive kit out through the window to him—only a couple of waterproof rolls, which held rugs and bare necessities; then locking up the bulk of our worldly goods behind us, slipped out of the Villa Valentina, mounted our mules, and were off across the white sand-dunes bordering the sea.

Tetuan lies forty-four miles to the south-east of Tangier: people with much time and little energy have made a three days' march of it. A range of hills rather more than half-way makes a natural division, and on the top of this watershed a *fondâk* (caravanserai) stands for the use of travellers during the night: here it is usual to camp.

We were an odd little procession as we left Tangier. Our mounted soldier, Cadour, led the way, in a brown weather-worn jellab, which he pulled right up over his head like a Franciscan friar: his legs were bare, his feet thrust into a pair of old yellow shoes. He carried his gun across his saddle in front of him, inside one arm: it was in a frayed brown canvas case, which had holes in each end, out of which both stock and barrel respectively protruded. With his other hand he jogged incessantly at the mule's mouth. Take him all in all, a soldier's was the last trade he outwardly impersonated. Behind him rode R. and myself, shaking down by degrees into our saddles, glad not to have before us eight or ten hours' jog across rough country on provincial side-saddles, which, apart from the strained position, are inconvenient for slipping off and on again. Behind us followed the two baggage-mules with our tents, etc.: loaded as they were, Mohammed and Ali had climbed upon the tops of their great packs. A mule carries as much as he can get along under in Morocco: the man climbs up afterwards, and does not count.

Two hundredweight, with a Moor on top, is a fair load for a long journey, marching seven hours every day. Enough barley should be carried for each night's fodder: the ordinary mule and pony live on barley and broken straw, beans when in season, and grass in the spring to fatten them. Sevenpence a day will feed a mule, and hire comes to three shillings a day. Good mules are not bought easily, and are worth, on account of their toughness, more than ponies, fetching £12 any day. Ours were but second-rate hirelings, and we made up our minds to buy later on, when starting on a long expedition. A mule should be chosen chiefly for its pacing powers, doing four and a half miles an hour on an average for seven hours a day, without turning a hair or tiring the rider, whose comfort depends on an easy pace. The longer the overlap of the hind-shoe print over the fore-shoe print, the better the pace. Moorish horses are wiry little beasts, but you seldom see a handsome one: either they are ewe-necked or they fall away in the hindquarters; their feet are allowed to grow too long, and their legs are ruined through tight hobbling. Nor is there much inducement to a Moor to breed a handsome foal, liable to be stolen from him, if seen by a governor or agent of the Sultan's. Naturally he breeds the inferior animal he has a chance of keeping, and puts a valuable mare to a common stallion, branding and otherwise disfiguring a colt which by bad luck turns out good-looking.

The slender desert-horse, the *habb-er-reeh* (gust of wind, as they call him), with the small aristocratic head, a nose which will go into a tea-cup, perfect shoulders, and diminutive sloping hindquarters, is seldom met with and hardly ever used, except quite in the south of the country, where he is given camel's milk to drink.

People as a rule start off on their day's march with the dawn, after a light breakfast of coffee, beaten-up eggs, and dry biscuits; halt about ten o'clock, supposing they are near water; and, if necessary, do two or three hours more, comfortably, before sunset. But we had made a late start, and the sun was far up as we jogged along one after the other, leaving behind the sands, the orange gardens, and the gimcrack Spanish houses, at every step the open country widening in front of us.

We followed a narrow path, one of the countless footpaths which zigzag in and out, and wind away to every point of the compass, like ants' tracks from an ant-hill. Donkeys, mules, countrywomen, eternally pass and repass along the polished ways, with the everlasting burdens of charcoal, faggots, vegetables, and flour : life in some form moving along them there always is.

Towards the edge of the horizon, clumps of dwarf palm and coarse grass slanted in the breeze : here and there grey rocks stuck up on the hillside like fossilized bones, and met the blue sky. A stream was meandering, hidden under deep banks, on our right. We wound along the wide valley, doing our best to keep the mules going at a respectable pace, and finding that there was quite an art in accomplishing it on a hireling. Cadour cut in behind, and supplemented our sticks and heels with Arabic words of much effect, his own mule's mouth suffering badly from his jogging, remorseless hand.

A raven, "a blot in heaven, flying high," sailed over our heads up in the blue, and then, leisurely dropping, sat on a rock and croaked at us. Morocco is a country of circling kites and keen-eyed hawks, whose easy, buoyant flight and vibrating "hover" in the hot air are things

OURSELVES AND BAGGAGE.

[*To face p.* 34.

of undying fascination. Now and again a puff of east wind—life-giving—would stir the whole countryside and pass on, leaving us glowing under a sun which warmed every cranny, and made the section of air just above the flat fields rock with heat. Two countrywomen toiled towards us under their bundles—a couple of figures swathed in yellowy white; they gazed at us as people gaze who have few interests in their lives, then smiled and spoke, gesticulated, and laughed again: a herd of goats was outlined on the hill above; the goat-herd called to another far-off brown-clad figure, and the echoes filtered down to us: a rabbit dashed up out of a palm-bush and scuttled away: and then there was silence profound, and we paced on eastwards, talking and singing a song sometimes, while the sun climbed right-handed.

There is no life like it—that life of the open air and its absolute freedom. Monotonous it would certainly be to many people: small and uneventful matters, and a palette set in greys and browns, charm but a few, for whom solitary rides and waste places are "things in common," and chance meetings and little incidents by the way suffice.

Two or three miles outside Tangier stretch rich undulating lands between low hills: a few divisionless fields bear witness to both primitive and erratic farming, and give that regretful air to the landscape which land not "done well by" always imparts.

The writer has lately read a somewhat pessimistic letter upon the state of Morocco. Morocco is a decadent empire, it is true: primarily, because the two races to whom the country belongs live, and have always lived from time immemorial, under a tribal system; and secondarily, because those same races, Arab and Berber, hate one another with a racial hatred. These two reasons by themselves augur badly for the land they live upon, implying a state of armed neutrality, no cohesion, and no settled peace.

Under a tribal system the tribe is the unit, not the individual—"one for all, and all for one": it follows that transgression and retribution are both upon a wholesale scale, and alike disastrous towards the consolidation of a united nation.

The government in a country cursed by the tribal system must in the very nature of things be despotic: lawless tribes need the tyrant's hand of iron. To the fact of his being a despot the Sultan owes his security, coupled with one other reason. Arabs and Berbers alike are fanatics: religion is the air they breathe, the salt of life. The Sultan is descended direct from the One Great Prophet; consequently the Sultan is acknowledged as lord. His policy is an Oriental one: tribe is played off against tribe, one European power against the other European power; the empire is isolated; innovations are prohibited, lest European civilization should oust Moorish eccentricities. So much for the Oriental policy of "the balance of jealousies."

Despotism breeds despotism. While every Moor below the Sultan ranks as equal, the fact remains that Government officials are all in their own sphere little despots, governing districts many days' journey from Court, with every chance of robbing and oppressing those under them, until the day of reckoning comes, when the Court, hearing how fat their fine bird has grown, summons him to the capital, and the process of plucking and imprisoning their wealthy servant follows.

Life exists upon life, from the *sheikhs* (farmers), who live upon what they can squeeze out of the peasants, to

Moorish Government

the *bashas* (governors), who exist on tithes, taxes, and extortion wrung from the sheikhs and townspeople, up to higher officials, who receive no salaries, and line their pockets by a process of bleeding the bashas and others ...... thus *ad lib.* Even the gaolers—also unpaid—earn their living by extorting money from the prisoners. The whole system of government reacts upon itself; for the venalty of the officials drives the tribes to redress their wrongs at intervals by raids and open rebellion, to punish whom there follows slaughter upon slaughter, and the country is laid waste.

Hence the principal reasons—wheels within wheels—which account for the Morocco of 1902 : its prehistoric customs, its uncultivated acres.

No reformer, no missionary, will alter the condition of Morocco. The Moors themselves have made it what it is; but since for an Ethiopian to change his skin is no light matter, there is small probability of the Moors themselves unmaking it.

A gloomy prospect, yet one which, taking the case of the people and looking upon it from a " happiness " point of view, must not be altogether judged from a European standpoint. The likes and dislikes of Moors are not the likes and dislikes of Europeans, and most of them view their good times and bad times with equal calm, as merely the will of Allah. Besides which, anything in the shape of law and order and daily routine rasps their raw nature. Just as a Moor prefers to eat to repletion when there is food, and to go without when there is not, so he would choose a desultory and irresponsible life, alternating between perfect freedom and excessive tyranny, to any regular humdrum form of government which Europe could offer him.

The country people we met, if hard-worked, had at

the same time cheerful enough faces : their enjoyment of life probably equals that of the English labourer.

On the whole, it is possible that, when the day comes—as it must come—that an effete and inadequate people goes to the wall, and civilized blood occupies their room, it may bring good, but that good will be tinged with regret—certainly in the eyes of those selfish mortals to whom one country, neither wire-fenced nor scored by railways, nor swept nor garnished, but coloured to-day by the smoke of many thousand years, still offers palmy days. Thus giving thanks to Allah for things as they are, after the manner of the country, we jogged along, looking out for a halting-ground : it was between twelve and one o'clock, and time to stretch our legs.

The river and some oleander-bushes, with green lawns between them, offered all we wanted. Cadour took off his brown jellab, and spread it for us to sit upon. There we lunched and waited for an hour. Some oxen were ploughing close to us, driven in a desultory way by a figure clad in a pair of once white drawers, and a once white tunic with a leather belt. All which this husband-man wanted being corn enough to supply himself, and no surplus to fall into the sheikh's hands, the field was naturally small. A well-to-do farmer might rise to growing a little maize or cummin or millet or fenugreek for exportation, perhaps some broad-beans, chick-peas, or canary-seed; but the duties are heavy. Wheat and barley have been forbidden export : the infidel shall not eat bread of the true believer's corn.

Our Arabic at that time was *nil*; there was no chance of a word with the ploughman unless through Mohammed. Such a mere scratch of a furrow as he made, into which the grain would be casually thrown, with never a harrow or substitution for one ! Allah provides, and there is no

reason to interfere with his arrangements : " B·ism Allah."
Thus will the fields be reaped, the corn ground, the bread
made, the loaf eaten, with the same old invocation muttered
beforehand : " B·ism Allah " (In the name of God).

The two little oxen drew the patriarchal plough, hewn
out of a log of wood, and shod with an iron point, entirely
by means of their heads, to which it was fastened with
dried grass-fibres across their foreheads and round their
horns, making a sort of large straw bonnet on top of
all which they held high in the air or sideways, with expressions of extreme disgust. In the middle of the field,
yoked by the bonnet to a second plough and a fellow-ox,
the companion had inconsiderately lain down, to the great
inconvenience of its foolish partner, which remained
standing, with its head forced into the most unpleasant
angle downwards, and the stoical expression of a true
Mussulman underneath its bonnet.

On the opposite side of the stream some sheep, suggestive of the lean, tough mutton we fed upon, were
searching round for anything in the shape of pasture :
flocks of small cows and calves were on the same quest
between the palmetto-bushes : somewhere a boy in charge
was no doubt asleep.

By this time Mohammed was impatient to be off: the
bits were put back into the mules' mouths, we got into our
saddles again, and pushed on. In wet weather the track
must be a bad one to follow : innumerable streamlets,
which have eaten out deep gullies in the clay, have to be
crossed, making the going hard upon heavily laden beasts,
and after heavy rains impossible. We slipped about a
little. Mohammed and his man had their hands full with
the two baggage-mules, which they had long ago given up
trying to ride. The slopes became more bleak : far away
in the distance Cadour pointed out our destination, a white

speck on the top of a range of hills, to be seen for a moment and lost sight of the next, as we dipped down on to lower ground. Another hour brought it very little nearer: fresh irregularities between opened up continually, meaning *détours* to the right or left. A few plover wailed over some marsh: in such places partridge, hares, golden grouse, and quail ought to be found; but since every male possesses a gun of sorts, from the peasant hoeing beans upwards, and is not troubled with game laws or ideas upon preserving, they become rarer.

We passed clump after clump of white narcissus in full bloom, and marigolds in yellow patches; but as we neared the hills the country grew wilder, and short scrub, palmetto, and cistus took the place of coarse grass.

At last we were at the foot of the pass, and the end of our march was all uphill, steep in places, the scrub turning into respectable bushes, with almost a "jungly" aspect. The baggage-mules were pushed and urged ahead. At last, about five o'clock, the sun setting, we reached our camping-ground, up in the teeth of a rising wind.

Standing by itself, the caravanserai—called a *fondâk* in Morocco—was a white-walled enclosure, with a great open space in the middle and colonnades all round the insides of the four walls, where men and mules huddled and slept unconcernedly. There is also one room to be had; but filthy, of course, such quarters always are, and dear at any price (the rate for accommodation is not large). One look into the walled enclosure, crowded with transport animals and their drivers, was enough, and we turned to see to the pitching of the tents outside.

The panorama of hills in the west had a red, lurid light, such as Julius Ollsson loves to paint: across the stormy glow trailed a few white wisps of smoke where the peasants were burning wood on the hillside for charcoal. Making a *détour* of the fondâk while there was light to see, we chose the west side for our camp, apparently the most sheltered; but the place is a temple of the four winds and gusty upon a breathless day.

It was quite dark before the men had things ready, hampered as they were by the gale which was getting up and the want of light. We tried to keep warm, and watched the first star come out from a knoll; at last took refuge in our wind-shaken tent, unpacked, and sat ourselves down with outstretched legs, wrapped in a medley of garments, round the little camp-table, lit by the flicker of two candle-lanterns, the flaps of the tents snugly fastened together from within, awaiting Mohammed's first culinary effort.

By-and-by from out of the chaotic kitchen-tent, pitched in the dark, filled with confused commissariat, and further blocked by Cadour, Ali, and their small effects, Mohammed emerged, and handed in through an opening in our tent chicken and eggs cooked in Moorish fat. After a long interval tea followed, and fruit. We sat listening to the wind, writing up a diary and talking till bed seemed the best and only warm place. The gale woke me after an hour or two: the tent, torn by raging gusts, threatened to give at every moment. I got up and took a look outside. A wild, gustful night indeed, of glimmering stars and a great white half-moon—cold too: the mountains stood out sharp; there was little cloud; round our tent a guard of men from the fondâk—always supplied, for the safety of travellers—were sleeping on the ground, heads and all wrapped up in their jellabs,—the moon shone on the queer bundles, and on our five mules, picketed opposite the tent door, backs to the wind, munching their barley. Neither of us got much sleep; roused periodically by the hammering in afresh of our strained tent-pegs, by the men's voices, which would relapse into silence for half an hour, and then break out again; above all, by the flapping and rattling of the canvas. For a moment there was a lull, and we heard the mules feeding and the thousand sounds of the night; then a wild blast almost carried the tent away, and the monotonous undertone of voices would begin once more.

We were up early, spent little time over dressing in a stiff breeze, and turned out to look at the weather. Banks of cloud lay piled up in the wind, but rain never comes with the *sharki* (east wind). The sun was up—no chance of seeing it for the present.

Mohammed boiled eggs and tea, and in another twenty minutes we were ready to quit our exposed camping-ground.

From the fondâk to Tetuan the distance is only fifteen miles, half a day's journey. The day before we had done twenty-eight miles, and ought to have started at dawn, avoiding the pitching of our tents in the dark. To-day we were off betimes.

It was cold, and I walked the first hour or two, Cadour and R. riding behind with my mule, coming slowly down the steep, rocky ridge into the valley in which Tetuan lies. It was a bad bit of riding, a continuous descent, and the baggage-mules fell far behind: the rocky ravine was uncultivated and treeless, scrub and rocks only on the bare mountains. Sometimes a crest would have a saw edge against the sky, suggesting fir woods; but as a matter of fact every tree worth having which is not planted by a saint's tomb, and therefore holy, has long ago been made into fire-wood, no coal finding its way into the interior of Morocco, and mining being a thing unknown.

At last the slopes gave on to more level ground

Tetuan in Sight

and strips of cultivation: we had our first view of Tetuan, at that distance little more than a streak of white lying in the shelter of the hills.

It was better going; and R. having jogged on some way ahead, I waited for Cadour, climbed into my saddle, and caught her up. Here and there, perched on each side of us, far above in the mountains, wherever an oasis of green lay between sheltering cliffs, a village had sprung up, an irregular cluster of brown-and-white huts, thatched with cane, weathered to shades of brown, the whole pile hedged with grey aloes and cactus, on the steep mountain-side—also brown—where, unless looked for, they could easily have been passed over altogether.

These were the only signs of man; for Tetuan shared the speciality of the fondâk the night before, in vanishing behind intervening hills and never growing any nearer. But the mules this time were fresher, or we had learnt the art of keeping them up to the mark; they broke into a canter, and scampered across the rich-looking flats bordering the river Wád Martîl. The Wád Martîl is the proud possessor of one of the seven bridges which the Empire of Morocco can show—a somewhat quaint construction, but a *bonâ-fide* stone bridge: no carriage could have crossed it; the middle cobble-stones were so steep and rough that they amounted to rocks. But Morocco knows not carriages, and at least it was a bridge.

Once across, Tetuan was not more than a few miles off.

Seen from any height, it is one of the whitest cities in the world, and the whitewashed walls lend themselves to flat shadow as blue as the sky above. Tetuan has been described as " a cluster of flat-backed white mice, shut up in a fortress in case they should escape": it has also been likened to Jerusalem, with "the hills round about." For my own part, it was like nothing I had seen, nor was prepared then and there to classify—this heap of chalk, this white city. Not a particle of smoke floated over it: purity and sunlight alone were suggested by the outside of the platter. The Moor has a weakness for whitewashed houses, for long white garments, for veiled women: there shall be no outer windows in his house, nor in his own private life. Ugliness there may be, enough and to spare, inside these white cities—it oozes out sometimes; but as far as possible let a haik and a blank wall enshroud it all in mystery.

None can fix the age of Tetuan: once upon a time the city was on the seashore—now seven miles of flats lie between, and crawling mules and donkeys link the two, working backwards and forwards, week in, week out, jogging down with empty packs to the cargo-steamers, and labouring back across deep-flooded country half the year, under solid burdens, to the city. From the flat roof-tops the weekly visit of a merchant-vessel is duly looked for, and a long black steamer lies at anchor for the day in the narrow ribbon of blue sea seen to the east, near the white Customs House, which stands back from the beach.

Southwards Tetuan faces the Riff country, range after range of mountains, inhabited by that indomitable tribe, whose "highlands" are closed to Europeans. The river Wád Martîl, between Tetuan and *the Riff*, winds across the seven miles of flats to the sea, and is fordable in two or three places except in heavy rains; and days "in the mountains"—safe within sight of the city—promised us many an expedition, and opened up another world of heights foreshadowed and gulfs forbidden, where the hours were all too short.

CLOUDS OVER TETUAN.

[To face p. 44.

Tetuan

Behind Tetuan to the north, the mountainous Anjera country, wild, bare hills abut upon the very city wall.

The name *Tetuan* means in Arabic "The eyes of the springs," and all over the city water gushes out of the limestone rock—the hardest water, I submit, that ever mortal tried to drink. Such a supply is worth a kingdom to an Eastern city. Every tank, fountain, and *hummum* (Turkish bath) has its never-failing supply, gratis, from the heart of the hills. The little streets are watered by it, and the sewage carried off on the lower side of the city in a strong current, which—still useful—works primitive corn-mills under the wall on the south side, where a sack receives the flour from a couple of flat revolving stones. A miller was robbed the other night asleep by his sack: the door burst open, and he expected a bullet, but was let off with a clout on the head and the confiscation of his sack.

Having ground the corn, sewage and all is conducted over the land, and enriches the fertile apricot- and peach-orchards, corn-fields and vineyards. The great orange-gardens lie beyond in the rich river-deposit. There is no want of fruit round Tetuan: May sees pomegranates, apricots, peaches, figs, prickly pears, in due course; September brings the grape season; acres upon acres of gardens are covered with green muscats ripening on the dry ground, and protected from the sun by branches strewn over the plants.

West of the city, upon which side we rode in, there are fewer orchards and more fields. Since crossing the Wád Martîl a string of travellers had caught us up and passed us: a soldier as escort led the way; a rich Jew ambled on a fat brown mule hard behind; a muleteer and three starved mules laden with Isaac's worldly goods brought up the rear.

The muleteer, a happy fellow in a brown jellab, sang all the way, as he rode sideways on his beast. He begged a match from Cadour, produced a ragged cigarette from inside his turban, and lit it skilfully in the wind: he probably lived chiefly on cigarettes, kif, and green tea, eating when there was bread; he was lean and sun-dried as a shred of tobacco, would sleep in snatches and often, his jellab-hood over his face to keep off the sun or the dew.

We got very near a pair of snowy *ibis*, or cow-birds, as they are called, attending on two grazing cows. White as geese, parading about on black stilt-like legs, which raise them a foot or more off the ground, they have yellow bills and a slightly puffed throat, in flight extending their long legs behind them. Cow-birds wage war on the parasites of mules, donkeys, oxen, and sheep, hopping about the fields and dropping down on to their backs: they are never shot.

Morocco is by no means short of bird life. Only that morning, as we rode along, we saw several pairs of whin-chats, any number of crested larks, some plover, pied and grey wagtails, starlings, and a sand-martin. Starlings in Morocco fly literally in clouds like smoke, blackening the sky wherever they are surging and wheeling. A single shot into the middle of a flock has brought down from sixty to seventy of them.

We jogged up the last yard of rocky path, and found ourselves in front of Tetuan in rather less than four hours after leaving the fondâk, to the satisfaction of Cadour: it was an improvement on the day before. This ornament of the cavalry had now come out in a clean white turban, in view of entering the city: he puzzled us at this point by leading the way off the road to a white wall in the middle of the field, behind which travellers occasionally camp, devout people pray, and sheep are slaughtered at the time of the Great Feast. Here he produced our luncheon. But we, in the innocence of our hearts, would "lunch at a café" in Tetuan, after calling at the British Consulate and leaving our letters of introduction : this, with signs and a Spanish word or two, was brought home to Cadour, and we turned back, skirted the white city wall, reached a gate built in an angle, and rode in under the archway, passing a few figures in jellabs reclining and talking beside a great stone water-trough, which was running with fresh water.

Following one of the worst-paved streets upon Allah's earth, whose slippery rocks and pools of brown manure-water offered no tempting footpath, the first Union Jack we had seen for many a long day appeared above a wall and spoke *Britain*: towards it we made our way. A soldier in a long dark blue cloak and high-peaked red fez was sitting at the Consul's office door: he took our letters of introduction, and, without our being able to explain ourselves in Arabic, insisted on ushering us straight into the presence of the Consul—Mr. W. S. Bewicke.

We found him surrounded with papers and cigarette-ends: he would most hospitably take no denial in the matter of lunch, but made us come into the house at once. His long, narrow dining-room was flanked by a small kitchen; above, the same shaped, long, narrow sitting-room was flanked by a small bedroom; a flight of narrow, steep stairs divided all four rooms, and completed the Consulate: this simple plan is usual in a Moorish house of the sort, and admirably adapted for the Eastern habits of the people. The Consul considered it inadequate. A sunny, walled garden lay in front; big orange- and banana-trees, both covered with fruit, shaded precious seedlings; a large tank, filled with gold-fish, took up much space under the windows; and in the background a high cane fence penned in turkeys, geese, ducks, and chickens, scratching and squabbling under orange-trees. There are no grassy lawns in these gardens: they are are devoted to fruit, shrubs, and flowers, bisected into equal divisions by tiled or grass paths.

People in Morocco, as all the world over, collect curiosities *nolens volens.* Mr. Bewicke's dining-room was no exception. Guns from the Riff, eight feet long; brass powder-horns, knives, daggers, pistols, engraved and inlaid with silver, ivory, and coral; a long brass horn, once blown from the top of the mosque, sacred and difficult to get; copper vessels, pots, pans, jugs, bowls; blue china from Fez; quaint Jewish candelabra and lamps; brown and white native pottery,—all found a place.

A young Riffian named Mohr acted as butler, a coffee-and-cream-coloured boy, with a girlish face and a head with a close weekly shave, all except one long love-lock, which, combed out, fell over one ear in a glossy brown curl. It is worn by all Riffs as good Mussulmans, and serves a double purpose, that of scalp-lock when the head is decapitated by enemies and borne by the lock instead of by the mouth, and that of handle, by which Azrael, the Angel of Death, carries the body to heaven on the last day. Mohr wore a Riff turban of brown string, several yards long, wound round and round his head, a white tunic and belt: his legs were bare; and leaving his yellow slippers behind him on the threshold, he moved noiselessly round the table with gracious manners, and, when he spoke, made nonchalant gestures with his hands.

Had we come a few days earlier, we should have fallen in with a thousand men from the Beni Has'san tribe, who had come down to pay their respects to the new *basha* (governor) of Tetuan, and to offer him presents.

They had fired off a good deal of blank powder, and a stray bullet or two into the Consul's garden door; had rushed about the *feddan* (market-place), discharging their guns; and had thrown stones at some one. On their way to Tetuan the thousand odd had pillaged right and left, stealing fruit and robbing houses. Finding some women washing, they stole the clothes, and report said two women as well. At last twenty of them were caught and put into prison, after which the nine hundred and eighty marched back to their own country.

Lunch over, we walked with Mr. Bewicke into the city. While Tangier might be called an anæmic copy of a Moorish town, Tetuan has the strength of a *bonâ-fide* life-study, and all that is curiously beautiful, strangely obscure, is unsparingly suggested. The longer a European lives there, the more the paradoxes in Moorish life force themselves upon him, and the more tangible grow certain intuitions which his surroundings convey.

It is not only such contradictions as lie on the surface—the squalor of some filthy fondâk, the emaciated raw-skinned donkeys, the bent-backed women, rubbing shoulders with the white-scented robes, the sleek mules, the luxurious tiled houses—these a blind man could see: the under-currents which will puzzle an Englishman more the longer he lives there are known to those only who have dwelt much in Morocco, and they belong by every right to a life which is drawn to the letter in "The Arabian Nights."

The ramifications of the narrow streets in Tetuan would take a quarter of a lifetime to master, and then an unexplored alley might be found, though it is easy to walk across the entire length or breadth of the city in ten minutes. Down a dozen intricacies we dived with Mr. Bewicke, through a labyrinth, half dark in places, where houses built overhead shut out the sun. Looking along the narrow streets, the buildings jostle one another, and the flat blank walls slope backwards out of the upright, at every turn a haphazard colour-scheme in white and mauve and chocolate, in blue and ochre and cream.

Here a long dark tunnel opens into sunlight and shops on each side, with great vines trailed on trellis-work—like a pergola—overhead, and sunlight in blotches on the cobbled paving below: there, just beyond, the *Slipper Quarter*, and we find ourselves in the thick of the tap-tap of the mallets on the hard-hammered leather—dozens of busy little shops on each side, lined with yellow matting, and hung from top to floor with rows of lemon-yellow slippers for the men, rose-red slippers for women, embroidered slippers for the wealthy, crimson slippers for slaves, slippers with heel-pieces and slippers without. In each shop a man and boys at work: the white turbans and dark faces bending over the leather, the coloured jellabs which they wear, the busy hard-white-wood mallets in the deft brown hands, even the waxed thread, the red jelly which glues the soles together, the gimlets, the sharp scissors, have a passing fascination for the wandering Moor himself, who sits down lazily in front and talks to the workers. Still more for ourselves. Leather bags are being sewn next door and ornamented with work in coloured leather and silks. Within hearing of the "tap-tap" lies the skin-yard, and the skins are scraped and tanned and dyed and turned into slippers all in the same square acre or two, whence they depart many of them for Egypt and supply the Cairo bazaars.

A few steps farther, and there is a steady clanking of hammers on anvils, beating out hot iron—the *Blacksmiths' Quarter*. Not the old turbaned blacksmiths nor boys with shaved heads, in tunics grimed with age, and leather aprons sewn with red leather, nor the primitive bellows and quaint iron points, all being beaten out for the ploughs, are the features of the Blacksmiths' Quarter; but the sheep. Every forge has its sheep, every shop its pen like a rabbit-hutch, made out of the side of a box, where the sheep lives when it is not lying just at the threshold of the shop in the sun, beside a half-finished meal of bran in a box. Sheep after sheep, tame and fat, take up half the room in the street: there are sometimes a few hens, often a tortoiseshell cat curled up on a sack, but to every shop there is always a sheep fattening, as no other animal in Morocco fattens, against the *Aid-el-Kebeer* (the Great Feast), when every family kills and eats its own mutton.

The little shops in Tetuan group themselves together more or less. There is another quarter where sieves are made, a corner where baskets and the countrywomen's huge straw hats are plaited, another where carpenters congregate, and an open square where rugs, carpets, and curios cram the shops, and so on.

We left the warm heat from the glowing cinders and the cascade of sparks, and walked on into the *feddan* (market-place), which was teeming with women from the hills and villages round, come in to sell provisions.

The *Jews' Quarter* lies on one side of the feddan, shut in by a gate at night and locked—a squalid, noisy, overpopulated spot, where the worst-kept donkeys and most filth are to be met with. Tetuan is a clean city: on every animal killed the "butchers" have to pay a tax; the tax goes towards the sweeping of the streets once a week, and towards their paving—that is, if the basha is conscientious: the last basha ate and drank the tax.

A gutter runs down the middle of the streets, where

chickens are killed, and the heads and uneatable parts of flesh, fish, and fowl thrown. Mules and donkeys walk along the gutter, while foot-people flatten themselves against the walls. A well-laden mule fairly absorbs the width of the little streets.

The condition of these wretched transport animals is not due so much to wanton cruelty as to neglect, and to a callousness bred of long familiarity. A Moor will not trouble to prevent his beasts having sore backs and fistulated withers and raw hindquarters, any more than he sees that his children are warmly clad and suitably fed. Fond of both, he is foolish and apathetic, treating his mules roughly, cramming them with unnecessary food or neglecting them, and invariably working them till they drop.

One or two little cafés we passed round the feddan, and banished any connection between them and lunch for ever and a day.

A little room in the shade hung with yellow matting, no chairs, but a wide divan at the far end, where a few Moors sat cross-legged or reclined, smoking long pipes of soothing kif, and eating the pernicious haschisch—this constitutes a café. A few of the Moors are playing cards; the rest look on. A dome-shaped pewter teapot, filled with a brew of steaming tea, stands on a low table, with a painted glass beside it half full of mint, which a freckled boy in a coarse jellab fills up from the teapot to the brim and puts to his lips; then he lights a cheap cigarette. A great urn, with an oil lamp under it, stands in one corner.

No self-respecting Moor patronizes these cafés: he is the most fanatical of Mohammedans in a land reputed to be more strictly religious than any Eastern country. In public he observes his Prophet's laws, only indulging *sub rosa* in smoking—" eating the shameful," as it is called.

Mohammed knew very well that Eastern peoples drink to get drunk, and smoke and eat opium for the purpose of intoxicating their senses. *Kif,* a herb something like hemp, produces this effect on the brain. He therefore forbade both.

When a Moorish " swell " wants to amuse himself, instead of passing the time at a café he goes out for the day into the country. There is generally an expression of perfect satisfaction with life as he finds it, on his lineless biscuit-coloured face and in his brown agate eyes—a content seldom expressed under the top-hats in the Park. Time is to him no " race " : he drifts easily down the years; knows no other home than, it may be, Tetuan ; nor is conscious that Tetuan sleeps, as it has slept for ages, curled up, underneath the towering hills, white, petrified, like Lot's wife.

Still down more streets, and on towards the Belgravia of the city we walked, leaving steaming little hot-fritter shops, where *sfins* are fried in oil and eaten with honey, where cream tarts may possibly be made and honeyed cakes, and crisp pastry prepared with attar of roses, and candied musk lemons, and dates mixed with almond paste. We left the fried-fish shops and fried spitted-meat shops behind, whence emerge *kabobs*—second only to *coos-coosoo*—and a smell indescribable ; and we wound down tortuous alleys, past quiet windowless houses, whose great painted doors, yellow and brown, studded with enormous nails and knockers, spoke respectability.

Never a straight street for six yards. Here an angle with a door ; turn down under an archway : there a tiny branching alley, which we follow : here another door ; plunge down the opposite way. A woman passes us with a friend, walking as only women in Morocco walk—figures in creamy haiks of the finest wool, which swathe them entirely from top to toe like a sheet, a pair of eyes barely showing between the folds. At the bottom of the haiks a flash of colour obtrudes, tomato in one, beetle-green in the other, and filmy muslin over both, which in their turn allow a glimpse of ankles wrapped round in snowy linen folds—rose-pink, gold-embroidered slippers completing the whole, suggestive of a tea party.

A yard farther and we pass *El-Jama-el-Kebeer* (the Big Mosque), which, unlike that at Tangier, stands with its doors wide open, but in front of which no infidel may linger. There was a vision of a cool tiled courtyard and splashing fountains of white marble and clean yellow matting, of endless tiled pillars vanishing into shade. There are saint-houses in the city where women are allowed to pray, but only upon one night in the whole year in El-Jama-el-Kebeer—a field-day among the wives and concubines, who flit like white moths through the darkness in flocks to worship, carrying red-and-blue lanterns.

At last we reached the house of the Moor upon whom Mr. Bewicke intended us to call—a specimen of the best Moorish houses.

Alarbi Abresha has been nicknamed "the Duke of Westminster"—the wealthiest man in Tetuan. A slave responded to the hammer of the great knocker, demanded who knocked, and then opened the door. Alarbi Abresha was out; but his son, a youth badly marked with small-pox, received us, dressed in a jellab of pale blue, tasselled, and worked in white. Mr. Bewicke asked after *the house*. No one in Morocco inquires after the wife or family distinctively.

A long passage led us into a large *patio* (courtyard), in which orange-trees were growing. It was open to the sky,

ALARBI ABRESHA'S HOUSE.

Photo by A. Cavilla, Tangier.

A Moorish Courtyard House

the floor tiled with shining tesselated tile-work; a marble fountain rippled in the middle: the dado round the four walls, the three rows of pillars which on all sides supported the gallery above—all were tiled in the same mosaic of small saffron-yellow, powder-blue, and white tiles, which are baked, coloured, and glazed in primitive potteries outside the city, and made only in Tetuan and Fez. A Moorish house is the essence of purity and light, with its whitewashed walls, its absence of all stifling furniture, and its capability of being sluiced down from top to bottom every day with rivers of water by barefooted slaves.

"The Duke" had spared no dollars to make his house beautiful. Of the triple row of arches, supported by the pillars round the patio, the outside row was a plain horseshoe, the inner toothed, the inmost carved. Through an avenue of pillars the rooms all round the patio look out upon the fountain and the orange-trees. Slaves occupied them. The kitchen also and the hummum are always on the ground floor. We were taken up to the first floor by the tiled staircase, with a plaster fan-shell ceiling, and were shown into the best room—the room belonging to the master of the house. The tiled floor was hidden by an ugly modern French carpet in strips: white and coloured mattresses were laid all round the walls upon the floor instead of chairs. Two immense brass bedsteads stood in recesses, blue silk four-posters; a great cushioned mattress on the carpet beside the bed is reported to be used by the wife; a slave will often sleep in the same room. The lower half of the whitewashed walls was hung with ancient silk brocaded hangings, a long-forgotten relic of the old wandering life as nomad Arabs, and still used by Arabs for the insides of their tents. The richer the owner, the better his silk hangings: the design is invariably a succession of horse-shoe arches, more or less embroidered, and giving the rooms a warm, luxurious air. In the mosques very fine mats are used; in ordinary houses, cafés, and shops, yellow matting lines the walls. Above the old hangings the Duke had hung a line of immense and tawdry gilt-framed mirrors. There were clocks in the room to the number of ten, some of them going; two inlaid cabinets; three cases of artificial flowers under glass; a great wooden coffer—the wife's property—holding a wardrobe of clothes; a gun on one of the walls; a rosary; a thermometer made in Germany: these were the only knick-knacks. Moorish rooms combine bedroom with sitting-room, but are devoid of washing-apparatus, tables, chairs, books, or pictures. Bathing is done in the hummum or in the courtyard of the mosque; of books there are none; while pictures Mohammed forbade, as inclined to lead to idolatry. Query: have many artists been lost to the world in fourteen hundred years among a sect numbering a hundred millions?

The ceiling and woodwork of the room were painted in barbaric, gaudy hues, which mellow with age and "tone" like a faded Kashmir shawl. A row of tiled pillars divided the room lengthwise, and raised the inner half a step above the outer: it was immensely lofty, lighted by the great double doors only, which stood wide open on to the patio. Glass is not used in Morocco: the windowless rooms are aired by the unfastened doors which look on to the patio, itself open to the winds of heaven. The outside world can have little idea of the life going on within the courtyard house: there is much seclusion therein, in fitting harmony with the spirit of Morocco.

Fireplaces do not exist, though from December to March the thermometer has sometimes, on single occasions, touched freezing-point at night. Earthenware pans of

A Moorish Household

charcoal, used for cooking, can be carried upstairs for warmth.

The other rooms in Alarbi Abresha's house were all more or less replicas of the best room shorn of its gilt. As the laws of the Medes and Persians, so is the arrangement of the matresses (*divans*) round the walls inside a Moorish house.

A Moor does not spend his day indoors. He eats and sleeps at home, but is otherwise sitting talking with his friends in the city, or in his shop, or out at his garden-house or fields.

He eats in any one of the divanned rooms in which he happens to be at the time, his rule being to "sleep where you will and eat where you will." A slave carries in his dish of meat on a tray, and puts it on a table four inches in front of the divan. Beef, mutton, and chicken are cooked in oil till they fall apart and can be eaten with the fingers. He eats vegetables and fruit, murmurs a "B˙ism Allah" beforehand and a " Hamdoollah " (God be praised) at the end ; washes his hands ; drinks green tea, or begins his meal with it and bread of fine white flour. His wife has the refusal of the dish after her lord, never eating with him ; and the slaves follow her. As many as five dishes may be brought up at a meal ; and the master of the house, sampling each, chooses which he will eat, and sends the rest away. If he has a guest, it is the height of politeness to select small pieces off the dish and put them within the guest's reach, or, still better, into his mouth.

Moors, unless they are wealthy men, eat "by the eye"—that is, not according to what they require, but according to that they see set before them: frequent hiccups express gratification at hospitality received, accompanied by "Hamdoollah." The amount which a Moor can eat is prodigious. There was a man at

Fez who was reverenced as a saint by his neighbours, because he had been known to eat a hundredweight of *coos-coosoo* (porridge) and a whole sheep at a sitting.

Alarbi Abresha, Junior, meanwhile, took us on into his father's guest-house, a suite of magnificent rooms, decorated in execrable taste, the barbaric glories of the old Moorish style giving place to modern French vulgarity. A courtyard house can be a strange mixture. Its woodwork, possibly *arrar*, a cypress of beautiful grain, scented like cedar, cinnamon-coloured, and immensely hard (out of which the Roman patricians cut their precious tables, valued at their weight in gold if as much as four feet wide: beams of arrar put into the Córdovo Mosque by the Moors a thousand years ago still exist); its old silk hangings; its tiles, kept polished like jet, and never desecrated by anything harder than a slippered sole,—all alike are the finest relics of a taste which ruled in the construction of the Alhambra, where Mauresque design is seen at its best. The aristocrats of Tetuan are descendants of the old Andalusian families, who, having left Morocco and invaded Spain, settled there, built the Alhambra, were in the course of time driven back over the seas, and took refuge in Tetuan and other coast towns. Their very title-deeds, together with the keys of their houses in Granada, are still in the possession of their descendants in Tetuan.

While the best work in the courtyard houses of to-day harks back to the brave days of Spain, the Moor of the twentieth century has less of the vitality and originality which distinguished his forefathers, and he is apt to mix cheap up-to-date decoration with the patio and the windowless wall, of which the Duke's guest-house may stand for an exemple.

When the great door had shut behind us, and we

were outside in the street again, it seemed both narrow and prosaic after the sunny patio, with the yellow-fringed orange-trees almost branching into the rooms, and the fitful accompaniment of running water, dear to the Moorish ear.

In the course of the afternoon Mohammed, Ali, mules, and baggage put in an appearance, and we found them waiting in the feddan, anxious to put our tents up in the middle of the noisy, crowded sok, where the wind, which had dropped but little, was whirling dust round in clouds, and where we should have been the centre of a staring throng—at the same time, an ideal place in the servants' eyes, suggesting cafés and conversation the whole night through. The camping-ground which "the infidel" selects is an insoluble puzzle to the Moor, and they went off mystified and disappointed, under orders from the Consul to pitch the tents outside the city.

Later on we followed, by a street redolent and sweet with honey, of which a great quantity had just come in from the Riff country, leading to *Báb-el-Aukla* (the Gate of Wisdom), so called because the elders of the city, the wise men, used to sit outside on some of the great rocks: a fine two-storied, square-shaped gateway, with a pointed arch and toothed ornament above it. Three little windows overlook the arch; the black noses of small cannon protrude in a long row out of the white parapeted walls; a flagstaff tops the whole, and flies the crimson streamer of Morocco. A line of sea-green tiling beneath the cannon breaks the flat wall, where the heads of turbulent tribesmen hang occasionally, sent over from some neighbouring raid by the Sultan's orders, and first salted by the Jews in the city, *nolens volens*. The cobbles were slippery under the gate. The huge, heavy wooden doors, studded with iron bolts, are barred and locked every night half an hour after sunset. Inside, looking back, just at the parting of two streets, a great white wall faced us, topped with green tiles, grass-grown ; below, a horse-shoe arch, somewhat in relief, belted with coloured tiles, defaced by age, contained a long solid stone trough, into which two spouts of water gushed—never dry in this city of springs. Mules and donkeys and country-folk all stop and drink, and the front of the trough is carved.

Báb-el-Aukla is the finest gate in the city.

Go where you will in Tetuan, at every turn water bubbles into time-worn and artistically moulded troughs and basins, under quaint arches, tiled in blue and brown and white. In the narrow winding street-ways, between the houses, half dark, still the bubbling of water is heard, and the shining wet trough seen.

As we left the city and walked down the sandy road which leads to the sea, our tents lay a quarter of a mile off, two white spots, pitched on grass just off the road, the mules picketed by them.

We had a somewhat light meal at six o'clock, Mohammed's chicken turning out like hammered leather. He was no cook.

An Arabic proverb says, "What is past is gone, and the future is distant; and to thee is the hour in which thou art." It was obviously never intended by the Creator that mankind should make plans. Morocco may have its drawbacks, but it is at least one of those few and blessed spots where it is waste of time to plan : life is a matter of to-day, and

> To-morrow ?—Why, To-morrow I may be
> Myself with Yesterday's Seven Thousand Years.

Thus some time that evening, when, after coping un-

OUR CAMP OUTSIDE TETUAN.

[*To face p.* 60.

Decide to Stay On at Tetuan

successfully with the chicken, it struck R. and myself that Tetuan had attractions over and above the head of Tangier, we settled then and there to stay on at Tetuan as long as we liked the place, though the weather looked very much like rain, not at all like camping out, and we had no clothes with us to speak of.

Overcoming or ignoring these difficulties, we finally decided to pay off our three men, send them back by themselves to Tangier with the tents and camp outfit, write to the Villa Valentina, pay our bill, have our boxes packed up and sent over to us at Tetuan by muleteer, and move ourselves into the Spanish *fonda* (inn) inside the city. Thus were we left for the next six days with one clean collar apiece.

In Tangier there had been some speculation on the elasticity of the Spartan wardrobes which we had brought out from England, at a moment when the dread of a vast impedimenta happened to lie strong upon us. In Tetuan such panics bury themselves. The slimmest wardrobe will suffice. A country's own materials, whether home-spun of Kashmir or sheep-skin coat of Afghanistan, naturally meet its requirements best: deficiencies are easily supplied, and later on we lived in mufti off the backs of Tetuan sheep.

Lying in bed in the early morning before it was light, duck were to be heard calling up the river; and, breakfast over, we strolled down to the banks, where the thick green orange-trees on the opposite side bore a crop of cow-birds, sitting like a covey of white cockatoos on the tips of the branches among the golden oranges, so thick and snowy that the tree might well have burst into abnormal flower.

By nine o'clock the camp was struck, and we had burnt our ships: the last of the five mules, three men, and baggage tailed off out of sight along the road to Tangier.

Under a cloudy sky, prophesying rain, we walked into the city to look for quarters: better, perhaps, a fonda in Tetuan than a tent at the fondâk in wet weather.

CHAPTER III

DIFFICULTIES OF " LODGINGS " IN MOROCCO—A SPANISH FONDA—A MOORISH TEA PARTY—POISON IN THE CUP—SLAVES IN MOROCCO—EL DOOLLAH—MOORISH CEMETERY—RIDE TO SEMSAR—SHOPPING IN TETUAN—PROVISIONS IN THE CITY.

CHAPTER III

> This by God's grace is *El Moghreb*—Morocco—and here a wise man is surprised at nothing that he sees and believes nothing that he hears.

IT is not easy to find a lodging in Morocco: there are no *dâk bungalows*—no large white English residences, with the familiar and hospitable *Burra Sahib*, a retinue of servants, spare horses, and a spacious bedroom at the disposal of the unexpected guest. Hotels, except at Tangier, are impossible for any length of time, unless to the vagaries of Spanish or Jewish cookery the heart can harden itself.

We steeled our souls, assisted by the grateful sense of freedom from all petty society functions, which in the nature of things are unknown in a city where one vice-consul, six women missionaries, and a post-office alone represent the British flag—where there is no English doctor, no English church.

Tetuan met all our needs: the only question was where to live.

Immediately outside its walls lies a land of gardens and orchards. Every Moor who can afford it has a garden, wherein he cultivates grapes and fruit-trees,—a dim reflection of that Paradise of his, which must be chequered with acres of shade cast by great rocks and gigantic olive-trees; which must be abundantly watered by running brooks of milk, honey, and wine; whose soil shall be flour, white as snow. The Moor's Garden of Eden reserved for the faithful after death bespeaks abundance and repose, differing but little from a certain Heaven of Epicures, wherein *pâtés de fois gras* were eaten to the sound of trumpets. Somewhere in his garden outside Tetuan he builds himself a garden-house, to which in the summer he migrates with his wife and slaves and the children of both, his divans, carpets, and kitchen utensils: the town house is locked up and stands empty while he spends four or five months under his vines and figs.

At the time we arrived in Tetuan—early December—not a garden-house but still lay empty; and naturally in their direction our longing eyes turned—an impossible desire, it was said, thereby clinching the resolve to make a superhuman effort to bring it to pass: between living in the city and a garden there could be no choice. In the meantime a Spanish fonda must constitute a make-shift until that came which is laid down for those who wait.

Inside Tetuan two hotels presented themselves. With fonda number one we could not come to terms; it was not attractive-looking: we took a high-handed line and left. Fonda number two, after much haggling in Spanish, agreed to take us both at the modest sum of seven-and-sixpence a day, all included. No sooner was the bargain struck than a messenger arrived post-haste from fonda number one, to say that they would take us at our own terms. Their golden opportunity was lost. Report said fonda number one might be a trifle cleaner, but fonda number two had the better cook: the inside man carried the day in favour of number two.

It was one among many flat-roofed whitewashed houses in the Moorish Quarter, in a street barely six feet wide. There was no outlook except from the roof-top, where

A VEILED FIGURE OUTSIDE THE GATE.

[*To face p.* 66.

the washing dried : there were no windows, the rooms depending for light upon double doors opening on to the tiny tiled patio—except in our own case, where the second room allotted to us was built over the top of the street, and had two windows cut in the walls by the Spanish occupants, neither of which quite shut, and provided us with an ample supply of air. The room beyond possessed dilapidated doors, which gave upon the patio. The patio was, of course, open to all the rain of heaven as well as to all the sun : it was the principal sitting-room of the family, where, downstairs, on fine days, they plucked chickens, made bread, washed, sat and received callers, did needlework and chattered ; on wet days creeping disconsolately round the lake of water in the middle of the tiled floor, where the rain dropped—splash—taking refuge on one sheltered seat in company with three dogs, a cat, and a tame chicken, or retiring into the dark little rooms which surrounded the lake.

The family comprised Spanish parents, married daughter and husband, three unmarried sisters, a brother, and a lodger—an old Spanish music-master. The fonda was run by the married daughter, a lady with a temper, who made everybody else work : her mother and one sister cooked ; the second sister was busy with a trousseau and a young man ; the third and prettiest—Amanda—waited on us. On the whole we were not uncomfortable, in spite of the Spanish element. Our rooms were clean : one afternoon we found a chicken sunning itself in a patch of sunlight on the floor of one—nothing worse. Dinner was sometimes, and Amanda was always, lacking in certain points to a critical eye. Sometimes it was a skirt, sometimes a petticoat, she wore : except on high days, it was doubtful and dependent upon chance threads and pins. All Amanda's blouses were low-necked, whatever the time of day : the stains and slits and remnants of torn frills were unique. She wore her sleeves turned up, and silver bangles on her arms. Amanda never buttoned her boots, and often put in an appearance with bare feet.

But Amanda was redeemed by her head-dress and her manners. She wound a crimson shawl gracefully over her dark head, after the fashion of a mantilla, with an effect beyond reproach. Amanda had a gracious way of putting things : she bore herself with infinite dignity, and a *je-ne-sais-quoi* which pointed to a mixed ancestry ; she had well-shaped hands.

At seven o'clock in the evening her knock preceded preparations for dinner, while she munched something or hummed a tune meanwhile. Seas of thin soup invariably preceded a dish of shapeless masses of "soup-meat," garnished with boiled peas. The third course consisted of chicken or partridge : on less happy occasions foreign and "shudderous" dishes appeared ; a peculiar jelly shell-fish was the lowest ebb—that and pork we resented. Last of all, a tall glass fruit-dish would arrive, the standard sweet—*flan* (caramel pudding). Then a long pause. Finally, Amanda's step, with a great plate of hot toast and a tall tin coffee-pot : black coffee was the best part of the meal.

A day or two after settling into the fonda we were asked to our first entertainment in a Moorish house. Hadj Mukhtar Hilalli wanted Mr. Bewicke and ourselves to "tea" with him.

As in the case of "the Duke's" house, so here, all the womenkind were hidden away on account of the Consul. Mohammedans are jealous and suspicious of their wives and daughters to a degree, and strongly resent, if not prevent, an Englishman's going up on to the flat roof, lest he have a view of fair occupants beyond or below.

Nevertheless, the wives always contrive to peep out of some loophole and see all there is to be seen.

Hadj Mukhtar Hilalli received us all three alone, as a matter of course, and led us upstairs to his best room. Like many others among the better class of Moors, our host had a shop and himself sold groceries. At the same time his sister is the wife of one of the Ministers; and as there is no respect of persons in Morocco, Hadj Mukhtar Hilalli might be called upon himself any day to fill a high official position, and be obliged to go, raising money, if he had not wherewithal to support the post, which, if a lucrative one, would soon repay the outlay.

Trade at Tetuan, and apparently everywhere else over Morocco, is not what it once was: the old flintlocks, inlaid with silver wire and lumps of pink coral, are unknown since the last gun-maker died; snuff-nuts, even slippers, do but a small business. Living is more expensive than it was: it cost Hadj Mukhtar three shillings a day to feed himself and the whole household, he said.

The room into which we went—our host leaving his yellow slippers in the doorway, and motioning us all to sit down on the divans round the walls—was hung with a silk dado, tiled in mosaic, and overlooked a good-sized patio with a running fountain.

Our dirty boots compared unfavourably with the Hadj's clean, bare feet, which, as he sat down cross-legged on the white and embroidered cushions, were hidden underneath his voluminous garments; whereas ours, not to the manner born, contracted cramp, unless stuck out in an ungainly way.

A gorgeously upholstered bed filled up one corner of the room; a gun hung on the wall. There was nothing else.

Three little sons of the house and Mr. Bewicke's soldier-servant having followed us in and seated themselves, preparations for tea—already waiting, arranged in front of the divans on four brass trays, standing on four low tables a few inches high—began.

Hadj Mukhtar Hillali, sitting on his heels in front of his tea-table, making tea with his thin brown hands, and presiding over it all with true Oriental dignity, was a veritable Moses or Aaron reincarnated. Women and men alike mature rapidly in this country, putting on flesh and becoming matronly and aldermanic without at the same time growing lined or aged: a wealthy man of twenty-five is portly and slow of movement—the result of Eastern habits coupled with the climate.

Hadj Mukhtar Hilalli, barely forty years old by his own account, had a white beard and moustache, no wrinkles, eyes of mild blue and benign expression, equally guileless and unfathomable.

Talking in Arabic to Mr. Bewicke, he drew the tray close to the low divan in front of him, saw that his sons provided cushions for our backs, and proceeded to wash the green tea in a bright nickel pear-shaped teapot, with water from the great brass urn which stood over a charcoal-burner: the washed tea was then transferred into a twin teapot, which the Hadj generously filled with immense lumps of sugar out of a glass dish standing on a tray by itself, stacked high with great blocks split off the cone with a hatchet. Heavy with lump sugar, a handful of mint and bay leaves was also crammed into the little remaining space in the teapot, the boiling water out of the urn was turned on over all, filling up every chink, the lid shut down upon the steaming fragrant brew, and the teapot set back upon the brass tray, the centre of a ring of tiny gilt and painted glasses.

The eldest son—a boy of fourteen, dressed in red,

A Moorish Tea Party

and wearing a leather belt embroidered with blue, and a fez-bag fastened thereto to match, whose head had evidently had its weekly shave that afternoon—lit a lamp underneath a little incense-burner, filling it with sticks of sweet-scented wood, till an odoriferous blue smoke rose from it. With much care he carried the burner to us, and put it inside our coats, thoroughly impregnating every thickness with warmth and odours of cedar-wood. It was taken last of all to Mr. Bewicke's soldier, who manipulated it correctly as a Moor, putting it inside his flowing apparel, and sitting down with every fold closed in round him like a miniature tent, the burner smoking away inside. A scent-spray was then handed, with which we anointed ourselves in Moorish fashion, inside our hats, up our sleeves, and round our necks.

Meanwhile, Hadj Mukhtar Hilalli poured out tea with a great elevation of the teapot, raising his arm and showing greens and blues mixed to perfection underneath his *k·sa* —a white woollen or silk robe worn only by gentlemen— which, semi-transparent and gauze-like, fell in white waves over his shoulders on to the divan. Under the k·sa was a long garment with wide sleeves and buttoned all down the front—a *kaftan*—of sea-green cloth, embroidered with gold. The kaftan just revealed a waistcoat of a shade of blue, with gold and green buttons and embroidery. Underneath this, and above his white cotton shirt and drawers, he probably wore a woollen jacket. But greens and blues and gold were alone visible. Sometimes several kaftans or several jellabs are worn one on top of the other, all colours mixed, particularly if the owner is travelling. Moors are a wool-clad people for the most part, due to the wet winter climate: the men's brown woollen hooded jellabs keep out the rain more or less, and the women's white woollen haiks answer the same purpose.

The Hadj turned up his sleeves as he made tea, the underside of them being embroidered for this purpose. It was ready by this time, and brought us on a brass tray by the eldest son. Though the little glasses are not capable of holding much, the violent sweetness and the flavour of mint prevent the uninitiated from doing justice to the regulation three cups which courtesy demands should be drunk. But it grows, even upon the European, that steaming golden-brown beverage, fresh and fragrant with sweet thymes, while something in the climate of Morocco tends to make sugar acceptable after a few weeks. We supplied ourselves with sponge cake, pounds of which were piled on a brass tray in front of us: sweet biscuits, toasted nuts, almonds, and raisins abounded on the same lavish scale; while a wicker basket, like a large waste-paper basket, was full of thirty or forty round cakes of bread, several sizes larger than a Bath bun, made of the finest semolina flour, flavoured with aniseed and baked a warm biscuit colour.

The Hadj pressed third cups upon us, but with the innate breeding of every Moor understood the limited capacity born of early days in Morocco. A Moor is nothing if not courteous, and, whatever his real feelings, conceals them under polite speeches. He will, as somebody has said, "cut your throat *most politely, most politely*," or with profound urbanity offer you a cup of poison.

Our host had sipped a first cup before allowing the tea to be handed round—a custom observed to assure the guest that the teapot was free from poison, and that no deadly drink was offered us, containing seeds which should propagate a horrible disease in the intestines, destroying life sooner or later. Poisoning is only too common among the Moors themselves, cases occurring almost every day in the country.

A Moorish Tea Party

Once, when Sir John Hay was having an angry discussion with a governor—Mokhta—coffee was brought in. Mokhta, as usual, took the cup intended for the Englishman, and put it to his lips, making a noise as though sipping it, but which sounded suspiciously like blowing into it, and then offering it to Sir John. Not fancying the bubbled coffee, he declined, saying to Mokhta, "I could not drink before you. Pray keep that cup yourself," and helping himself at the same time to the second cup, which he drank. Mokhta put down the cup which he had offered Sir John, and did not drink it.

Some one in Tetuan dies every year of poisoning. Wives frequently kill their husbands. No two brothers, both in ministerial offices at Court, would dream of sitting down and eating together without precautions beforehand, on account of *the marked pieces* in the dish. One brother, as he dines, may invite the other, who happens to enter, to join him in the meal; but he will reply, "I have already dined." *He dare not.*

Meanwhile, Hadj Mukhtar Hilalli talked away in Arabic to Mr. Bewicke, who translated for us. He said that Menebbi, the Minister of War who went over to England with the last embassy, and who is practically Prime Minister, lost a considerable amount of influence during the short two months he was away, but that he was rapidly gaining ground, and might be said to be completely restored to favour again. Menebbi is the only one of the Sultan's Ministers who is likely to help him to reform the Government of Morocco. A clever, crafty brain, the whole Court under his thumb, it yet needed but an absence of eight weeks to generate in that hotbed of Eastern intrigue such a tissue of false evidence and lies as nearly cost Menebbi his position, if not his life. His enemies possessed the Sultan's ear; every Menebbi had been removed from the army; he had probably not a single friend left in Morocco. With the fickleness of their race, his name was cursed at every street corner; and when spoken of, the people said, "There *is* no Menebbi." Hurrying back from England, the tidings of his fall reached Menebbi when he landed at Mazagan: he was to be arrested. But the man they had to deal with was one of those few who make a full use of every opportunity life ever offers. From Mazagan to Morocco City, where the Court was, a distance of a hundred and forty miles, he had a relay of mules and horses posted, and he rode without stopping. There were dead and sorry beasts left on the road that day. Menebbi rode up to the cannon's mouth, so to speak: he need never have gone to Morocco City, but that would have meant his sinking into private life and his banishment from Court; he preferred to "play to the uttermost," and he staked life and fortune on the card he held. Things in Morocco City hung on an eyelash: the great man galloped in from Mazagan, went straight to the palace, never paused a moment, straight to the Sultan's private door, straight into the presence itself. And who shall say what Menebbi said to the Sultan through that night which he passed with him—what false accusations he refuted, what diplomacy he used? Next day Menebbi was not at prayers; he was "sick": in other words, he had tidings of a plot to kill him on his way to the mosque. However, in time he righted himself: now his enemies are under his heel, and Menebbi breathes again.

The Hadj spoke of the great wish the Sultan has to visit England—an impossibility, for in the eyes of his fanatical subjects he would be countenancing the unbelievers, and his throne would be handed over to a successor: the throne

The Sultan of Morocco

to which he succeeded, for the first time in the history of Morocco, without having to fight his way to it—a fact owed to the Wazeer's sagacity. Keeping the death of the old Sultan secret for a few days, the Wazeer meantime bribed and forced the Ministers to accept the young heir as Sultan, hurried to Fez, summoned every citizen to the mosque, had the doors locked, proclaimed the news of the Sultan's death, and surprised or forced the whole mosqueful into swearing allegiance to the present ruler.

So far the Sultan knows only two or three places in his whole kingdom, and has practically spent his life at one—Morocco City, or *Marrakesh*, as the Moors call it. Nor would his journeys be reckoned blessings by the unfortunate country through which he passed. Only able to move with an army, that army, without any commissariat or transport, feeding itself upon its march, wipes corn and food off the face of the land as a sponge wipes a slate. " Where the Sultan's horse treads the corn ceases to grow." He seldom travels with less than thirty thousand followers; and, supposing he is passing through a turbulent tribe, fights his way as he goes, leaving ruin and desolation behind. " They make a desert, and they call it peace."

Hadj Mukhtar Hilalli had travelled considerably farther afield than his sovereign ; he knew Genoa, Marseilles, Egypt, and of course Mecca. The Mussulman pilgrims passing through Constantinople on their way to Mecca this year are, he told us, very numerous, the Sultan having ordered the fares on the Massousieh Company's steamers to be reduced one-half for them. He thought that about two thousand Moors would be leaving Tangier in the early spring for the pilgrimage, returning some three months later. Neither the Hadj's sons nor Mr.

Bewicke's soldier joined in the conversation, but continued steadily to consume tea, all eyes and ears.

At last the trays were removed; and there being no co-religious eye to shock, Hadj Mukhtar indulged in a cigarette, while we puzzled him with a few tricks of balance and reach, which pleased him quite as much as his boys: everybody tried their hands, and finally the Hadj sent his eldest son for an old, heavy sword, and, squatting on the floor, showed us a clever piece of leverage with it and his thumb, which it was in vain to try and imitate.

Watching our failures, he produced a snuff-box, a small cocoanut-shell, ornamented with little silver and coral knobs, with a narrow ivory mouthpiece, a stopper, and an ivory pin fastened to the cocoanut-shell to stir up the snuff inside—Tetuan snuff—noted for its pungent flavour. Hadj Mukhtar jerked the grains through the narrow mouthpiece into the hollow of the back of his thumb, where all Moors lay it, then lifted his hand up to his nose.

Near the door hung his rosary of ninety-nine beads, reminding the pious Mussulman of the ninety-nine attributes of God. Each of the ninety-nine beads corresponds to the name of some holy man, and as the bead is passed along with the hand the saint's name is murmured. Curious that the use of rosaries in the Spanish Church is said to have been borrowed first of all from the Spanish Moors.

The eldest son of our host was, his father told us, looking forward to beginning the Fast of Rámadhan this year—fasting, as he was only a novice, for half the day instead of the whole of it: evidently as much importance and excitement were attached to the prospect as later on would attend the boy's marriage. This same boy of fourteen is learning to write in Latin characters, for a Moor a most unusual and advanced step: at present he was only wearing a little red fez cap, not having reached the age of turbans, with all their dignified symmetry. The Korān was all the literature the boy would ever know. Strange that a strong and sober people should have for ages confined their studies to the Korān, an occasional Arab poet, and a sacred treatise or two. There is, as I have already said, no literature, no art, no science, in Morocco, and no architecture—the Korān forbidding, it is said, research or study in any line except that of religion. Geography is entirely unknown. Like Moors in general, Hadj Mukhtar may have heard of London and Paris, and might know the names Germany and Russia, besides Mecca; but none of the former would have any connection or "place" in his mind, and Morocco must be, he is confident, the finest country under the sun. If it were brought home to him that his country is in a decadent condition, he would reply that at least it is good enough for him as it is; and that if Europeans were allowed to exploit it and to settle therein, the end would be prosperity for the Western civilization, and a knuckling-under on the part of the Moorish—which is true.

We talked on upon one and another subject till it grew late, but before we left our host took R. and myself to see his wife, downstairs, in a smaller room. Five wives are allowed by Mohammed, but few Moors in Tetuan were rich enough to afford as many, and contented themselves with slaves. We were not impressed by the very plain, sallow-faced lady, with a black fringe and hard brown eyes, who shook hands with us, and from her likeness to the eldest boy was probably his mother.

The second son was evidently by a slave: there was no mistaking that likeness—a fat, happy individual, the greatest contrast to another slave, who, though well dressed, was pale and miserable-looking. Two or three other corpulent, smiling blackamoors made up the sum-total of the party in the downstairs room—most comfortable, lounging on the cushions, they looked, no mean advertisements of Hadj Mukhtar's "table." The principal and favourite wife possessed a noisy sewing-machine, which she proudly displayed.

Every Moor's establishment has its slaves—so many, according to his income: in Tetuan they are sold privately, and frequently exchanged one for the other, while the wives are as easily divorced. Every year something like three thousand slaves come into Morocco, chiefly from the Soudan: a few are stolen from Moorish tribes; the rest are brought in by Moorish traders, who catch them in various ways, such as scattering sweetmeats, or in hard times corn, round the villages, up to neighbouring coverts, just as a poacher at home entices pheasants with raisins, then pouncing out and carrying them off.

As there are no such things as Moorish women-servants, negresses and slaves of various types step into the gap, and the evil of this influx of black blood is seen in the deterioration of a fine race, and the increase of the type which tends towards thick lips, low foreheads, and sensual tastes. The slavery of Christians in Morocco, once common, has been by treaty abolished since the day when the savage Sultan Mulai Ismael had eleven thousand Christian slaves in Mequinez employed in building his walls, whose bodies, when they succumbed, were mixed in with the stones and mud of the buildings. Slaves are not ill treated in the present day, though now and again one may be flogged to death as the result of fault or the malice and slander of a jealous fellow-slave: as a rule they live happily; and if a female slave bears a male child to her master, by a law in the Korān both mother and son are *ipso facto* freed, though they continue to live on in the same house.

The last thing Hadj Mukhtar Hilalli showed us was his hummum, cunningly arranged to flank the kitchen fire at the back. A tiny room; but four of his wives and slaves could, he explained, take their bath in it at once. There was a small stone slab inside as a seat, and hot air came in by means of a pipe in one corner. The *hummum*, or Turkish bath, is partly enjoined by the Korān and partly taken for its own enjoyment; it is a feature of every Moorish house of any pretension, and largely used by men and women.

The evening was a dark one, and we picked our way back to the fonda by the light of lanterns: it is impossible to go out at night in Tetuan without carrying one; the streets are wholly unlit, and the refuse-heaps and central gutters unpleasant traps.

Next morning R. and I strolled out of the city in the direction of Ceuta by way of the *Báb-el-M'kabar* (the Gate of the Tombs). Just beyond this gateway congregates in the road *el doollah* (the drove)—that is to say, the mules and donkeys belonging to any one in Tetuan who has no work for them on that particular day. They are all left by their owners at this spot in the care of a tall, tattered Moor, whose business in life is to look after them; and there they lie in the sandy road or lean up against the hot wall or each other, one of the saddest sights on God's earth, some of them infant two-year-olds, all of them overworked and starved. About midday the drover drives his charges off to the nearest grass— such as it is—and the ragged squad troops along the stony track without bridles and without spirit to abuse its freedom. They have none of them packs or saddles, unless their sore backs are too deeply aggravated to allow of exposure to the flies and dust; and in due time, one by one, the old or the dying drop tacitly out of the ranks; a couple of days—the scavenging dogs' work is done—and only a tangled knot of bones is kicked away from the roadside by the feet of the living generation, which have picked up the scantiest feed, and are straying back citywards again in the late afternoon, to be called for outside the Báb-el-M'kabar each by its owner.

El doollah had not started; and leaving them all in the road below us, we passed the little knots of country-women who sit by the Báb-el-M'kabar selling myrtle for laying upon the graves, and wound our way uphill through the old Mussulman cemetery, with its quaint domed tombs and toothed, arched doorways, cracked, decayed, and yellow with lichen, half hidden among the tangle of bushes and wild flowers on the rough slope.

The older of the tombs are probably those of the first Moors who fled from Spain in the days of that great *trek* back to Morocco: a much later and very conspicuous dome belongs to a brave lady, who, not a hundred years ago, did her best to defend Tetuan against the Spaniards, fighting side by side with the Moorish troops, and, in the course of the siege, accounting for half a dozen Spaniards, thereby earning for herself in due course a Joan of Arc reputation and a public sepulchre.

The cemetery was overgrown with *ayerna* root, one of the commonest weeds in Morocco, poisonous when it is eaten raw, though it is possible, after boiling the root for ten or twelve hours, spreading it out to dry in the sun, and grinding it in a mill, to make a sort of bitter bread out of the flour, and to subsist upon that. This the poor

A MOHAMMEDAN CEMETERY.

[*To face p.* 80.

The Mueddzin

do to a great extent, whenever corn runs short and they have nothing but roots and grasses to fall back upon: their pale yellow faces and emaciated bodies tell a tale of the ayerna root. We grubbed some up with a little difficulty in the stiff clay soil with nothing but sticks to help. Fifteen inches down we found the root, a small whitish bulb, the size of a bluebell root.

There is much desolation about the old cemetery, with its crumbling ruins; but the sun struck a key-note of splendour, and turned the lichened stones into nuggets of gold.

A black raven sat on a grey rock above us and croaked; below lay the white city—white beyond all English ideas of whiteness. Two tall minarets, with simple straight lines, only a mosaic of green tiling let into their flat faces, cut the peaks of the mountains beyond. At a quarter past twelve a little white flag slowly mounted to the top of each mosque; an infinitesimally small black figure appeared against the sky; then leaning over the parapet and looking down upon the humming city, a cry broke from the figure, and was carried over to us upon the wind— a cry which rose and fell, most musical, most sonorous: "Allah Ho Akbar—Allah Ho Akbar." The black dot moved round the parapet, and east and west and north and south chanted the great summons to the Faithful to prayer. And then the little white flag was hauled down.

On the other side of the river the neutral-coloured villages could be picked out by their white saint-houses. Morocco is stuck as full of saints' tombs—fuller—than England of dissenting chapels. They stud the land. Moors rid themselves of much valuable energy in the erection, by countless thousands, of tombs to the memory of the eccentric or pious dead; and distances are measured, tracks marked, not from church to church as in Spain, nor from village to village as in England, but from saint-house to saint-house, each of which is village-green, club, or public-house rolled into one, where the men gossip, the pious read, travellers halt, offerings are brought the dead saint, and sick children arrive to be healed—all at a little whitewashed building with a dome like an oven outside, and a horse-shoe arch, an olive- or a fig- or a palm-tree, a flag-staff hung with morsels of rag, and often a spring of water. At four cross-tracks, instead of sign-posts, heaps of stones, cairns, are to be found, placed in such a way as to indicate the direction in which the next saint's tomb lies.

A saint-house or two spot the green plain below the cemetery, which merges into the seven miles of flats stretching from the city to the sea, the haunt of wild duck, plover, and snipe, among wastes of coarse grass, marsh, and red tangle. Coils of grey river lie upon the flats: the very flatness over which the stream snakes is at once most strong—serene.

As we walked down the hillside, a brown figure upon a flat-topped tomb was silhouetted against the plain: he raised himself, and then again prostrated his body to the earth, his face set to the distant belt of blue sea, worshipping towards Mecca.

That afternoon we visited Semsar, a village two or three hours' ride from Tetuan, up in the mountains to the west. R. had a sedate brown mule with no idea of exerting himself: my mount was a clever little grey, nervous and rather handy with his heels, nearly kicking me more than once when I dismounted or mounted carelessly. We rode, as usual, on the high-peaked Moorish saddles, covered with scarlet cloth, such as every Moor uses—the stirrup-leathers of twisted scarlet silk, several thick saddle-cloths underneath, the girths never drawn, the saddle only kept from slipping over head or tail by scarlet britching and breastplate. It is impossible to mount unless the stirrup is held. After repeating the sacramental word "B'ism Allah" (a Moor mounts and dismounts in the name of God), with a man at his stirrups, he sinks without an effort into his saddle, amidst a furbelow of white robes, which he has afterwards arranged carefully for him. Possibly for this reason he gets on and off as seldom as possible, hugging the convenient maxim, common among the Moors, that mounting and dismounting fatigue an animal more than carrying a burden. He rides with his knees up to his chin: he is a natural horseman, and looks at home in his practically girthless and quite shapeless saddle, which must have given him a pang, if ever he galloped for his life in front of his enemies, and reflected that his safety was dependent upon the breastplate. A man, before now, has, as he rode, unwound his waistcloth, and twisted it round his horse's neck, for further security against the saddle's slipping back.

Mr. Bewicke and his soldier rode with us: the latter a dark, lean-faced, unwholesome-looking man, unable, like so many of his countrymen, to grow any hair on his face—an obsequious individual too, inspiring little trust; below his long blue cloak he wore brown riding-boots, embroidered with orange, and fastening up the back with orange-thread buttons.

My little grey bustled along; but once or twice, when the road fell away into a steep drop, his weak hind legs gave under him, and he "sat down": we soon learnt the effect which merely shaking the feet in the great angular stirrups has on mules whose sides have often been in touch with the sharp points, and jogged forward wherever the bad road allowed.

We had left the city by another of its six gates—the *Báb-el-Toot* (Mulberry Gate), the old name pointing back to an energetic past, when mulberries, silk-worms, and silk-weaving flourished around Tetuan—when the cultivation of sugar-cane, cotton, and rice in Morocco was more than a memory.

Following for a time the road to Tangier, we branched off to the right, and took a rough path winding upwards, passing a spring where women wash clothes, three parts walled in, to prevent their being seen.

A little higher up and one of the countless saints' tombs came in sight—better known in this case as the Robbers' Tower, where brigands congregate at sunset, and from an excellent coign of vantage. keep a lookout on the Tangier road, to drop on any unfortunate so foolhardy as to be on it late in the day. After dark no Moor from Tetuan would walk near this sainthouse.

Only a few weeks after this very ride a man was murdered on the Tangier road, why or wherefore no one knew, except that his body was found, brought into Tetuan, and buried without further investigation, since his relatives were neither rich nor powerful enough to institute a search and demand compensation.

Robbery in Morocco is almost sanctioned by Providence; it is made so simple. The lonely tracks, the absence of police, the inconveniences of travelling, and the innumerable wells scattered over the country, almost sunk for the reception of inconvenient bodies—one and all tempt a man to turn brigand; and yet Europeans are seldom attacked, in view of the fine imposed upon the tribe in whose territory a crime is committed.

Thus the borders, where several tribes meet, are always unsafe country, one tribe disposing of bodies which they have done to death by depositing them in the territory of the next tribe. But even in "Christian-ridden" Tangier a German was knifed three years ago walking home, as was his custom, at dusk. He happened to have no money on him. His murderer was given up to justice— that is, the basha of Tangier said some one must die, and together with the fine the tribe outside Tangier produced a man, who was duly executed, though whether he was the murderer ......

Meanwhile, we were leaving the millet-fields behind us—stubbles, an occasional stalk three feet high, no lying for birds—and were in a country of wild lavender and stunted bushes: these consisted chiefly of cistus or else palmetto, a little dwarf palm, the fruit of which is eaten by goats, and the root by natives as a vegetable, while its fibrous leaves make rope and baskets and a hundred things. A bleak undulating country, which ran up into rocky blue gorges and grey peaks on the right hand. The path was almost blocked at one point by an immense cairn on the top of a ridge—a holy pile, upon which the devout Moor in passing casts a stone, because from this spot the mountain can be made out on which the venerated shrine of Mulai Abdesalam lies, in Beni Anos, the goal of thousands of pilgrims each year. Though it is within a day's ride of Tangier, the country for miles around is forbidden to any European, and two Englishmen only have penetrated into the sacred city of Sheshawan, which lies in the same district. Mr. Walter B. Harris and Mr. Somers, at different times, got inside, but only at sunset, and after lying in hiding all night had to flee for their lives at dawn.

Gradually we reached wilder and more rocky country, recalling Scotland as far as the open moorland went. If fir-trees were planted on the sheltered slopes, the fir-pins should, in conjunction with the natural soil, form land capable of growing vines—an idle dream in the Morocco of to-day.

Between two hills in front of us towered a cliff of rocky red limestone, which might once have formed the bed of some vast stream. Semsar lay where the waters should have struck the rock beneath as they fell: a more sheltered village could not be, facing south-east. The cliff above is still riddled with the remains of an old silver-mine, worked years ago by the Portuguese: the ladders and scaffolding inside have fallen to pieces, and after penetrating along dark tunnels on hands and knees for a certain distance an open shaft intervenes, and further exploration is impossible.

Semsar, nestled into its crevice, takes more or less the local brown; but among the thatched huts, rising one above the other like an uneven pile of mud terraces, a few walls were whitewashed, and of course a white village mosque stood guard over all on the top of a hillock. There is something a trifle "animal" in these villages, rough clusters of bee's-comb or ant-heaps or beavers' lodgings as they might be, assuming exactly the shade of their surroundings, as nests the colour of their hiding-places, or as the khāki-coloured sand-lizard, desert-lark, and sand-grouse of the great Sahara take on the yellow-ochre tone of that desert.

A friend belonging to Mr. Bewicke's soldier had ridden out behind us. He owned a garden at hand, and asked if we would go in and look at it. We stooped low under a white stone doorway, an imposing structure, invariably the entrance to every garden: the door generally painted Reckitt's blue, and kept locked with a key eight inches long, while on each side of the gateway the cane fence is tumbling to pieces and offering useful gaps to marauders—

A Moorish Garden

a curious inversion of the rule in Spain, where to this day they bar the window heavily and leave the door open.

Though to all appearance the owner was a hard-working Moor, the garden at any rate bore no great signs of expenditure of labour. We found ourselves in an overgrown wilderness of orange-trees, peaches, pears, figs, plums, damsons, cherries, white mulberries, quinces, jasmine, all overgrown and stabbed by the interloping prickly pear—a good fruit, too, in its way, and a "useful beast" as a hedge.

Half of his oranges were always stolen, the owner said; the remaining half brought him in from sixty to ninety shillings a year, selling perhaps at a shilling or two the thousand. He had evidently not the capital to get the half of what such fruitful soil could give with Gibraltar at hand for export, nor the means of securing to himself any money he made; and it is poor work putting money into the hands of the nearest extortionate sheikh. Yet his garden was, and is to every Moor, a source of great satisfaction and content: truly a field of the slothful, a garden where the mystic finds rest and heart's ease, and the two things which appeal most to sun-baked men—shade and water. It is enough in such a spot to drowse away the sunny hours amidst the hum of bees, the rattle of the tree-beetle; to muse upon some book of whose drift only a faint idea is intelligible, content to leave its problems in the limbo of the insoluble, where most of life's questions seethe harmlessly enough; then, turning, give thanks to Allah, who has made gardens for mankind, and doze again.

Farther on the path led us across streams banked with maiden-hair fern like rank grass. Water had worn the rock into grotesque shapes, a cavernous arch in one place, the banks, like a tunnel, almost meeting over our heads in another. Immense blocks of stone barred the way; it was not easy riding, but the mules climbed up and down rocky staircases with much tact, while we sat holding our breath.

Over one of these obstructions the breastplate of my saddle, which had only been fastened to begin with by three stitches of string, burst, and I found myself almost over the grey's tail: such a common occurrence that no Moor goes out without string and packing-needle handy; but this was past mending on the road, and I changed on to the soldier's mule, whose top-heavy saddle was no fit at all, and, shifting all over its back, required careful balance on the rider's part.

The road was only a few feet wide, and so overgrown that, as we jogged one after the other, trying to dodge grey arms of fig-trees, lying on the mules' necks under dark masses of foliage which shut out half the light, hatless, the stiffest bullfinch at home would have been ears of corn compared with what we went through.

At last, however, it came to an end, and the trail opened out into the village of Semsar. Nobody was to be seen; dogs barked as usual; some kids bleated inside a hut. We rode by the crazy hovels; a woman carrying water emerged, and a boy with a baby. Beyond the last brown erection we came to a saint's tomb. This meant the village green without any "green." Two or three country people sat in the usual meeting-place among trodden-down weeds, talking and smoking their long pipes, congregated round one busy man, who was chopping a log into a plough with an axe. Around the tomb was a group of olive-trees, preserved leaf and stick and all, not a branch even of dead wood off the ground removed, by reason of the sanctity of the spot. However small a grove, it would otherwise have been cut down, as afford-

A Ride

ing cover to robbers and *ginns* (evil spirits). Thanks to saints' tombs the traveller in Morocco still meets with clumps and occasional woods of olives. The sunshine glowed on their hoary twisted branches, and flecked the gnarled trunks; the grey foliage cast patches of dense shadow on the brown earth under the mammoths, whose broken lines and odd elbows supported such masses of quiet colour and solemn shade. We wound our way to the left among the huts. Of any road between them there was none; the mules could barely climb over some of the boulders among the refuse.

Once quit of the "green," we saw no one again, and got much mixed as to direction. Finally, we struck a path with a descent into a pool and below a fig tree, which, having made ourselves small, we circumvented, and discovered that it meandered in time to the outside of the village. Following, we wound southwards by a gorge along a rocky stream, which has the reputation of rising suddenly after rain, and not long ago drowned three mules.

Stepping-stones are not provided in Morocco, and it is generally a case of plunging through a stream to reach the opposite side. Near a city with good fortune a Jew may pass, the chance may be worth waiting for; but no Mohammedan Moor would carry an infidel across on his superior back.

In time a different path led us back to Tetuan, and we rode in by the Mulberry Gate at sunset, as the mueddzin was calling upon true believers to worship.

On fine days we made many such excursions, and exploited the country for miles round. Showery and doubtful days were devoted to the city and shopping.

Shopping in a foreign city tends towards the accumulation of white elephants, which, safely landed in England, work havoc in an English home. Long flint guns from the Riff, and old blue dishes from Fez, and orange-striped rugs from Rabat look strangely out of place with wall-papers and oil paintings. The East will never sit down with the West, and the adjuncts of either are bound to "fight." And yet we shopped.

There are fewer more interesting ways of studying the outside life of the people; a little gossip and less reliable information are all thrown in to the bargain. The little Tetuan shops are a species of club, for each Moor has certain shops at which he habitually sits and may be found with more or less certainty. While the owner and his goods remain inside the shop, there is room for two people outside on the sill or doorstep, and a couple of fat leather cushions are provided for them. Even Mr. Bewicke was in the habit of sitting every day at Hadj Mukhtar Hilalli's shop and hearing the news, between four and seven o'clock every evening.

He interpreted for us in our early days. We spent a whole morning buying *humbells* (striped carpets) at a shop where the owner was sitting on the floor playing chess with a friend and drinking green tea. All over Tetuan draughts and chess are played constantly on little boards, either on the doorstep or inside the shop. The game had its origin, like bridge and polo, eastwards of England, and was introduced into Europe after the Crusades, together with baths and other civilized habits. Our shopman looked exceedingly bored at the interruption. However, after much bargaining, we bought a humbell, having to point to everything we wished to buy, for no Moor likes a Christian to come inside his shop, because of his dirty boots. A Moor is either in a pair of clean yellow slippers, or else they are on the doorsill, and his feet are bare: he tosses all his silks, towels, embroideries,

OUT SHOPPING.

[*To face p.* 90.

carpets, on the floor, and sits among them, while the purchaser stands outside, points to the shelves and heap, and trusts to the owner's divining which particular silk handkerchief is wanted.

In another shop we found a second humbell, chiefly black and orange, the property of a taciturn individual in a snow-white *selham* (hooded cloak), a turban to match, with scarlet peak, a dark blue garment underneath the selham, and a complexion like cream and roses. He lay at full length on a pile of many carpets. We stopped in front of the shop. Neither rising, bowing, nor bustling about to show off his goods, the white figure lay still, looking dreamily through and beyond us. We were bores. In reply to a question of price, a long sum was murmured. At last we expressed a decided wish to inspect the humbell, and, slowly rising, he condescended to lift it from a shelf, his looks suggesting that he would prefer being left alone. Again we asked his lowest price. Twenty-one shillings. We offered sixteen. Without deigning to answer, he solemnly folded up the humbell and put it away, then folded one by one the goods which littered the floor, and stacked them above the humbell on the same shelf. Still standing in front of the shop, we repeated our offer of sixteen shillings. He shook his head decidedly, made a deprecating gesture, and prepared to sink again on his couch. Mr. Bewicke forbade us to offer more; we walked away. A voice said in Arabic, "It is yours," and the humbell was thrown after us; the sixteen shillings were received with a sigh as the shop-keeper resumed his couch.

Tetuan makes many artistic "towels," which form the ordinary dress of the countrywomen underneath their old enfolding yellowish-white woollen haiks; but for quite the majority a towel as skirt and a towel as cape are sufficient for all purposes. There is the rare addition of a pair of cotton drawers.

The strong substance and fast scarlet dyes make these towels no mean substitutes for curtains, except that, like native goods in general, they seldom quite match, and distract the soul which demands "pairs" in all and everything.

A Jew we visited in the Jews' Quarter had a fine carpet for sale, made farther south, something like a Persian, the ground whitish, with harmonious reds and greens. For a long time we sat and tried to bargain in his odd little den up a dilapidated staircase and nearly pitch dark: he wanted £5. The pattern was a little small. We came away without it. Some of the old *kaftans* (robes of coloured cloth or satin or silk brocade, embroidered with gold or silver, buttoned down the front and with wide sleeves) were well worth buying: none are made like them nowadays, for common material is used; unfortunately the best are often in tatters.

We visited the Slipper Market, and, sitting on the doorstep of one of the shops, gave directions for two pairs—blue velvet embroidered with gold, and milk-coloured leather embroidered with green. Size, price, and colour were duly discussed; rain came on, we sat on the doorsill sheltering, and the basha—Tetuan's governor—was criticised. The slipper-maker had not a good word for him. To begin with, it seems he has no money, is of no family, and aristocratic Tetuan refuses to "hob-nob" with him. He dislikes Tetuan after Fez, whence he was transferred, and where he made more money. The other day a neighbouring tribe sent him a present of so many dollars. At the same time they owed him certain taxes, in lieu of which he accepted the money, but pointed out that the present must follow in due course. None ever arrived, and the

Tetuan Market

basha sent his brother-in-law and a soldier to the tribesmen to ask an explanation of its non-appearance. The brother-in-law was tactless, incensed the tribesmen, and provoked them to bastinado him, whereupon the soldier lost his head, and fired his gun off into the air. He was promptly disembowelled.

The brother-in-law returned to the basha, stiff, but alive; and the country people give it as their verdict that the basha is a rapacious man. They threaten that they will no longer bring their produce into Tetuan to market, but will hold their own markets at some place chosen by themselves out in the country, and Tetuan shall come out to buy. Such a proceeding would be most inconvenient; for Tetuan is dependent for all its supplies on the country people, who hold their markets on Sundays, Wednesdays, and Fridays in the feddan, where they sit upon the ground packed in hundreds, their chickens, eggs, butter, and produce in general in their laps and at their feet. Their beef and mutton are but second-rate, and the shapeless lumps of lean, tough meat take double as long as an English joint to cook, and make but a poor show in the end, hacked by the unskilful butchers past all recognition. Goat and fish are to be had, sometimes partridges, hares, and rabbits, occasionally a haunch of wild boar. Fish came in on certain days when the wind was favourable: there was then a rush on the fish market, and almost a free fight over the great panniers full of shining silvery sardines, and over the bodies of the sellers seated on the ground. The successful carried off a handful each, and the cafés and fish shops were soon frying sardines for dear life, while the little streets were thick with the steam of native oil and butter. Some big fish, four and five feet long, came into market sometimes, and a small boy would be hired by a purchaser to carry one home across his shoulder, its great head hanging down behind, and underneath a pair of thin brown legs like little sticks hurrying along the street.

Bread in Morocco is "passing heavy," flavoured with aniseed and full of grit. Vegetables are to be had in abundance.

The slippers, which had been promised in three days, appeared in three weeks. Whenever we passed the shop we asked after them: always the same answer—*Mānana* (To-morrow). "No, there was no butter to be had to-day, but *mānana*." "No, the pillows were not finished yet, but *mānana*." "The boots left to be soled were not ready, but *mānana*." Tetuan lives upon *mānana*: it is the reincarnation of JAM YESTERDAY, AND JAM TO-MORROW, BUT NEVER JAM TO-DAY.

Equally exasperating was the habit of every shopkeeper of locking up his shop and going off to pray or eat or chat. If a shop had to be revisited and purchases exchanged, the owner was invariably out, and the door fastened with lock and key. At 12.15 a.m. nobody could ever be found, but was presumably at the mosque. Again and again we visited the same shop: one day the owner was at a friend's shop, the next at home, and so on. We gave him up, to see his sleek cross-legged figure seated inside the little cupboard the very next time we passed.

Walking by a saint-house on the outskirts of the city, devout and impoverished women were often to be seen there, visiting the shrine and carrying with them small vessels of food, which they placed on the ground for the spirit of the holy man to eat. The window of the shrine was tied with a hundred scraps of rag and dead flowers, bits of wood, and paper and oddments of all sorts. Empty earthenware bowls later on, and pariah dogs skulking around, licking their lips, told a tale; but if asked if

SHOPS IN TETUAN.

[*To face p.* 94.

Moorish Auctions

they really thought their saint would come up out of his grave and eat the food prepared for him, it was open to the Mussulman to answer the Christian, "And do you really believe that your dead friends come and smell the flowers you plant on their graves?"

Small-pox kills a great many Moors, and an incredible number are marked by the disease. It is looked upon much as measles are in England: cases are never isolated, and children are all expected to have it. Each year it is prevalent, and people may be passed in the street with it out upon them; but every four years it breaks out seriously, and a large percentage of the population dies.

Last of all, in our shopping days a few things we bought by auction. No auctioneer is employed as in European countries, but the owner and seller himself perambulates the street or courtyard with his goods—a mule, or a frying-pan, or a carpet—calling out each successive bid which he receives on his article, pushing his way and jostling the motley mob of market people, peasants and loungers, silks and rags, until he has got his price, and hands over to its new owner his late possession.

CHAPTER IV

THE FAST OF RÁMADHAN—MOHAMMED—HIS LIFE AND INFLUENCE—THE FLOOD AT SAFFI—A WALK OUTSIDE TETUAN—THE FRENCH CONSUL'S GARDEN-HOUSE—JEWS IN MOROCCO—EUROPEAN PROTECTION.

CHAPTER IV

Manage with bread and butter till God brings the jam.
Old Moorish proverb.

WE had not been long at the fonda before the Fast of Rámadhan began. Rámadhan, ordained by Mohammed, takes place in the ninth month of every Mohammedan year, and lasts for twenty-eight days, during which time the Faithful fast from dawn, when it is light enough to distinguish between a black and white thread, to sunset. It alters by a few days every year according to the moon, and when it falls during summer in scorching hot countries the agonies of thirst endured mean a penance indeed.

Rámadhan begins when the new moon is first seen. Tidings were sent from Tangier to say that it had been observed there, which tidings Tetuan handed on to the farthest mountain villages: a gun was fired from the Kasbah at sunset, horns were sounded, and Rámadhan began. It sometimes happens that Tetuan does not see the new moon till the day after Tangier has seen it at the beginning of the fast, in which case the Tetuan people are guilty of "eating the head of Rámadhan": this year it was not so. During the twenty-eight days of the fast, every night, or rather every early morning at 2 a.m., the householder was awakened by the crashing of his knocker on his door and a shout bidding him

"Rise and eat": the mueddzin at the same time from the top of the mosque called the hour of prayer, and long brass horns brayed to the same effect.

The month was almost over before we had learnt to sleep through it all. As the fonda was in the Moorish Quarter our door was not exempt. Far away up the street the knockers clanked, nearer and nearer every moment, then the man's footsteps, then our own knocker sounded like a sledge-hammer, and "Rise and eat" followed: the man went on to the next door, and back again shortly up the opposite side of the street. And every Mussulman arose in the dark and had a large meal. Again at sunrise the big gun boomed from the Kasbah, the concussion shaking our ill-built room, and we woke once more.

No doubt the original motive of fasting and abstinence in the Old Testament was the promotion of sanitary conditions. It is not good to eat pig in hot countries: thus pork was "unclean," and is to-day in Morocco. Nor is the consumption of much spirituous liquor wise when the thermometer marks a hundred and one: hence the Korān forbids the use of strong drinks. The same motive underlies the fast, which rests and relieves systems over-fattened and little exercised. But the "all or nothing" theory which governs the uneducated and knows no moderation runs a benefit into an abuse. Rámadhan had its disadvantages. Tetuan was revelling at night and in a sodden sleep through the day; work was slipshod and at sixes and sevens; men were irritable and quarrelsome; every one looked indisposed; and the excuse for it all was always Rámadhan. Worst of all, the country-women still tramped four and five hours into market with loads, and children a month old, only half nourished at the time of the fast.

A CLUSTER OF COUNTRY WOMEN.

[*To face p.* 100.

The Feast after Rámadhan

But Rámadhan came to an end at last: Morocco breathed again. The day before the fast was over everybody was smiling, and Tetuan had but one hope, that the new moon would be seen that night, and thus the month of penance come to an end. After the letter from Tangier had been received next morning, which said that the new moon had been seen there, the gun from the fort thundered, the basha went in gorgeous state to the *Jama-el-Kebeer* (Big Mosque) on a white mule, all caparisoned in blue, and read aloud the letter, the city was uproarious, and the mountains echoed again, for soldiers were sent posthaste up the valleys, and fired all day at intervals to notify to the fathermost villages that Rámadhan was over.

And the next day! The first day of the *Aid-el-Sereer* (Little Feast)! Everybody was in shining white, if not new, apparel, and all Tetuan was abroad. That among a people clad so largely in white and in gorgeous colours means a great deal, and the streets of Tetuan might have competed with the Park on the Sunday before Ascot. The Moorish crowd was almost entirely a male one, dressed like peacocks: satins embroidered with gold and silver prevailed.

And if the snowy haiks and turbans and the resplendent shades of the kaftans were the first point about the feast, the sweetmeat stalls were the second. A Moor is a born sweet-tooth, and at every corner of the streets a board was stacked with creamy mixtures in which walnuts were embedded, with generously browned toffee full of almonds, with carmine-coloured sticks, with magenta squares of sweet peppermint, with blocks of nougat inches thick. And the joys of the feast seemed amply to compensate for the fast.

Mohammed ordained many minor feasts and fasts. Rámadhan stands out chief of the one: *Aid-el-Kebeer*

(Great Feast), falling two months and six days afterwards, is chief of the other.

The three reforms which Mohammed instituted were temperance, cleanliness, and monotheism, at a time when reform was badly needed. He was born in Mecca five hundred and seventy years after Christ, an Arab of the tribe of Beni Has'sim. Christianity was not unknown around him in his day.

Always somewhat of a visionary and introspective turn of mind, when he was about forty years old he became deeply interested in the subject of religion. Living in the imaginative East, in a hotbed of mysticism and superstition, it was easy for him to conceive himself a chosen vessel of the Almighty, and to assume by degrees the rôle of prophet, in the honest belief that the words he uttered came direct from that God whose mouthpiece he conceived himself to be. A small band of followers by degrees collected round him, and in the ordinary course of events his end would have been that of a saint with a tombstone white; but, added to the saint's fanaticisms, Mohammed possessed the talents of a leader, and the ambition which accompanies those talents.

Men and more men were attracted to him; he instituted among them a ceremonial of prayer, feasts, and fasts, and built a mosque at Medina, in which they worshipped. Persecution from their fellow-countrymen followed as a matter of course, and Mohammed's disciples, who began to call themselves Mohammedans, turned to him as their chief. The one "able man," he naturally assumed the position of a theocratic ruler, and led them against their enemies; while the words he spoke were committed to memory, constituting later on the Korān.

As a general Mohammed was successful: battle after battle was fought and won, reverses were amply compensated for, and men flocked to his standard, while deputations from surrounding tribes poured in upon him, acknowledging his supremacy, and asking for instruction in his creed.

That creed was admirably adapted to suit the manners, opinions, and vices of the East: it was extraordinarily simple, it proposed but few truths in which belief was necessary, and it laid no severe restraints upon the natural desires of men; above all, its warlike tendencies captivated the men of its day, and war, which at first had been necessary in self-defence, was still carried on, and gradually came to be looked upon by Mohammed and his followers as a lawful means towards spreading their religion. In the name of a *Holy War* the conquerors offered their defeated enemies the option of death or embracing the new religion, while the women and children taken in battle were sold as slaves, after the manner of the time.

And the Prophet's influence deepened and extended. Meanwhile, his sayings, or "the Korān," were written down from time to time by one or other of his followers, on palm leaves, on stone tablets, on the shoulder-plates of goats and camels, and even tattooed on men's breasts; while his ritual was strictly carried out—prayer with absolution, frequent washing, fasting, almsgiving, the pilgrimage to Mecca, and the recital of the formula "There is no God but God, and Mohammed is his prophet."

Prayer was offered up five times a day, as now, by every true believer—at sunrise, at midday, at three in the afternoon, at sunset, and two hours after sunset: the *adzan* (call to prayers) was chanted at each time by the mueddzin from the minarets of the mosques. The first thing in the morning at sunrise the call ran, " God is great; God is great. Mohammed is his prophet. Prayer is better than sleep. Come to prayer; come to prayer." The believer, obeying the summons, washes, enters the mosque, and repeats from four to eight short prayers, with genuflections between each.

Mohammed strictly obeyed the forms of his doctrine, and himself performed the yearly pilgrimage to Mecca and the ceremonies round the Kāaba. He was familiar with at least part of the Gospels, but his knowledge was possibly scant and distorted: he was unfriendly towards Christians. For the Old Testament he had a profound respect.

As far as can be gathered he was a sober and meditative man: he sought neither state nor riches for himself, when either might have been his for the asking. He looked upon women from a point of view not unlike the characters in the Old Testament—a distinctly Eastern one. He possessed five wives, and probably concubines—bondwomen in much the same position as Hagar of old.

Mohammed instituted the veiling of women, with corresponding restrictions on domestic intercourse, as a check upon undue sexual licence—the curse of hot climates.

There is no reason to believe that Mohammed was not honest in the conviction that his mission was divine, and that, if he countenanced vindictive revenge, rapine, and lust as a means towards the furtherance of his teaching, he justified the act in his own mind by what he believed to be revelations from a spirit other than his own.

A great character has perforce its great faults, and the courage and ambition which made so mighty a leader were naturally enough the rock upon which that leader split, blinding his eyes and distorting his point of view, leading him into compromise and error. But though self-

Mohammedanism

deceived and fanatical, it is improbable that Mohammed was insincere. By the spirit of his day he must be judged. His day believed in him.

He died early in the seventh century, sixty-three years old, saying, " Verily I have fulfilled my mission. I have left that amongst you, a plain command, the Book of God, and manifest ordinances, which, if ye hold fast, ye shall never go astray." Within two years of his death the Mohammedan armies had overrun Syria; Egypt was in their possession, and the whole northern coast of Africa.

The scraps which contained in writing the sayings of the dead Prophet were all collected by his chief amanuensis: his followers appointed three judges to overlook the work. The new collection was written in Mohammed's own pure Meccan dialect, and every spurious copy was burnt. So carefully was this done that there is but one and the same Korān throughout the vast Mohammedan world.

Mohammedanism satisfied the East for two reasons: first, because it was a warlike religion, and therefore appealed to warlike tribes; secondly, because, deeply underlying it, was the strong, calm spirit of fatalism, that world-old foundation-stone on which many a man has come to anchor. The very word Mussulman means, " One who has surrendered himself and his will to God."

ISLAM is the belief in one God,
> one Prophet (Mohammed),
> the immortality of the soul,
> the resurrection of the dead,
> the day of judgment,
> angels,
> a devil.

There are no subtle intricacies in such a creed, no

mysterious contradictions to puzzle the uneducated mind ; it amply satisfies a simple people ; and probably no other dogma makes so many converts.

In Morocco to-day the Mohammedan religion is interwoven with the whole fabric of life. To the Moor Allah is always present, is behind every decree of the Sultan, and enters into the smallest detail of his own private life to such a degree that barely a single action is performed without invoking the sacred name. Religion is, according to the temper of the individual Moor, "a passion, or a persuasion, or an excuse, but never a check": for a man may commit any sin under heaven, and "Allah is merciful; Mohammed is his prophet; all will be forgiven." And this is not hypocritical : the larger soul includes the smaller—that is all.

It follows as a natural sequence that, because Allah is as much part of a Moor's life as the air he breathes, he is forgotten. The repetition of words bulks so largely in Mohammedanism, that, as with the Jews of old, the letter of the law has killed the spirit. The evil of Mohammed's religion lies in its essential antagonism towards progress and civilization : scientific investigation is forbidden ; a proverb runs, "Only fools and the very young speak the truth." Thus Mohammedanism will never advance or regenerate Morocco ; for these tenets are Government policy.

At the same time there is in Mohammedan society a certain negative virtue which contrasts strongly with the gross immorality existing in Christian countries. The conditions of what is lawful for a Mohammedan are wide enough to content, and extremes offer no temptation. Polygamy, divorce, and slavery are all allowed, and war upon unbelievers is enjoined as a duty. And yet "social evils" and the lowest depths to which humanity falls are

Mohammedanism

almost unknown in Morocco; while what is held to be sin is rigorously punished—adultery by stoning (a father has no hesitation in shooting his daughter himself), robbery by mutilation, and so on.

Unlike many Christian churches, a Moorish mosque is never closed: the sanctuary is always open. It is council-chamber, meeting-place, and for travellers at night resting-place. There are no priests in the European sense; but the *basha* (governor) or the *kadi* (judge) reads prayers on Fridays, a sermon follows, and letters or decrees from the Sultan are given out in the mosque after service.

The treatment of Mohammedan women, against which so much has been written, is after all Oriental, and nothing more. The Korān speaks of woman as an inferior being, an incomplete creation, needing no education, to be rigorously and jealously guarded all her life, and who after death may or may not be admitted into the Mohammedan heaven. Her function, if rich, is to bear children, and to be treated like a petted lap-dog: if poor, to work as a labourer. But interrogate the wife of a rich Moor on the subject, and she will not have the slightest wish to educate herself, but will affirm emphatically, " We have children and enough to eat. Why should we want to learn anything? "

It is manifestly absurd to compare Mohammedanism with Christianity, which are each the outcome of a distinct race, divided by that greatest barrier—a racial gulf.

Christianity, it must be confessed, bearing in mind the Christian renegades with whom the Moor has traded, is looked upon by him for the most part as a thing beneath contempt. It had five hundred years, before Mohammed was born, in which to impress itself on the East. It signally failed. And yet only a few years after Mohammed's death his religion had taken by storm Egypt, Turkey, Arabia, Persia, Turkestan, parts of India, the Malay Peninsula, the north coast of Africa, and parts of China, introducing monotheism, and impressing temperance and cleanliness on uncivilized millions, but never advancing beyond that point. It is borne in upon one that, in spite of missionary effort, Morocco will change its religion for that of Christianity when, as its own proverb says, "The charcoal takes root and the salt buds." The East, when it adopts other tenets, will exchange its own for a wider and a more universal cult than that which modern sects and parties are endeavouring and failing to introduce to-day.

While we were in our small quarters at the fonda, the weather by no means came up to the high standard it is said to reach in December. A few sunny days, when we could bask out of doors, were grudgingly sandwiched between many wet ones, and again and again the Rámadhan sunrise gun awoke us to gouts of almost tropical rain, a fiery sunrise followed by an hour's brilliant sunshine, the herald of a shamelessly distorted April day. The little gutters down the middle of the streets ran like torrents, carrying off chickens' heads and cabbage-stalks; hail scoured the pebbles; outside the city "the dry land was over your boots"; the road to the sea was impassable, and the rivers between Tangier and Tetuan were unfordable; snow lay in patches on the mountains; half the vale was inundated; the river could be heard a mile away; both our windows leaked; and down in the little patio, where the family sat, the waters were out.

From the west coast at Saffi terrible reports arrived of the havoc the weather had made of the city. The lowest barometer ever seen had preceded sheets of rain,

Photo by A. Cavilla, Tangier.]
A TYPICAL MOORISH STREET.

Flood at Saffi

and a solid *hamla* (flood) had entered the gates from the valley above, filling the narrow streets in a few moments to a depth of seven and eight feet, and carrying everything before it: men, women, children, and cattle were swept in a torrent through the water-gate out to sea, sometimes a hand stretched out above the eddies. Then the gate became blocked with floating *debris* and bodies, and the flood rose to ten feet in the principal street. The townspeople who survived took refuge on their roofs. The vice-governor was drowned. Houses, shops, mills, and mosques were gutted as if by fire; furniture and household goods were ruined; the Saffi shopkeepers were beggared. For many weeks after the survivors starved upon roots, in spite of a subscription raised in Tangier to relieve them.

The rain apparently was something like a waterspout. Happily Tetuan was exempt from waterspouts, and on days when the rain gave over for a time we rode, or, picking our way along the muddy streets, drank tea with some Moor.

One dull afternoon we sampled the state of the roads outside, R. on a donkey, and Mr. Bewicke and myself on foot. Walking out by the Gate of the Tombs, we bore to the left, and dived into the narrowest of narrow lanes, shut in with tall cane fences and high mud-banks crowned with prickly pear, the shape of whose fat, fleshy leaves recalls moles' paws.

The donkey was an unusually large one, and its pack rolled more than packs in general: before we saw the last of Tetuan its rider had many a fall off her unsteady perch; and if there is truth in the Moorish saying that "one does not become a horseman till one is broken," R. may claim to have qualified. It shied and bucked and came on its nose over rocks; but this time Mr. Bewicke's boy, Mohr, directed its ways, and thoroughly enjoyed cudgelling it along with a stick, helped by its rider's switch, cut from a quince-tree, which often as not hit Mohr instead of the ass.

By-and-by we met a countryman, his wife, and a donkey. The woman, who wore little except two striped towels, and a handkerchief round her head, staggered along under a great load of faggots. She was stunted and wrinkled, removed mentally but few degrees from the three-year-old weather-beaten donkey which minced along in front of her, also loaded with faggots. The woman had strips of rough leather bandaged round her legs to protect them from thorns. Her feet were bare. Her husband sauntered last of all, presumably looking after the donkey: he had no load. Another time the donkey also might be exempt, while the woman was still burdened; and the man, when asked why, if he would not carry the load himself, he did not at least put it upon the donkey, would reply, "Because it is too heavy for the ass."

A little farther on and a magnificent Riffi passed us, walking along at a smart pace into the city, his face "old oak" colour, framed in a turban of dark red-brown strings of wool. He wore a chocolate-coloured jellab, embroidered at the edge with white, and sewn with tufts of red, violet, yellow, and green-coloured silks: a tall, wiry fellow, with a back like a ram-rod, a thin face, and keen, defiant eyes. The light glittered on his long, brass-plated Riffi gun: a red leather pouch full of bullets hung at his side. He was a great contrast to the labourer who passed us afterwards, also bound for the city—an old and grizzled monkey-faced man, with his head tied round with a ragged red cloth gun-case. His jellab hung in tatters, but he also carried a gun, and by a string a brace of partridges and a wild duck, which "bag," after some bargaining, became ours for the sum of one-and-sixpence.

Among the brown jellabs and varied turbans European clothes were forcibly out of their place: a people like the Moors, childlike, patriarchal, whose lives embody one of the oldest and perhaps best ideas of a simple existence, may well hate the sight, on the face of their select country, of prosaic tailoring and hideous head-gear. The traveller in his boots, where boots are things unknown, passes the muffled women with their silent gait, the picturesque ruffians with their swinging stride, and is unable to help feeling not at home and something of a blot on the landscape.

The lane we wandered up had been, and was still in places, a watercourse, and we struggled along the steep chasms gouged out of the soft soil, and clambered over rocks which had withstood the torrent.

By-and-by a red door intervened on our left, fitted into an imposing whitewashed arched gateway, with a mounting-block on each side, and the great brass ring-shaped knocker in the middle of the door which the Moors have left all over Spain—the garden-house of the French Consul. In another four months, when all aristocratic Tetuan would migrate in a body into their "summer-houses," and by their mutual presence reassure each other as to their safety, the Consul would move out of the city: at present he would look on such a step as sheer madness.

An old negro slave, with a beard like cotton-wool, was at work in the garden, and, opening the door, let us in to look round. A wide gravel path led up to the dazzling walls of the house, spotless as a sheet of glazed cream-laid note-paper, the window-frames and door picked out with Reckitt's blue. A white railing in front edged the terrace, the steps of which were tanned by the damp salt air a fine rusty ochre. The house inside was built on the invariable Moorish lines—kitchen and inferior rooms on the ground floor, one great lofty room above, and the flat roof over all. A garden-room flanked the house on the south-east, the front open to the garden, pillared and arched with the old white plastered " horse-shoe." In underneath the arches were shade and cool tiling, and outside more tiled ground suggested steaming brews of fragrant green tea, tiny glasses, low tables, and long divans spread under the sky.

It was a grey day, and height beyond height on into the Riff country was cloud-capped, while *shar d'jebel* (the hair of the mountain, as the Moors call snow) whitened a few furrowed peaks. The flats lay below to the left, and a horizontal blue pencil line was scored beyond them. Cow-birds stalked about the garden among some new vines which the old negro was putting in.

We sat down on the terrace, looking at the view, and the silence of the place was above all things most striking. A cavalcade of mules tailed away in the distance in single file along the faint track to the sea; the packed white city lay to the right, but no voices reached us; here cart-wheels, railway-trains, threshing-machines, and busy farm life were not. It would have been hard to age and wrinkle in such a spot—Adam and Eve might have felt at home.

It was also a weedy one, this Paradise: a tangle of greenery spread underneath the oranges, hanging like yellow trimming on a green fabric, choking the vines and a few scarlet geraniums. Labour, in such indolent and self-possessed acres, was a crude and gauche idea.

The greybeard with the marmoset face and leathern apron let us out at the red door: he had a history. His master, a prosperous Moor, once offered to free him:

the old slave refused the offer, on the score that he was quite content as he was. However, his master urged him to accept, and he was eventually given his freedom. But later on the master lost all his money, and ruin was before him. His old slave came back. "See here, my master; here am I. Take me; sell me"; and he finally persuaded the man to sell him. He seemed contented enough as the property of the French Consul, who is a Moor.

We passed a party of closely veiled women, as we strolled citywards, taking advantage of a break in the wet weather to visit their gardens, carrying a great key, and accompanied by two or three ink-black slaves, fine upstanding women, well fed and clothed, looking good-tempered to a fault, whose children, by the same husband and master, would rank equally with those of the wives.

Mohammedan women, though veiled and supervised, have at least their gardens to saunter out to and visit when the tracks allow. Jewesses in Morocco deserve infinitely more pity. Their one recreation seemed to consist in walking as far as the Jewish cemetery, ten minutes outside the Gate of the Tombs, and attending to the gravestones of their friends.

The cemetery is gradually absorbing one side of a rough red-earthed hill; it has no fence of any description round it, and the flat pale-blue and white tombstones spread over the ground look in the distance like so much washing out to dry. The stones are all alike, oblong lozenges, inscribed in Hebrew.

Here, especially on Fridays, the women's day, Jewesses congregate, flocking along the cemetery road — the mourners in ponderous black skirts, vast breadths of crimson silk let into the fronts and embroidered with gold, white shawls over head and forehead, a yellow sash-end edged with red appearing behind, and completing their mourning. Some of the shawls are family heirlooms, and only parted with for five-pound notes.

Loud checks and gaudy colours adorn the Rahels, Donahs, Zulicas, and Miriams not in mourning, as well as the white shawls; and the procession troops to the cemetery, sallow, sad-eyed daughters of Jacob, talking a mixture of Arabic and Spanish, with a few English and Shillah words thrown in.

Of all life's unfortunates, the Jew in Morocco was once, next to the negro in the West Indies, the most persecuted and degraded of God's creatures.

In Tangier and the seaport towns, where the Christian representatives countenance and support him, the Jew, subject to certain restrictions, is in the present day a flourishing member of the community; but in the interior his fate is still a hard one.

There is a Jewish tradition that when Shalmaneser, King of Assyria, conquered the Israelites, the tribe of Naphthali took refuge in the interior of Africa, and spread to Morocco. Jewish tombstones are certainly to be found dating as far back as twelve hundred years, and one synagogue possesses fragments of the Old Testament written on parchment, while there is a population of from four to five thousand Jews in the Atlas Mountains who have lived there since time immemorial.

Perhaps the wandering Jew merely drifted into Morocco just as he drifts all over the universe, and he would have taken refuge in North Africa more particularly when Spanish persecution became intolerable.

Once in Morocco, the Moors permitted the Jews to remain because they were useful to them; but upon certain conditions. They are confined to a certain quarter of the city—the Jews' Quarter, the Ghetto in fact—which is shut and locked by a gate at sunset, barring them from the outer world. In their own quarter they may do as they like, except ride a horse; the horse is considered too noble an animal to be ridden by the Jew: outside they may not ride at all, not even a mule, but are obliged to trudge barefoot through the slush of the rest of the city, summer and winter. They are compelled to wear one costume—a long black gabardine and a black skull-cap. Few Jewesses care to leave their quarters by themselves, for fear of insult. No synagogues or public places of worship are allowed them, and they must address Moors as *Sidi*, or " My lord."

But these customs are fast dying out. There is one which universally obtains: the Jews' Quarter is known as the *Mellah*; Mellah means "salt" in Arabic,—the Jews are compelled to salt the heads of conquered tribes killed in battle, and of criminals, which are afterwards nailed on the city walls as trophies and warnings.

In Tetuan the Jews are influential and well treated: many of them wear European clothes. On Saturday— the Jewish Sabbath—a young masher (a Mordejai, or Baruch, or Isaac) would boast a pair of brand-new yellow shoes and white socks, but wear at the same time a dove-coloured gabardine down to his heels and a mauve sash round his waist. Claret-coloured gabardines were fashionable, and a black skull-cap inevitable.

Though Tetuan was lax and liberal in its treatment of the Israelites, wealthy families of whom it possessed, the Mellah was at once the noisiest and filthiest quarter of the city, teeming with children (unlike the Moorish quarters, where there are few), who played and fought, laughed and cried, by fifties down the three principal arteries of the quarter, whose few feet of walking-space were lined with small and dirty greengrocers' and butchers' shops, their stock-in-trade encrusted with flies. On hot days the Mellah stank; on wet it was deep in black slime.

Once upon a time it ran close to the Jama-el-Kebeer; and when a hundred years ago the Sultan who had built the big mosque sent his envoy to examine it, all was approved of except the proximity of the Jews' Quarter. "Can a mosque be admired near Jews?" was speedily answered by the Tetuanites, who turned the Israelites neck and crop out of house and home, giving them another piece of ground walled in and sufficiently removed.

The sons of Abraham are only tolerated all the world over. As a nation, Moors loathe them. To a pig, which they count "unclean," they give the epithet of *jew*: out pig-sticking, when the pig breaks, the beaters shout, "The jew! the jew!" To begin with, having forced his presence on an unwilling people, the Jew retains his own exclusiveness, neither marries a Moor nor eats with a Moor, nor treats him as anything else except unclean. Not only this, but by unscrupulous cunning Jews contrive to exercise a maddening oppression over a people with whom they have chosen to cast in their lot, swindling, extorting money, and playing a hundred low tricks upon the very race on the produce of whose labour they live: at the same time their exasperating patience and cringing humility, court contempt and insult.

The poorest Moor in Tetuan is a gentleman: the richest Jew is not. But he has his good points: a great sense of brotherhood, a strong bond of freemasonry among the Jewish nation, undaunted energy, and an unshaken faith in their religion are all admirable points in themselves. Energy in Tetuan was concentrated in the Mellah. The best workmen were all Jews. A hundred things were sold by them which no Moor made.

Photo by A. Cavilla, Tangier.]
A STREET IN THE JEWS' QUARTER, TETUAN.
[*To face p.* 116.

Thus in their Ghetto live the Chosen People, the Separate People, of strange and ancient customs,—leaving the hair uncut for a year after a relative's death, sitting on the floor, and not on a chair, for a week after; twisting a pocket-handkerchief round the waist on the Sabbath in order to save "the work" of carrying it; slitting the button-hole of the waistcoat in time of distress instead of "rending the garment"; eating *adafina* on the Sabbath, an indigestible dish of hard-boiled eggs, meat, and potatoes prepared overnight and left on the fire till next morning.

There is no end to ceremonials throughout a Jew's life: the first at his circumcision, the next when his hair is cut for the first time, the next when he goes to the synagogue for the first time, and so on.

When a Jew was buried in Tetuan, the uncoffined body, wrapped in sheets on a wooden bier, might only be borne out of the city by the *Báb-el-Je'f*, literally the Gate of the Unclean Dead—that is, the Jews' Gate.

The mourners howled and the male relatives cried aloud; friends followed, talking and smoking cigarettes. It happened sometimes that the grave was not ready when the cortège reached the cemetery, and that the party would sit down on the hillside while it was lengthened and deepened; from time to time the body would be measured with a walking-stick, and the result compared with the grave.

It is impossible to write about the Jews and omit one certain point. Before the traveller has lived a week in Morocco he begins to hear of *protection*, and he carries with him vague words—"protected Jews" and "protected Moors"—which one sentence can explain. *Protection* means that a European living in Morocco, a Portuguese, a Frenchman, an Englishman—it matters not—has it in his power to make the Jew or the Moor desiring protection a nominal citizen of that country, Portugal or France or what not, and can allow him the rights of a citizen and the protection of the same; while it follows that the Sultan and the Moorish Government have no more power to touch him than they have to touch a French or an English subject, the protected Jew or Moor being outside their jurisdiction, and only answerable to the consul of that country which has given him protection, whether Germany, France, or any other. The advantage of protection is to guarantee thereby the safety of property. It was instituted a hundred years and more ago, to obviate the difficulties and dangers incurred by Europeans in trading with Jews and Moors in a country so badly governed as Morocco. Supposing that a European went into partnership and traded with a Jew or a Moor who was unprotected, in course of time, when the Jew or Moor became rich, the Moorish Government would hear of it, and set to work systematically to bleed him. Naturally the European partner would lose money in the general robbery. Therefore *protection*.

There is scarcely a Jew of property in Morocco who is not protected, and there are hundreds and hundreds of protected Moors; but though many Moors have enjoyed security for themselves and their belongings by this means, others less fortunate, more especially some years ago, have only escaped the talons of Moorish despotism to fall into the clutches of European swindlers, adventurers who have dared—themselves somewhat beyond the reach of their own home government—to fleece the unsuspecting Mohammedan, bribing some basha to imprison him for the rest of his days.

A European consul has before now "sold" his Moorish protected partner—that is, he tells him that, if he does

The Corruption of Protection

not produce so much money within a certain time, protection will be withdrawn. The wiser course for the Moor is to pay the sum. If protection is withdrawn, the Moorish Government and the European blackleg will divide his worldly goods between them.

Such risks are minimized every year, and protection is greatly sought after by Moors and Jews. From the French they get it easily enough. The system is a bad one: that it prevails at all is a proof of the corruption of the Moorish Government.

CHAPTER V

PLANS FOR CHRISTMAS AT GIBRALTAR—A ROUGH NIGHT—THE STEAMER WHICH WOULD NOT WAIT—AN IGNOMINIOUS RETURN TO TETUAN—A RASCALLY JEW—THE ABORIGINES AND THE PRESENT OCCUPANTS OF MOROCCO—THE SULTAN, COURT, GOVERNMENT, AND MOORISH ARMY.

CHAPTER V

Why curse? *Mektub.* (It is written.)

IN spite of the attentions of Amanda, as December drew on and the weather showed no signs of clearing, we began to hanker after a week at Gibraltar, which should combine Christmas and the purchase of camp outfit for use when the rains passed over. It was not difficult to tear ourselves away from the fonda; for it became less easy to tolerate the proximity of the old Spanish bandmaster, with his bad tobacco and long-winded stories; nor were our landlady and family over-refined. We had not come to Morocco to live amongst the scum of Spain: could Tetuan be swept clean of the Spanish element, it were better for it. In fine, amusing and even interesting though our quarters had been for the time, circumstances pointed towards a move into others, the interval being spent in a run across to Gibraltar.

The steamers which call at Martine, down on the seashore, and bring goods to be carted up to Tetuan, six miles inland, are as mysterious as they are rare. One is supposed to call on alternate Tuesdays, weather permitting; another occasionally calls in the intervening weeks; none come direct from Gibraltar, though all are supposed to go straight back there after touching at Ceuta. But there are many buts. Worst of all, the river at Martine has formed a bar, and Martine is a "bar port": this prevents landing in a strong wind.

We pinned our faith upon the Tuesday boat, not realizing its uncertainty; for if the boat had not enough cargo on board to make it worth while her calling, or if she had too much and time was short, or if the weather was bad, she had no hesitation in missing Martine and Tetuan out of that fortnight's round altogether.

We did not want to ride forty-four miles to Tangier with the "roads" in the state they were, even if it had been practicable; nor almost as far and a worse track to Ceuta: either would have meant sleeping a night in the fondâk up in the hills, or in a Spanish lodging-house of doubtful repute: therefore we planned to go by boat from Martine, engaged rooms for a week in Gibraltar beforehand, and, with the optimism born of ignorance, doubted not but that we should get away on the steamer.

Packing up overnight and breakfasting at eight, we were soon ready to mount our mules and ride down to the shore to catch our boat. It was a matter of two and a half hours from Tetuan down to Martine: the track need not be described—this speaks for itself. Our luggage, tied with complicated rope-knots, was judiciously balanced upon one mule, and we had said good-bye to Amanda and family when a message arrived from the steamships agency to say that the steamer was not in.

After taking counsel, however, the luggage was dispatched down to Martine; a muleteer badly marked with small-pox climbed on the top of our worldly goods, and the mule jogged off: we would follow when the steamer was sighted.

Walking into the feddan in search of information about her, every Moor or Jew only replied with shrugged shoulders and extended palms. Who could tell? She

REFUSE GOING OUT OF TETUAN.

[*To face p.* 124.

might come in at eleven, she might not. "Ift shallah" (Allah will show). As she had two hundred and forty tons of cargo to unload, the agents thought she might stay till the following day before starting for Gibraltar: on the other hand, the previous night had been a rough one, and it was quite possible she had passed Martine altogether, and did not intend to call for another fortnight.

It was a sunny morning: there was nothing to be said but "Mektub" (It is written), and nothing to be done except sit in the sun and await events, after the fashion of the brown figures in jellabs also sitting in the sun against the south wall of the feddan where it is highest and nearly always dusty.

Wandering up and down, Spaniards were to be seen in one café shuffling filthy cards and drinking spirits, while in another, behind a great vine which held in its arms a rustic trellis porch and seats, Moors lay on their elbows, tumblers of tea swimming in mint in front of them and long kif-pipes. A Riffi sat on a stool in the sun, leaning against the vine, nursing his gun; his single long black lock fell down by his ear, glossy and tied in a knot at the end. Next door a gunsmith was at work in his little shop sand-papering a gun-stock: a sheep was penned inside against the Great Feast, and more sheep in the grocer's beyond. On the opposite side of the great square a Jew was selling enamel ware to one of the five lady missionaries. Then meat came hurrying by, just killed outside the Mulberry Gate and still warm. Red-and-white shapeless carcases were balanced on a donkey's back, kept steady by a sanguinary Moor who sloped along behind: the donkey knew its own way well, across the wide feddan, down a narrow street, and into the meat market. Thither hurried the lady missionary to buy a joint. If cooked before it has time to get cold the meat is tender, otherwise it must be hung.

It did not seem long before the bell on the top of the Spanish Consulate rang out twelve o'clock. There was no sign of any steamer—the steamships agent had given her up; and not wishing our luggage to lie on the beach all night—for gumption was not one of the characteristics written on our pock-marked boy's face—we sent a messenger off on the two hours and a half ride down to Martine to summon him back.

About one o'clock, just as we were sitting down to lunch in Mr. Bewicke's room, the news arrived that the steamer was signalled. All doubt was at an end: we lunched complacently, allowed time for coffee and a button-hole out of the garden, mounted the mules, Mr. Bewicke his white pony; the gardener, Madunnah, following behind on foot, carrying our sticks and umbrellas, which burden was increased half-way through the city by a bracket, but lately coloured in garish tones, vermilion prevailing—it bled somewhat, but was to serve as a Christmas present at Gibraltar.

Over the cobbles, under the Gate of Wisdom, out on to the sandy track, and along the sea road we rode, the mules refusing at first to pass some sacks of grain which lay in the middle of the path waiting to go down to the beach. There is a gate tax on every loaded animal which passes under the Gate of Wisdom, to avoid which the sacks are carried just out of the city on men's backs, set down, and picked up in time by mules.

The first mile or so was not worse going than usual. Coming from the right by a trail which led across the river, a string of women bore towards us, bringing wood into the city from villages miles away—scrub off the mountain-side. Their rough heads were bound round

Our Projected Journey to Gibraltar 127

with weather-stained coloured handkerchiefs: listless eyes looked straight out from under lined foreheads. On each side of their doubled-up backs protruded rough wood-ends— these kept in place by a rope over the shoulder, grasped in knotted hands above copper-coloured muscular arms. The bit of towelling round the loins, brushed by the wind, left bare a species of knees and legs, carved by two thousand years of toil into humanized Norman piers, buttressed with muscle, in which ankles have no lot nor part, which have carried and still carry unreasonable loads from childhood to the grave. These women walked in single file, as do the mules and donkeys. And this is partly due to the space which the wide bundles take up on each side, partly to bad paths, and partly to entire lack of initiative. Why should they strike out a line of their own, these "cattle" and "beasts of burden," as they call themselves? The old way comes easier.

Thus life has moved across Morocco, without deviation, down immeasurable years, and moves so to-day, along innumerable trails worn afresh by bare feet after every rain-storm, footprint into footprint, padded hard and smooth, narrow and polished.

The flats, after so much wet weather, were under water, and the lower down the road dropped, the deeper the country grew. Our mules struggled along at a slow walk, and we constantly diverged off the track, circling to this side or the other whenever a field looked an improvement upon our muddy quagmire, generally to find that it was very little better and sometimes worse.

About half-way we met our luggage and messenger. The pock-marked boy had taken our effects to the shore, had found no steamer, waited a short time, then calculated that he would be late getting back to the city, and ran risks of robbers, to say nothing of *ginns* (spirits) lurking in the wells by the road, so turned his face homewards.

We were in total ignorance, and so of course was he, all this time as to the movements of the steamer: once out of the city, the level of the road is such that nothing can be seen of the sea until a couple of hours' riding, lands people right on the beach itself. With every hope that she still lay at anchor, we turned our "pock-mark" round, and the poor mule faced the bad road down to Martine for the second time that day.

Madunnah handed over the bracket to crown our baggage, and plodded bravely on, often well up to his bare knees in mud and water. A brace of duck forged across the sky above our heads; some plover called and called again mournfully, wheeling above the irresponsive marshes and brown fallows; a string of mules moved like mites over a cheese in the sandy distance. We passed the Wad-el-Martine in heavy flood, its yellow yeasty depths swirling between the soft red banks.

At last a couple of stone bridges came into sight, isolated in a waste of water, remnants of the old Portuguese road, and in normal times affording a dry path over two dykes. We plunged through unseen holes and among stony pitfalls up to the lonely landmarks and dry ground for a few yards; then more floods; but after that the last mile or two became easy enough, the land rose, and dry sandy dunes, with tough bents flattened in the wind, conduced towards a jog, almost a canter. Goats, picking up a bare living, scattered as we hurried along, past the white Customs House and an old wharf on the river, away to the beach. Behind us the mountains were black and purple, heavy rain-clouds were gathering, and directly we topped the crest of the sandy shore a strong east wind met us full in the teeth straight off the sea. But there as large as life lay the steamer, a long way out, on account of the bar and the wind, with a choppy sea running between.

A cargo-boat was vainly trying to cross the bar, towed by a long green boat which six Moors were rowing. She made no headway, shipped water which deluged the cargo, and seemed half aground on the bar. No other boat or boatmen seemed to be available: the steamer was not within hail. Certainly there were three more cargo-boats lying in shelter in a corner of the river-estuary a little way off the land, but some men in one of them seemed half asleep—at any rate, they were out of our reach, and deaf to our shouts and gesticulations to the effect that we wanted to be rowed on board the steamer.

We waited and waited; Madunnah yelled himself hoarse; but the cargo-boat still rolled on the bar, lashed by the waves, and the men still strained at their oars and paid no heed to our cries. Twice we thought they meant coming to our signals, but each time they were only trying fresh manœuvres.

Rain came on, a sharp easterly scud; the pock-marked boy drew his jellab over his head; the mules turned their backs to the squall; but Madunnah still stood at the edge of the waves, gesticulating wildly with our sticks and umbrellas at the impassive rowers. Sunset was upon us. At a fire of driftwood on the beach a short distance off R. and I tried to warm ourselves.

Suddenly the long green boat left the cargo and pulled towards us: the sea was rising, and looked anything but encouraging; breakers were showing their white teeth on the bar; but the green boat drew nearer and came in at last, or nearly so—for she stopped short off the shore, and, half aground, lost her rudder. Still none of the crew paid the faintest attention as we hailed them in Arabic, English, and Spanish across the few yards of water which put them just out of our reach. They had something else to do except attend to three mad Britishers—let them rave.

The cargo-boat, deserted by the long green boat, had stuck worse than ever: darkness was coming on, and she was in a bad case. The men in the "long green" roused the half-sleeping Moors in the companion boat, and it was evident that both meant going out together to tow the belated cargo in.

Our voices carried less as the wind rose, and it was evident even to Madunnah that words were wasted. The rain drove in torrents; it was bitterly cold, and growing darker every moment; as the two boats turned their heads towards the wave-swept cargo we realized that it was night, that all chance of getting on board was at an end for that day at least, and we set our backs to the sea.

There still remained one alternative and a last chance of getting to Gibraltar for Christmas Day: the steamer might not leave till the following morning, and, taking shelter for the night in the Customs House on the beach, we ought to be able to get on board at daybreak. We turned off to the left through blinding gushes of rain, and headed for this refuge.

The Customs House was much like a caravanserai: an open space in the middle was enclosed by sheds for mules and asses; a rough stair led to the living-rooms, above the sheds, which opened on to a flat white roof. We stumbled up on to the roof; then in under a low doorway into a little wooden lean-to, where an old Jew caretaker was living. The rest of the place was given over

A MOORISH PRISON GATE.

to a family of Israelites, who had come down to "the seaside" from Tetuan for change of air.

Much to our relief, the old Jew caretaker assured us that the steamer would be landing cargo till noon on the following day: he offered us everything he had in his power for that night, and promised to see us off in a boat the next day. Committing us to his care, Mr. Bewicke left us and rode back to Tetuan with the mules and Madunnah; our baggage was stowed away under shelter; and the old Jew, finding a light and improvising two seats out of boxes and matting, sat us down at his little table, with a bit of frayed linoleum on it and a glass.

The roof leaked and the rain beat on to the linoleum, but we were in snug quarters after the beach, and our friendly host began boiling up a great black kettle in a tiny inner room, assisted by a Moor. He was very rheumatic, the old man, also very deaf, and Martine must have been a damp spot for him (the river and marshes close at hand, and east or west wind, both of them heavy with moisture—nothing would dry, hung out in the air at Tetuan); nor were his quarters rain-proof.

He hobbled backwards and forwards, muffled up in a worn grey handkerchief, with a fortnight's white stubble on his chin, and an aged greenish overcoat down to his slippers.

From the recesses of a bunk in the next shelter, where he slept, he produced some pink china cups; then returned with a plate of bread, hardened to the consistency of biscuit, and smelling strongly of aniseed. After that he made tea in a little brown earthenware teapot—sweet green tea with mint—and we soon thawed under a succession of cups. Still he stumbled about, hunting out of a cupboard a small basket of eggs, and in the next room a great stirring and beating-up followed.

By-and-by the Moor who had been assisting him appeared with an omelette; it was dark brown, mixed thick with aniseed, chopped ham, and parsley; nor was it easy to dispose of it.

Our kind host ended up by pressing gin on us.

Warmed and fed, but unfortunately unable to sustain a conversation with him either in Arabic or Spanish, and having exhausted the few words at our command, the next best thing was to make ourselves comfortable for the night. Lighting a candle, the old Jew paddled across the wet roof, and we followed him, dimly distinguishing beasts feeding in the stalls down below, to a small room on the far side, where some sort of preparation had been made for us: a rug was spread on the stone floor, and a bedstead had a blanket laid upon it, while our baggage was piled in a corner. Putting on overcoats and rugs, we sat down on one of our trunks—it is unwise to place confidence in unknown beds in Morocco; but when, driven by sheer weariness, we lay down as we were on the blanket, we slept unmolested.

A Jew on the other side of a thin partition which did not reach the ceiling, snored heavily and awoke us at intervals. About six next morning, what sounded very like the steamer's whistle blew repeatedly, but we paid little attention to it, the old Jew and Mr. Bewicke having both assured us the boat would leave about twelve o'clock. Morning had dawned when we burst open the wooden shutters of a little window much swelled with damp, and looked out across the sand-dunes at the sea.

There lay the black hull of the steamer at anchor: the wind of the night before had dropped; a flaring sunrise and stormy sky lowered behind the Riff Mountains, which were black.

Dressing was short work. The Moor handed us in

at the door a tin basin of water, and in a short time we were ready for the next move. At that point R. craned up to look out of the high window. When she spoke, I could hardly believe her words. . . . *The steamer had weighed anchor and was moving.*

There was no mistaking it: the black hull had swung round, and was making for the open sea, with a flag of smoke trailing behind her; and away she went to Gibraltar.

We rushed out upon the flat roof and up a rotten ladder minus three rungs—all unheeding—which gave access to the roof above our room, gaining nothing thereby except a panoramic view, with the departing boat in the middle distance. Already she stood well out to sea: the Customs House was a quarter of a mile from the beach: there was nothing to be done: to blame our kind old host would have been as ungrateful as it was useless, and regrets were equally unavailing. True it is that the wise man fends for himself and makes no arrangements second-hand in Morocco, where every one is *casual* and every plan is *casual*. Had we found out when the ship's papers were going on board, and arranged with the agent to call us and take us in his boat, we should have eaten plum pudding in Gibraltar. Apparently the steamer had been signalling for the last hour to the effect that she was going, that the weather was bad and the sea rough outside, and that she would not venture to stay and dispatch her cargo—none of which facts the deaf and decrepit old Jew had grasped. He hobbled out, and would hardly believe his eyes.

We sat down to some weak green tea and the same dry aniseed-flavoured bread as the night before, and, thus fortified, reviewed our course of action, which had few complications, there being no other steamer before Christmas, and the ride to Ceuta or Tangier barred by reason of the flooded streams and general state of the country. The "open road" pointed towards Tetuan and our old quarters in the Spanish fonda, of which we had taken only the day before such joyful leave. It was inevitable, that next move; and should be made quickly, to judge by the look of the weather—the clouds were growing lower and blacker every half-hour.

Animals were a difficulty—our mules had gone back to the city the night before; but it would have been hard work wading across the flooded acres for seven miles; and there was our luggage.

Eventually we raised a seedy little rat of a pony, which R. rode; a ragged donkey, on which half our goods was balanced; while the other half went on a mule, with me on the top of all. We turned our backs on the hospitable white Customs House and the ill-favoured sea with a muttered imprecation.

In Tetuan a wealthy man was building a house. It was at a standstill for want of plaster. The plaster had already come in on the steamer *three* times, and three times she had gone away without unloading it. The boat we had lost had made a fourth endeavour, and we learnt afterwards that Mr. N——'s ill-fated plaster had formed the cargo in the wave-washed boat of the evening before. Wet through, it set as hard as a stone in the sacks, and was useless: it lay like rocks on the beach. The bar at Martine has been tolerated for unknown ages: there is no reason to think that the Moor will rouse himself into making an effort and trying to facilitate the landing of passengers and cargo.

We left upon our right as we rode along, some hundreds of yards from the sea, the remains of what years upon years ago was a fort, built somewhat as forts will be built in the near future—with a view to concealment. The outside wall facing the Mediterranean was crescent-shaped, and but four feet high at most, the sand sloping up nearly to the top, and overgrown with vegetation, so that little or no fort showed at all. There were a few loop-holes, through which men could shoot from the inside lying down; there was a well in the centre of the fort, and a small bomb-proof building, with an arched roof many feet thick, where powder had been kept. A primitive construction, this harmless-looking little crescent facing the sea—once upon a time bristling with dare-devil Moors and their long guns.

Half-way to Tetuan we passed *the* cart, the first and last I saw in the place: its antediluvian body was set on two demented wheels, which rolled out of the upright like a tipsy sailor. The cart was Government property: five mules of different sizes, drew it up in a string from the sea to the city, through the quagmire, laden with flour and kerosene oil and stores of all descriptions, a couple of Moors toiling alongside.

R.'s "rat" was not too surefooted, and some of the floods were deep: once it came on its nose, but a second time sat down in a hole in the middle of a sheet of water, leaving nothing for its rider but to slip off and wade out, walking afterwards wherever the track allowed, to raise a little circulation underneath drenched clothes. A certain melancholy possessed the flats as well as our vexed selves that stormy and ill-fortuned morning. In places the tops of the grass-blades alone showed in a green watery waste, except where tall dark rushes made a heavier mass, or where the tufts of red-brown tangle lay in warm lines. The sea behind us was an angry purple; the Riff Mountains were steel-blue; the nearer hills now black, now gold in fitful sun-gleams, now crossed by a rainbow.

Only in the north there was a great break, and a light like brass, behind Ape's Hill. Tradition has it that a subterranean passage leads thence underneath the Straits to the Rock of Gibraltar, and is used by the monkeys as a means of transit from Africa to Europe.

Our miserable beasts were several hours toiling up to Tetuan: the rain came on, and with the wind straight off the snows it was as cold a ride as I remember.

The next morning we went to the French Steamship Company's office for the purpose of recovering our passage money from the agent, who had insisted upon our buying tickets beforehand. This fat, greasy Tangier Jew, of no chin, and flabby, suet-pudding face, flatly refused in plausible French to return us our cash, gesticulating, contradicting himself, pretending to misunderstand us, all in the same breath, and needing nothing so much as a good kicking. Since the money would only go into his own pocket, we fought the point, and, after being most insolent, he was obliged to promise that if the French Consular Agent in Tetuan judged it right, he would hand over the money.

To the French Consular Agent we went: a Moor, whose office was in the French Post Office—a solemn, dignified man in a flowing blue jellab, over the same in white, both hoods drawn up over his head, showing a long olive face of the true Arab type, black eyes, black beard and moustache. He wore white socks and yellow slippers—a most courteous individual. On hearing our case, he simply sent for the Steamships Company Agent, and told him to hand over the money. We sat and waited with Mr. Bewicke, who was interpreting for us. Presently a step, and, much out of breath, the plausible Jew himself arrived, in a long great coat and billy-cock. He took a seat, and stated his case in Arabic to the French

The Weak Moor

Consular Agent. There could have been no greater contrast than between the vulgar excited Israelite and the stately Mohammedan. The Moor sat with folded arms: occasionally he raised one hand to emphasize a quiet monosyllable. But alas for the steadfastness of his race! Perhaps he disliked being mixed up in the matter. At any rate, having said that the money was to be refunded, he allowed the Jew to argue the point, and, we gathered, was telling him finally that the whole question had better be referred to the company itself—a dim and visionary Steamships Company on the other side of the Mediterranean: it augured badly for us.

But at this point R. spoke in French, and reminded the Jew that he had promised to refund the money if the French Consul so judged, that the Consul had given judgment, and that if the Jew still refused he was no longer a man of his word. Strange to say, this quickened a dormant conscience underneath all the dishonesty, or it pricked the Jew's pride; at any rate, after a torrent of protestations, from his tight waistcoat-pocket he produced a pile of dollars, and handed them over to us. The money had taken an hour to draw: as far as actual value went it was not worth it.

The French Consular Agent, the dignified Moor, had to all intents and purposes failed us at the critical moment, since he would not exert his lawful authority over a French-protected Jew. But a Moor's faults may be summed up in one word—*weak*. As in the above instance, refusing to face circumstances or to follow one definite line of action to the end, he invariably acts on the principle of "going roundabout." In the course of time evasion has come to appear to him the best line to pursue, and he has sunk like a stone into a slough of compromise, a tarn of apathy.

Such weakness, incompatible with Moorish fanaticism and courage, is due probably to tyranny.

Living under a tyrannical government and religion, both of which, welded together, form the one dominant factor of his life, the Moor is afraid of each, and stands in dread of the ruin it is in their power to work in his life. Not only this, but he lives in fear of his countrymen and their long guns, of his wives and their poisons, of evil spirits.

Morocco, as has been said, accepted Mohammedanism of necessity, not from choice, at the hands of the conquering Arabs, and it is accepted to-day, as the corrupt Government is accepted, with a shrug of the shoulders and "What God wills cannot but be." Weakened by blind submission, and at the same time holding nothing for which they have fought or wrought—no truths made adamant in the furnace of persecution, no Magna Charta won on the sword-point of patriotism, all of which are so much tonic and discipline to a nation, breeding grit, developing backbone—the Moorish people are paralyzed by a despotism which allows no originality of thought and action; they are no longer capable of "running straight," but, suave and polite to a fault, lack that species of courage which conduces towards plain-speaking.

After all, who and what are to blame except the people themselves? One writer curses the religion, another curses the Government. *Cui bono?* Climate and the fertility of soil may have influenced the races called Moorish, but the Moor himself is alone responsible for his Government and his religion.

Historians from time to time have had something to say about these tribes, and tradition boasts a legion tales respecting them; but the most able writer upon Morocco in old times was Leo Africanus, a Moor himself, who, when all

Photo by A. Cavilla, Tangier.]

A PEEP OF TETUAN.

[*To face p.* 138.

his countrymen were expelled from Spain in 1492, fled to Fez.

Twenty-five years later he was captured by Christian pirates and taken to Rome. He became a Christian, and he published his great and reliable history about the time that Henry VIII. was successful in Flanders and Scotland, when Wolsey obtained a cardinal's hat, and Catherine of Arragon had not been ousted by Anne Boleyn.

The aborigines of Morocco were without doubt Berbers, and to-day Berbers occupy four-fifths of the country, in spite of the invasions of other nations. First on the list of the invaders came the Phœnicians, the earliest civilizing agency. The Romans followed eighty years after Cæsar had landed in Britain, and annexed Morocco, Christianizing its people. Next to invade the country were the Vandals, who turned out the Romans, remained among the Berbers for over a hundred years, leaving red hair and blue eyes behind them. Then six hundred and ninety-eight years after the birth of Christ the deluge of Mohammedan conquest burst over Morocco, and hordes of Arabs, burning with a fanatical missionary spirit, swept over the land. At the end of eleven years the resistance of the Berbers was overcome, and they adopted Mohammedanism as lightly as they had adopted Christianity under the Roman rule.

About two years afterwards a body of them crossed over into Spain under the one-eyed chieftain Tarik, and laid the foundation of the Moorish supremacy in Europe. Thither this band of pioneer Berbers was followed by the Arabs: the two races mingled and built up together an empire in Spain said to surpass all its contemporaries in learning and refinement. The Spanish named them indiscriminately *Mauros*, and *Moors* they have been ever since; but the name Moor can be traced back as far as

23 A.D., when Pliny and Strabo speak of the *Maurusii* and *Mauri*.

A reflection of their empire's greatness shone even in Morocco itself: libraries and universities were founded in Fez and Morocco City. But at the same time the benighted country knew no settled peace; it was torn with civil war between the Arab and Berber tribes, until the Berbers finally mastered the Arabs, and forced them to confine themselves to certain districts.

Meanwhile, in Spain the Moorish Empire, which for seven hundred years had remained firmly established, keeping alive Greek philosophy, building the Alhambra and making an indelible impression upon the Spanish nation, crumbled and fell, or, more properly speaking, was expelled from Spain after a year of bitter persecution. Thousands of Moorish refugees flocked back across the Straits to the land of their progenitors, and settled in Tetuan, Tangier, and the cities on the coast, buoyed up with the lingering hope of returning, when fickle Fortune smiled again, to the glories of their old houses in Granada, and to that land which had chosen to cast them out.

As may be imagined, the government of Morocco soon fell into their more capable hands: they amalgamated more or less with the Arabs and Berbers—their own kith and kin—and the country became known to Europe as Morocco.

In due time a certain Moor, a *Sharīf*—that is, a direct descendant of the Prophet Mohammed—as head of the Mohammedan Church, gradually united under himself Arabs and Berbers alike, and was acknowledged as their Feudal Lord, Religious Chief, and Sultan. The present Sultan is of the same holy line: hence his title of *Sharīfian Majesty*.

A Berber and an Arab may easily be distinguished

Berbers

from each other. Berbers, taken as a whole, have square frames, high cheek-bones, small eyes, and are great walkers, not horsemen. The mountains are to them what the plains are to the Arabs, and they prefer an agricultural life to any other.

Leo Africanus describes them, and his picture in all essentials holds good to-day: "They are strong, terrible, robust men, who fear neither cold nor snow; their dress a tunic of wool over bare flesh, and above the tunic a mantle, round their legs twisted thongs, never anything on the head. They rear sheep, mules, and asses; and they are the greatest thieves, traitors, and assassins in the world."

From personal experience let this ryder be added: that they make good servants, faithful up to a certain point, to be trusted up to a certain point; but they are rascals.

In Tetuan many more Berbers are to be met with than Arabs: the Riff tribe is Berber, and Tetuan is full of Riffis.

Until the last thirty years the Berbers owned only a nominal allegiance to the Sultan; to-day he could pass through little of their territory without an army at his back, and into the Riff country he has never been at all.

Among the Berbers there is plenty of throat-cutting as a legal punishment, and murder on the score of private vengeance, while Government oppression is rampant. As for travellers journeying across their country, only certain "roads" are "open" and safe: a Christian, with proper precaution, is seldom attacked on the way to Fez or Morocco City—a Jew occasionally. Off the beaten track and anywhere in the Riff country his life would not be worth a *flus* (small copper coin).

The Arabs have given the Berbers a name of their own—*Shillah*, which means "Outcast," referring back to the days when they drove them out of the plains up into the mountains; and it has stuck to them ever since.

Travellers descant upon *the noble Shillah race*. The dialect which they speak is called Shillah: the Riffis at Tetuan spoke Shillah among themselves, but soon picked up Arabic of a sort, and a little Spanish.

The Arab differs in every respect from the Berber. One of the finest types among mankind, he has a tall, spare frame, aquiline nose, fine eyes. He is kind, hospitable, dignified, abstemious, a poet, a gentleman, and a horseman. He is capable of great things, and of all Orientals has most impressed himself upon the world. At the same time he is too often treacherous and bloodthirsty, inclined to be sensual and inquisitive.

Perhaps his faults have led to the extolling of the noble Shillah race at the Arab's expense. On this subject Mr. Cunninghame Graham writes, that certain travellers in Morocco must have "been humiliated at finding in the Arabs a finer type than their own, and have turned to the Shillah race with the relief that the earthen teapot must find when taken away from the drawing-room companionship of Dresden china and put back again on the kitchen dresser." For myself "earthen teapot" and "Dresden china" have both much fascination. I would trust either just as far as I could see him.

Thus Morocco is populated by two antipathetic races, who neither singly nor jointly have or can consolidate it into a thriving empire. The Arab cared only to convert a conquered people to Mohammedanism and to push his individual fortune, heedless of assimilating individuals

The Moorish Government 143

into one nation, as did the Romans. Great Arab chiefs there have been, but never a patriot. With the fatalistic spirit of the East, and a tendency to see life only from the personal standpoint, it followed that, when a holy war no longer fired the wandering and independent shepherds to fight and forced them to obey, they became "slack," remained stationary, or retrograded.

The Arab would not advance civilization in Morocco, nor would the wild and lawless Berber; the Moorish refugees from Spain had sadly degenerated; to crown all, civil war led to the destruction of the libraries and universities in Fez and Morocco City, and education was no more.

Ignorance begat worse government; decline and poverty followed one after the other. Corruption among the rulers spread downwards and ran through the country, until the whole body politic was unsound, and is so to-day.

Though the name of the Sultan, as Head of the Church, is held in reverence, yet many of the tribes would resist to the uttermost any attempt on his part to subdue them by force of arms, so unsettled is his empire.

He holds himself to be far superior to the Sultan of Turkey, who is not descended from the Prophet, but who, on the other hand, is the guardian of the sacred city of Mecca, and who possesses superior forces.

Second in rank to the Sultan of Morocco follow his ministers—the Chief Minister, the Foreign Minister, the Chief Adviser, the Minister of the Interior, and the Minister of Finance. Their duties are to carry out the Sultan's wishes, and, receiving no pay, they look to enriching themselves at the expense of their respective billets.

A body of secretaries come after the ministers, who write and dispatch the Sultan's decrees to distant cities, where their letters are read aloud in the mosques to the people by the governors. A special body of messengers is employed under the secretaries.

Each district and city has its *kaid* or *basha* (its governor), whose duty is to read the Sultan's letter aloud and carry out his instructions, who oversees the city market, prices food, detects false weight, deals with robbers and murderers, and sees that the peace is kept.

As well as basha every city has its *kadi*, or judge of civil law, who settles all questions of land, of grants, divorces, etc.

We visited the Court of Civil Justice at Tetuan, a tiny room, carpeted with yellow matting, where the white-haired kadi, attired in white, sat like a magnificent white rabbit on a large red cushion on the floor, beside him a table six inches high, with learned-looking books, ink, parchment, and thin slips of wood for pens.

Below the basha or kaid come *sheikhs* (village elders), who may be called gentlemen farmers. They collect the taxes directly from the country people. A province is taxed according to what it produces: no one pays the sum demanded of him, nor at the time it is demanded, but eventually every householder in the district is judiciously squeezed to the uttermost farthing, and half of what he pays goes into the sheikh's pocket.

Morocco conceals its wealth in times of visitations such as these: money and corn alike are buried in the ground. Some of the people are imprisoned, some tortured, and eventually all disgorge, and are left with barely enough for their every-day wants.

It is a system typical of the East and its slipshod, rough-and-ready dealings: its great element of simplicity harks back to a life in tents, where red tape was unknown.

The highest officials are in the habit of transacting

The Harem

business at their street doors or in their stables: the basha invariably sits in some gateway near his house, hearing and judging matters which two or three gesticulating claimants explain to him. Private matters are public property: the man in the street chats with the Minister of Finance—for are not all men equal? The minister may have sold groceries at one time, before he was called upon to fill a position at Court. Who can tell what a day may not bring forth?

The Sultan—who is known as "The Lofty Portal, the Exalted of God, the Noble Presence"—has a body of servants and retainers round him: first of all "The Learned Ones," men who advise him, but make a point of ascertaining his wishes before they give an opinion, and are of no use at all except in conducting negotiations; next the officer who carries the great pearl-and-gold-embroidered parasol over his head; next an officer who flicks away flies; then a master of ceremonies, a headsman, a flogger, a shooter, a water-bearer, a tent-layer, a tea-maker, a standard-bearer, and a "taster" to see that no poison is given.

More closely connected than any of these with the Sultan is of course his harem, of both black and white women, who have been honoured by admission into the much-sought-after precincts. Some of them are Circassians, supplied by Constantinople: all are the best which money can buy, or ease and position tempt. When their numbers have been greatly swelled, certain of them are drafted on as presents to kaids and bashas.

The offspring of the Sultan's numerous wives are brought up in isolated sanctuaries, each boy in company with a slave of his own age, whom he calls brother. Girls inherit no rank.

One and all are married when they reach maturity, at a State function which takes place each year, the Sultan choosing their consorts. He gives his favourite son—whom he has named as his successor—a high command in the army or an important governorship: as long as the boy is too young for either, the Sultan associates him with himself in official receptions.

All possible rivals to the Sultan are disposed of, chiefly by banishment.

Guarding the intriguing and inflammable harem are eunuchs, imported at great expense from Abyssinia, and responsible for the Sultan's wives and concubines, whom "wise women" prepare to meet their lord. The late Sultan was in the habit of having his harem paraded in his garden on Thursdays, in order to select the most attractive, and spend Friday—the Mohammedan Sunday—in her company.

It is a curious fact that the Imperial Treasure, which is distributed between Fez, Morocco City, and Mequinez, of which no details are ever made public, can only be opened by agreement between the keeper, the governor of the palace, the trusted eunuch, and the head woman in charge of the harem. The secrets of its treasures are jealously guarded. It is probably impoverished.

Every one who approaches the Court is expected to make the Sultan a present, and his collection of offerings would stock a museum.

In the time of George I. we read of the Sultan's being sent "a rich crimson velvet sedan or chair for the favourite Sultana, and ten pounds of the finest tea at thirty shillings a pound." In the present day telephones, heliographs, gramophones, bicycles, motor-cars, guns, fireworks, and the latest inventions of all kinds find their way into Morocco.

The Eating Up of Rebellious Tribes

In return the staple Moorish offering has always been, and still is, Arab horses, with richly embroidered saddles and bridles.

It is impossible to estimate the strength of the Moorish army. The only regulars are under European instruction, Sir Harry Maclean (known as Kaid Maclean) acting as commander-in-chief. Their pay is something like a penny half-penny a day for infantry, fourpence for cavalry, a shilling for commanding offices. The ranks consist of private, sergeant, captain, centurion, and colonel, each officer having a lieutenant.

Every Moor capable of bearing arms in Morocco is liable to be *pressed* for service.

In May, when the country is dry, each basha or kaid is ordered to collect troops in his own district: then is Tetuan deserted, and every boy and young man absents himself. How the lady missionaries hid their house-boy! Tetuan sent off two hundred men, under a colonel, while we were there, which were to help punish certain rebellious tribes. Often these expeditions are for the purpose of raising taxes. In any case the tribes against which the Sultan's troops are sent are said to be "eaten up." Long before it happened it was known and talked of.

"Ah, yes; the Beni M·Saira would be eaten up in April."

The Tetuan two hundred were sent to help eat up the Beni M·Saira tribe, some of whom had abducted two Spanish children a year ago. The children had driven their pigs on to land belonging to the tribe—a thing abhorred of by Mohammedans, to whom pigs are unclean. Expostulation was not heeded, and the Beni M·Saira resorted to strong measures, and kidnapped the children. They were sold from family to family beyond hope of recovery, and it would be hard to say what was their fate. Of course they were never seen again. Tales were circulated which said that the girl had been turned into a dancing-girl, and taught to dance upon hot ashes, or she may have become slave and concubine to some Moor. She was sixteen years old, and the lady missionaries at Tetuan knew her well, and her ten-year-old brother.

The Spanish Government had complained to the Sultan, and now a year after the offence the Beni M'Saira were to be eaten up; there was to be a general raid upon their country: men would be killed, women taken as slaves, villages burnt, and corn destroyed. The worst part of the whole business is the fate of the prisoners on these occasions. These unfortunate men, suffering scarcely for their own misdeeds, are sent in chains to far-distant city prisons, whence they seldom emerge alive.

The colonel of the Tetuan contingent was an example of the rapid rises and the vicissitudes of life in Morocco. Only the other day he had been harbour-master down at Martine, but was accused of smuggling and turned out of that berth; he then took a café and sold drinks in Tetuan, when suddenly the Sultan's pleasure took the shape of making him a full-blown colonel in his troops. As in the days of Joseph, the chief butler is sent for out of prison and made much of: the baker is sent for and hanged.

The lucky colonel and his two hundred left Tetuan in bad weather: their pay was such that many of them, before starting, sold the bullets supplied them, in order to buy food with the money, preferring to fight without ammunition rather than on empty stomachs; but only *one quarter* of them got as far as El K'sar—the rest deserted on the road, to escape hunger and exhaustion from rain and cold.

A SAINT-HOUSE, TETUAN.

[*To face p.* 148.

Bribery and Corruption 149

The Oolad Moosa tribe were eaten up not long ago; their land was harried, their fruit-trees destroyed, and themselves killed, imprisoned, and enslaved. I was told by a Spaniard that he had seen five camel-loads of the heads of tribesmen brought into Larache while he was there. The Sultan offered three shillings per head. His soldiers sent up not a few heads which belonged to their own companions-in-arms. Consignments were sent off to various cities throughout Morocco, where the Jews, as usual, salted them, and they were set up over the gates and on the walls.

There is little or no artillery in his Sharīfian Majesty's army, though the few cannon he has, render him all-powerful against his rebellious tribesmen, who are only armed with rifles (principally French), which are smuggled into the country.

Soldiers are supplied with the same rifles and European swords: the native curved dagger is also used.

Pitched battles are seldom heard of. The troops entrench themselves strongly, gallop out in parties against the foe, fire a volley into his line, and gallop back again to reload. Pillage is the great element in this species of guerilla warfare.

In connection with the army are the *Makhaznia* (mounted police): they are practically cavalry. A few were quartered in Tetuan, and the basha employed them to take men prisoners and preserve peace and take messages and so on. The Makhaznia are paid for whatever they do by any one who employs them, and they often act as soldier-escort to Europeans.

The Government of Morocco has but one hinge—a golden one. Thirty thousand pounds was paid by the late governor of Morocco City for his billet, and a capable man would still make his fortune before he retired, by means of bribes and presents from every one in connection with him, and a little undue pressure and taxation here and there. But no governor is exempt from that war-cry in Morocco, "Pay! pay! pay!" And if he or a basha wish for the Sultan's favour, which in order to remain in office is most desirable, he will forward a present regularly to Court, though at every feast he is obliged to send another in addition. When a Sultan imprisons a minister, he confiscates all his money.

Bribes largely contribute towards filling the coffers of Government officials, from toadies down to unfortunate sufferers. A man has to buy himself out of prison: it costs a murderer about four pounds. Those who cannot afford to pay do not come out.

Not long ago a poor man whom we knew was suddenly appointed to fill a lucrative post under Government. He dare not refuse it, but he was head over ears in debt, and of course a large sum of money was due in return for the appointment. He borrowed from the Jews and took up office. In one year he had paid all his debts, he had paid the Jews, and built himself a luxurious house. And who can wonder at it? Customs-house officers can all retire after *three years* (if they choose), and live well. It is calculated that the Government gets exactly half of the duties.

Tetuan had a favourite tale of bribery. A man wanted to make sure of a case he was bringing before the basha. He knew that the basha had a weakness for mirrors. He was a poor man, but he bought the best looking-glass he could afford, and dispatched it. The case came on; the basha gave it against him.

"What!" cried the poor, discomfited loser; "did you not receive the mirror?"

"Yes," replied the basha coolly; "but immediately

The Looking-Glass

afterwards a very fine mule came along, and *he kicked the looking-glass into a thousand fragments.*"

So when a man is disappointed of his due, they say, "The mule has kicked the glass."

Another man had a brother in prison whom he wished to buy out: he took the basha a mule, and presented himself with his present.

"You shall not bribe me," said the basha. "Soldier! put this man into prison with his brother, and put the mule into my stable."

The man's family had a heavy bribe to raise.

CHAPTER VI

WE LOOK OVER A MOORISH COURTYARD HOUSE WITH A VIEW TO TAKING IT—WE RENT JINAN DOLERO IN SPITE OF OPPOSITION—AN ENGLISHMAN MURDERED —OUR GARDEN-HOUSE—THE IDIOSYNCRASIES OF MOORISH SERVANTS—A NATIVE GUARD—THE RIFF COUNTRY.

CHAPTER VI

> Ah ! Moon of my delight, who know'st no wane
> The Moon of Heaven is rising once again :
> How oft hereafter rising shall she look
> Through this same garden after me—*in vain !*

CHRISTMAS DAY in a Mohammedan city passed with nothing to mark it except deluges of rain. The fonda had not grown upon us; and when two Moorish houses in the city at last presented themselves, the result of weeks of inquiry, we decided to take one, if, as was apparently the case, a garden-house outside the city was not to be had for love or money. The Moors all told us it was impossible. The fact is, that they are chary of letting their houses to unbelievers: the thing is not encouraged in the land; indeed, they are liable to be imprisoned for doing so, unless they have "protection" from a foreigner.

All sorts of complications have arisen out of permission granted to Europeans to settle in the country: it depends on the European; he does something foolish, and legal or social or religious difficulties arise, and a storm in a teacup may end in serious dispute and a heavy indemnity to pay. So, naturally enough, the Sultan's advisers are averse to extending the limits of property owned by Europeans, and the barriers which they put in the way, debar ordinary people from running up villas and committing outrages such as half the world endures in silence.

In Morocco it is necessary first of all to obtain the consent of the Government for the purchase of land. Interest can sometimes do it, and the pill must be heavily gilt. The next obstacle lies with Moorish jurisdiction, which, with forethought, sets forth that all disputes relating to property shall be referred to native courts and settled by Moorish law. This opens a door to barefaced bribery and intimidation: some one will be fleeced. Last of all, Moorish workmen building for an Englishman or any foreigner are liable to persecution and arrest. Thus foreign labour must be employed. And how is foreign labour to be had? A Jew or Spaniard may not be available. It is scarcely less difficult to rent a house in Morocco, unless it is in Tangier.

Of the two which were thus unexpectedly offered us one was out of the question—it was damp ; but the other, standing empty in a long narrow alley in the middle of the city, was as sound as houses built of rubbish and thin bricks can be, and we went to look over it, well prepared to ignore petty defects.

It was entered, as usual, by a wide yellow door, studded with giant nails and a resounding knocker: a courtyard house—a most quaint and original construction in which to spend two or three months. From the ochre-coloured door we walked into a tiny tiled patio open to the sky, too small and insignificant for a fountain or an orange-tree: the kitchen and one other room where servants could sleep opened out of it, lighted only by their wide doors, which were never shut. So much for the ground floor.

A tiny tiled staircase led to the first floor. Four narrow rooms, windowless, flanked the four sides of the square,

A Courtyard House "Found Wanting"

and looked down into the little court below. Each room had double doors standing open for light and air. From the house-top above the first floor, on to which we went last, there was at least a view of a thousand flat white roofs, of pencil-shaped minarets, of turtle-backed mosques; but at the same time the sun itself could not be more dazzling to look at than was the impossible whitewash which besmeared all the roofs, and we soon left for our first floor, in whose four little dark rooms we proposed to live. Standing on the gallery which ran outside them, and leaning on the balustrade looking down into the minute patio, it was a case of the view below into that, and the view above up at the sky, and no more—a limited, and on wet days gloomy, prospect. Added to that, the orgies worked in the kitchen by a Moorish cook could not do other than proclaim themselves all over the first floor. True, the little patio embodied the Moorish conception of *al-fresco* seclusion, and a depth of shadow lay in the inner rooms within the thin shell of the white walls. And yet—and yet—the lines of old-fashioned Eliza Cook returned insistently, and refused to be silenced :—

> Double the labour of my task,
> Lessen my poor and scanty fare,
> But give, oh! give me what I ask—
> The sunlight and the mountain air.

And in the end the vote was given against the little windowless dwelling in the Moorish Quarter. No doubt a courtyard house is bizarre, but it has its imperfections.

A Scotch proverb has it that "Where twa are seeking, they are sure to find." In time we found. A certain Moor of Tetuan, named Ali Slowee, a Spanish protected subject, was guardian, uncle, and stepfather to a boy named Dolero. Dolero owned a garden-house outside the city, called *Jinan Dolero* (The Garden of Dolero). Ali Slowee heard of our wants and offered us his nephew's house, provided we undertook to give it up at the end of March. Than the unexpected, when it does come, nothing is so good. After a little difference over the rent (our landlord began by asking two pounds five a month, and came down to thirty shillings) all was settled, and New Year's Day, 1902, found us living in a whitewashed garden-house in Morocco, out in the country.

Moors have extravagant ideas of the sums English people will pay. Mr. Bewicke was offered a house and garden for seven pounds ten a month: some time after the landlord asked three pounds; eventually he came down to thirty-nine shillings.

Having handed a month's rent over to Ali Slowee, he had Jinan Dolero done up, whitewashed at least, outside and in, from top to toe—a rite performed on every opportunity all the year round in Morocco, like spring-cleanings at home. Tiles were mended, windows repainted, glass put in, and we followed,—the simplest thing in the world; " furnishing " takes no time in Morocco. Three mules carried out all we put into the empty little house—all our effects, that is to say, from the fonda. A few rugs were unrolled, camp-beds, table, and chairs put together, some nails driven into the walls, and in one hour we were " in." Gibraltar supplied the camp furniture; necessaries were raked together in Tetuan, including the dome-shaped pewter teapot, and the painted tins, pink and green and blue, for tea, coffee, and sugar, which mark the tramp of the European across Morocco, and are both of them for ever associated with sweet green tea and turbans. Mattresses we had made, and made ourselves, of moss, brought in by the country-women and dried; and an Englishman, A—— (one of

JINAN DOLERO.

[*To face p.* 158.

The Murder of an Englishman

the few who have become Mohammedans and settled in Morocco), lent several more, which made divans round our walls.

A—— has a little house close to Jinan Dolero, and occupies himself with his garden outside the city. He dresses like a Moor. In spite of it all, he is not welcomed among them as a brother, but goes by the name of "The Renegade." They probably divine that he adopts their religion as a part of the customs of the country with which he identifies himself, less for the sake of Mohammedanism itself than for the life which that religion inculcates.

Apparently men in such a position rarely benefit the country in which they settle, and often do harm, ending by paying the penalty of meddling with the manners and customs of another race.

Now, at the time of writing this chapter, A—— has paid in full. Only a few months after we left Tetuan he was shot one evening in his garden and killed on the spot, apparently from close quarters, probably from behind the hedge. The servants had gone home and found his body next morning. If they are to be believed, no one heard a shot. Men have been imprisoned and men will suffer death for the murder, no doubt; but whether the actual murderer is shot or goes scot-free, and what his inducement for committing the crime, probably half Tetuan will know and half Tetuan will tell, *and tell a lie.*

Some say that A—— was shot for the sake of his gun and his money. Others that he was shot by some Riffi brothers because he was in the habit of talking to their sister. Others that the murder was connected with his having lived at one time with a Moorish woman, from whom he eventually separated.

No one will ever know.

Jinan Dolero would have been called in the Riviera "a villa": it was a typical Moorish garden-house. We lived upstairs, after the manner of the country, in the airiest and lightest of small whitewashed sitting-rooms: its three windows, set certainly with head-splitting glass, looked south, east, and west, on sea, mountains, and city. The second larger room, in which we slept, had a thick white pillar in the very middle of it, supporting the ceiling. A store-room on the same floor did duty as larder, and a staircase led up on to the flat white roof.

Underneath us were kitchen, mules' stable, and two rooms for our two servants: a little staircase led down to them and on to the hall and front door. The floors were all tiled: a dip in the corner of each room and a hole in the wall carried off the water when they were sluiced down. Innocent of spouting, the water merely streamed down the outside wall. Each window reached to the floor, and an inartistic iron grille removed all danger of falling out. It was the sunniest house in the world, and an airy one, for the passage and rooms had loop-holes, a foot high and four inches wide, cut in the wall, through which air freely circulated. On the ground floor the windows were *nil*, but more loop-holes let in ample light. One was constructed on each side our hall door, that before unbarring at night we might know what manner of visitor we had, and even fire a charge through the aperture if the occasion warranted.

Our garden was another Moorish wilderness, another "Field of the Slothful," thick in a waste of weeds, blue borage, and yellow marigolds. But it was also a vineyard. Dead-looking branches of vines trailed among the weeds, which later on were cut down with a sickle and turned into green meat for cows. Splendid muscats, we were told, our vines would produce: branches are spread over them in the summer as a slight protection from the sun, but the grapes are left on the ground and often soiled; nor has a Moor the slightest idea of picking them, or of preserving their bloom. Besides the vines, there were fruit-trees in Jinan Dolero. Pink almonds blossomed first; the leaf and the flower of apricots followed; apples, peaches, and pears came almost at the same time; and we lived in a pink world. The fig-tree softened its hard heart last of all, and its ashy-grey arms burst into tender green leaf and infant figs; at the same time the pomegranates shot into warm red leaflets. There were lemons which were ripe on the trees on New Year's Day, and made many a lemon-squash: there was double narcissus in flower everywhere; it sprouted up in the grass paths which divided our garden, and got badly trodden down: there were rows and rows of beans, which scented the air: last of all, there were some red geraniums in flower.

A hedge of prickly pear ran down the east side of the enclosure, a tall cane fence effectually hedged in the rest, and the whole was entered by the inevitable locked and barred door, and whitewashed doorway, the long key of which, was a care in life, till we learnt that in Morocco every precaution is taken up to a certain point; matters are then handed over to Providence, and man, forbearing to meddle further, sits down and awaits their development.

Thus, with all their locks and bolts, garden doors were often left open, and the cane fences were full of gaps. But none of our lemons were stolen—not, at least, after we got rid of the guard of soldiers which for the first week the basha insisted on sending to Jinan Dolero every night. They ate them.

Fine days were never long enough in the little garden-house facing the mountains: in the mornings an opal light; the sunrise stalking across their summits, while a cloud of white mist would sweep down the valley out to the blue sea-line; all day bright light and dazzle, a wind soft and yet racy; at night an abrupt sunset, leaving for a few moments a rose-pink after-glow, followed by an intense silence.

The first thing in the morning, we always wandered in our garden down the grassy paths among the dew; measured the rain-gauge; looked at the sky; watched the birds, of which a flight, chiefly flocks of finches, invariably travelled over the little terraces of fruit-trees towards the river, taking our garden on the way, and feeding there for a while. A white jasmine almost hid our white steps and pillars: a rose grew with lavish prodigality; as Jinan Dolero stood there, in the middle of the Garden of the Slothful, a certain imperious dignity was given to the little white-walled structure by means of its magnificent situation.

Sometimes we breakfasted in the garden: we were never in to lunch on fine days, but rode and walked all over the country, occasionally with the lady missionaries or Mr. Bewicke, but oftener alone with the big grey donkey and a boy. There were Moors to see in Tetuan, and always something of interest: we came away from that corner of Morocco without having got through half of what might have been done. To live in a country, adopting some of its ways and imbibing a little of its spirit, is the only satisfactory way to "travel." Hotels with home conventionalities and English tourists never amount to the same thing. Either camp out or settle down for a month or two in a hut, with one of the country people to cook. There must be sport, or agriculture, or village characters, or architecture, or botany, or geology to study: bird-life and bird-watching are never-ending interests; the fields are never empty. Only by living its own life, can the country and its ways unfold themselves, and become understood and cared for, by the traveller who has time for, and a love of, such things.

As a whole, and seen in January before spring has begun, around Tetuan it is a tired and brownish-looking country: its colour is bleached and dried out of it, and it has the air of a sun-dried, wind-blown land, patched with pieces of brilliant greenery where corn has been sown near water. And yet it possesses the charm of strength and repose which simplicity gives; for it has been worried by man but little, rather allowed to straggle through the centuries at its own sweet will.

In the evening every Friday, to mark the Mussulman's Sabbath, the sunset gun boomed and echoed among the opposite mountains. Watching the grey turreted walls of the Kasbah bitten out against a primrose sky, with watch in hand, at last the weekly flash of red, then a puff of brown smoke shot out of the wall, and last of all, a reverberating roar, tossed backwards and forwards among the hills. It is long before the "thunder" dies away, and we watch a gigantic smoke-ring, sprung from the mouth of the gun, float lazily out to the south; while the mueddzin's cry from the top of the mosque rises and falls on the waves of sound, drifting now clear, now faint, over the garden.

When the sun dropped, the frogs began, from the cracks in the moist clay soil where they sat, all over our acre and a half, croaking in a wet, guttural chorus—the whole garden called; and the rattle of the tree-beetle which followed was one of those tropical sounds which recall the East. The frogs were tiny brown fellows, hard to get at. The owls would begin after the frogs—a brown owl, which flew noiselessly in the twilight among the fruit-trees and on to the edge of the roof, hooting long and low or chuckling oddly. Then stillness, and wonderful starlight nights, all through January. That month no rain fell. In February we had seven and a quarter inches, and more in March.

Having found Jinan Dolero, and furnished it after a fashion, we still lacked servants, and they seemed to be almost as difficult to meet with as houses—that is, trustworthy ones. Again, however, we were fortunate. A soldier-servant who had lived with a missionary happened to have nothing to do, and agreed to come to us with his young wife, Tahara. They both of them knew something of European ways, and were scrupulously honest. They brought a few oddments, a little looking-glass, a mattress on which they slept upon the floor of the room near the kitchen, and a few cooking-pots and pans of their own. We overcame their objection to sleeping outside the city at that time of year; but I believe they never liked it up to the last, though they comforted themselves with two guns (one of which belonged to the man, and one he borrowed) and the fact of a revolver as well, being all under the same roof with them.

They were both of them Riffis, and their own home was in the Riff country, two days' journey into the mountains from Tetuan. His name was S'lam Ben Haddon Riffi of Bekiona, son of Haddon and of Fettouch Ben Haddon of Bekiona. S'lam's wife was Tahara. He had served for a year in the French army

OUR SERVANTS, S'LAM AND TAHARA.

[*To face p.* 164.

S'lam and Tahara 165

in Algeria, in the 2nd Regiment of Tirailleurs Algériens; and having picked up a little French, we learnt, with a few Arabic words, to understand each other. He and Tahara spoke Shillah to each other.

S'lam was about twenty-six years old, Tahara about twenty. He was a sinewy, long-legged ruffian, well over six feet, and holding himself creditably. He had a pair of fierce, dark, restless eyes, little beard or moustache, the front half of his head shaved, and a few locks left long at the back in token of his being a " brave " and having slain his man in a blood-feud. The Riffi turban, of strings of dark red wool, was wound round his head; a white shirt showed at his neck; he wore a black waistcoat, a white tunic down to his knees, and red knicks, below which came his long hairy shanks, ending in a pair of yellow slippers.

A scarlet leather bag, hung by a red cord over his shoulders, a leather belt, and his gun, finished off our Moorish servant, who shot us partridges, roasted chickens, and was as good a hand at buttered eggs and coffee as I have ever seen.

Out of doors he always wore his brown jellab, embroidered with silk tufts of green and yellow and white.

Tahara was a pretty, pale, dark girl, with curious cabalistic Riffi marks tattooed in blue on her forehead and chin. She bound round her head an orange-coloured silk handkerchief; wore, except when at work, an embroidered yellow waistcoat, a pale blue kaftan down to her ankles, a sprigged, white muslin, loose garment, all over that; and a creamy woollen haik, when she went out or was cold, covered everything.

S'lam acted as butler, Tahara kept our rooms in order, and they were joint cooks. Their standing dish was mutton stewed in vegetables, or a chicken; and given time, four hours in the pot, on the pan of charcoal, it was quite a success. But they learnt many things in a Dutch oven lent by the missionaries, besides stews. They had eccentricities—as when S'lam prepared to put the toast-rack itself on the charcoal fire, with the bread in it, thus to "toast": the toast-rack we made ourselves, too, out of some old wire. They kept chickens, which S'lam brought home from market, either in their bedrooms for the night, or else in the kitchen, until their crops were empty and they could be killed.

Every morning S'lam was dispatched to the city with a basket, instructions, and two or three shillings. He stayed there an unconscionable time, visiting his mother, and sitting sunning himself in the doorway of a little Moorish café, returning laden before lunch. He never went into the city without his gun and best jellab, striding along with his long legs—a most picturesque figure. After dinner every evening he rendered his account, stalking into the sitting-room when we called, pulling up a chair, and sitting down at the table opposite R. From his leather bag, change was produced, and if the change was wrong, there was agony; but that only happened once or twice. A scrap of paper was brought out covered with Arabic writing, items of the day's expenditure, which read more or less as follows:—

Chicken	7d.
Milk	1d.
Four eggs	2½d.
Mutton	6d.
Apples	2d.
Vegetables	2d.
Bread three times a week	4½d.
Butter twice a week	9½d.

Charcoal for cooking purposes, and oil for lamps, added

three shillings to our moderate weekly expenditure. Living is cheap enough in Morocco, nor are servants' wages heavy. S'lam and Tahara had eighteen shillings a month and their food, which was simple indeed—a loaf each of native bread a day, green tea, lump sugar, and odds and ends from our meals. Our rent, it will be remembered, came to thirty shillings a month. Morocco suits "reduced circumstances."

Once a week, one of the little donkeys, which passed along our "lane" in droves, carrying charcoal into the sok, was waylaid, brought into the garden, and its three pannierfuls commandeered for us and stored in the mules' stable, where Tahara did the washing in a great tub bought from Mr. Bewicke.

Milk was left every morning by a Moor, who took it in for sale to the sok.

When the accounts were all settled up, S'lam would swing out of the room with a "Bon soir tout-le-monde," unless he stayed to give R. a lesson in Arabic, which he could write as well as read—an unusual thing, and marking him for a scholar in his country.

Blood-feuds among the Riff tribe are common enough. S'lam's father was shot when S'lam was a boy. As soon as he grew up, S'lam shot the man. He had left the Riff in consequence: he was a "marked man," they said; but he began to talk of going back again, and while he was with us he bought a new French rifle. In the Riff he might be potted at, he might not: he would risk that. The brother or son of the man whom he had shot would never trouble to journey far for the purpose of shooting him. Why should they? All in good time. Some day, when he came their way, they would put a bullet into him. Only women die in their beds in the Riff. "Sudden death, Good Lord, grant us."

Men in the Riff who have blood-feuds will not go out of their houses in the early mornings without first sending the women and children to look if the coast is clear: neither will they walk up a hedgerow nor in a wood, but across the fields, keeping well in the open, since murder is always committed out of sight, decently, and in good order.

A man living in Tetuan now, has a blood-feud with an enemy, who has been in consequence obliged to move to Tangier. Sometimes he comes over, secretly, by night, to see his mother, and lies hidden in her house till the sok is full of market people in the middle of the day, when he can go out into the crowd without running great risk,—though in the sok a quarrel sometimes arises; in a flash, guns are up at men's shoulders—bang—bang—and bullets ping into the soft walls, if not into some one or other. Only lately a boy was shot twice in the thigh, happening to be in the way in a scuffle.

S'lam and Tahara were often amusing, if not interesting: never commonplace or "well-meaning." One corner of the roof of Jinan Dolero had been left unwhitewashed, the whitewashers' ladder was still there, and one morning S'lam came to say in his best French, " Deux mesdames. Pour arranger en haut."

The two madams were the whitewashers—two black madams, clad in a couple of striped towels each, Ali Slowee's slaves, bought for, say, £7 each. A very ragged countrywoman who came and weeded the garden, and seemed almost devoid of intelligence, was also a madam.

S'lam was deft with a needle; he borrowed one of ours and a thimble, sat himself down in the kitchen, and stitched away at a large white garment "pour Maman," he said—sat up half the night, finished it, and took it to her next day.

S'lam and Tahara

He did not make a bad man-servant; but he was fond of tempting Fate by carrying trays, laden with china and glass, balanced on one hand; then he would stoop down and pick up a kettle in the other, there would be an ominous clatter, if not crash, in the tray amongst our crockery, and S'lam would murmur reproachfully under his breath, "O tray! tray!"

He bought a new jellab for wearing on visits to the sok; and after it had been proudly shown us, it was found, neatly folded up, placed on a hat-box in our bedroom. When we asked why it was there, he was taken aback. "Mightn't he keep it there? It was new: it was very clean."

One evening, when he came in to settle accounts, he said that he wished to write a letter. Would we give him a sheet of paper and envelope? They were produced. We were not quite prepared for it, when he at once drew up a chair, sat down at the table, and politely asked for a pencil. But it was impossible to snub so simple and well-meaning a child. I sharpened a pencil, and S'lam wrote diligently for quite half an hour, without a pause, from right to left, wonderful spidery characters: it was a long letter to his old master down in Morocco City. He held his string-turbaned head on one side, and was without embarrassment as he sat between R. and myself (one of us worked, the other wrote); indeed, S'lam might have spent his evenings in a drawing-room all his life. When the letter was finished, he accepted a stamp most gratefully, wished us "Bon soir," and departed.

Tahara had her eccentricities too, of which one was an extraordinary aptitude for annexing wherewithal to tie round her head in place of her own yellow silk scarf, which was kept for high days. One week one of our table-napkins was raised to this honour; the next one of our clean bedroom towels had taken its place round her dark locks.

I made her a present of a flannel shirt to wear, but the second day S'lam had appropriated that, and wore it in place of his waistcoat, unbuttoned.

Apparently, in the eyes of the Tetuan world, we were taking a most unprecedented and foolhardy step in sleeping outside the city in the winter: the Ceuta "road" near us was said to be famous for robbery and murder. For some reason or other a reputation clung to us of being fabulously rich. The Moors warned, the missionaries seriously expostulated with us. None of them would have done it, and Mr. Bewicke was put down as mad for countenancing such an action. But we had two men in the house at night; for, besides S'lam, a labourer was induced to sleep in the mules' stable for our protection, and we had a couple of rifles and a revolver. Now, since the news of the murder of A——, one wonders..... But *he* was alone: *we* had the safety of numbers.

To show how jealous Moors can be, and what precautions they take about their women, S'lam never allowed the labourer inside the garden gate unless he himself had come in. The man sat and waited on the bank. Then, after he was installed in the stable, the door between the kitchen and stable was locked and bolted. When we went out, Tahara was made to bolt every door; and if any one came to the house, she would only call down to them out of our bedroom window.

The first night we slept in our garden-house and for several nights after, the basha took upon himself to send us out a guard of soldiers, who were responsible for our safety. We never asked this favour, and were annoyed;

A Night Alarm

for they slept under our windows, talked and coughed the whole night, lay on the bulbs in a flower-bed, and stole the lemons. Seeing, however, that we did not pay them anything at all for the attention, the basha soon grew tired of sending them, much to our relief; for when, to prevent their depredations, we locked them outside the garden door, they broke down our fence, scrambled into the garden, and lay under the prickly pears, as being a safer place than the lane outside.

There has never such a thing been known, as a guard without a cough, or who do not talk. If told to be silent, they reply that they must talk to keep awake; for if they fell asleep, how could they guard? Occasionally, to show how much on the alert they are, guards will discharge their guns in the dead of night. Altogether Moorish soldiers at close quarters are not conducive to sleep.

We had an excitement one night, but it turned out to be groundless. Guns were fired from the garden-house below ours, repeatedly, about 10 p.m., and S'lam got into a fever of excitement, brought his rifle up into our sitting-room, and sat watching at one of the windows. He thought it was tribesmen come down from the hills to rob. At last the firing stopped, and R. and I went to bed; but S'lam was up all night, and Tahara brought their mattress upstairs and slept in our sitting-room for safety. It turned out to be Moors who had come out to sleep for one night, and were amusing themselves by firing rifles from the loop-holes and out in the garden.

There is an advantage in being in a country where game is not sacred. For instance, one evening after tea, standing on the steps outside our "bungalow," in the hush which came just after sunset, R. and I were startled by a familiar call over in the garden next ours.

S'lam was strolling about, and confirmed our supposition—a partridge. We went indoors and forgot about it; but ten minutes later the report of a gun brought us out again, and there was S'lam crashing over the great bamboo fence into "next door" with his rifle, scudding across our neighbour's beans, then stooping down over something; a second later and he was back again, across the palisade like a lamplighter, and striding triumphantly up our path with a partridge dangling from his hand—a red-legged Frenchman, which we hung long. This acquisition to the larder had to be applauded perforce, in spite of its being shot sitting, and on some one else's acres. As luck would have it, S'lam's great bullet, about the size commonly used for big game, had gone through its head: he naïvely explained the advantages of shooting birds through the head. But I think he was a fair shot. Most Riffis are.

I suppose that the Riff tribe is more or less an anomaly. Think, if you can, of a clan or a tribe who are pirates, wreckers, who encourage slavery, who count the vendetta an admirable custom, who have no laws, no governors, who acknowledge as their supreme head a Sultan who has never from all ages ventured within their borders—a tribe who have, as it has been said, "no fear, no anything, save and excepting their faith in One God and Mohammed as his Prophet, their own daggers, a Martini-Henry if they can get one, and failing that, a ten-foot-long Riff gun, coral-studded, ivory-butted, brass-bound, and deadly to handle"—a people who live in a country without roads, *and all within a few hours of Gibraltar*: have they their parallel, except among adventurers in the Far East, and those but a few upon distant seas?

To explore the unknown Riff country would be interesting indeed. No book has been written upon it except

TWO WOMEN FROM THE RIFF COUNTRY.

[*To face p.* 172.

from hearsay, and no European has penetrated across its length and breadth. The Riffis want no foreign interlopers among their sacred hills, and would "knife" the first who showed his face. It is but two days' journey eastwards from Tetuan, this select and exclusive country, and it extends about a hundred and fifty miles, with a population, it is reported, of one hundred and fifty thousand souls. Strange to think that no European pioneer, nor gentleman-rover, has ever exploited the Riff.

The law of the vendetta, is the law and the ten commandments of the Riffi, which, if he fail to keep, renders him in the eyes of his country-folk damned to all eternity, to be ostracised among men. A widow will teach her baby-son to shoot, and studiously prepare him for his one great duty, that as early as possible he may put a bullet into the murderer of his father. And thus the feud is nourished. Even the great-great-grandson of a man who has taken a life years upon years ago is not safe. He will probably meet with a dagger or the muzzle of a long gun one day.

But a people who inculcate such severe and cursory measures have their redeeming-points. It is a fact that cursing and swearing, so common among Moors, and polygamy and adultery, are seldom, if ever, met with in the Riff: for if one Riffi insults another, it is at the peril of his life; while the stain of immorality is wiped out at once by death.

The gun, pistol, or dagger is the Riffi's summary judge and jury. He submits to no authority. Questions on land, on inheritance, all legal questions, are settled in each village by the keeper of the mosque. He arranges marriages.

The Riffis are therefore a moral people: a man has but one wife; the women do not veil, and yet familiarity is not tolerated between the sexes; a young man will go out of his way to avoid passing close by a young woman whom he sees in the distance, lest he be suspected of behaving lightly to her.

The Riffis are an indomitable race, one which has never been conquered, magnificent raw material out of which to shape a battalion of infantry. Though acknowledged as the Kaliph of the Prophet and their religious head, the Sultan, as has been said, has never dared to put his head in this independent hornets' nest.

They are an industrious tribe, growing crops assiduously and rearing cattle: their valleys are fertile and well farmed for an uncivilized country. But these details must be taken for what they are worth. S'lam could say nothing but good of the Riff: how cheap living was, and how abundant food,—except when rain failed, and then there followed disastrous famine, and starving Riffis would come down to Tetuan, and lie in the caves outside the city, and live on roots, doing any work which offered; and some of them would die, in spite of the missionaries' kindness and unremitting efforts.

There are many legends about the Riffis: they boast one tribe among themselves who are said to be descended from the Romans; and there is no reason against the assumption, since the Romans were in Morocco after Cæsar's day. Another family claims to be descended from the inhabitants of Sodom. Some of them are quite fair—regular "carrots": Vandal blood may run in their veins. While, again, some people say there are Celts among them, with Irish characteristics and Irish words. Possibly. Pirates and rovers are apt to introduce foreign strains.

At any rate they have nothing in common with the Arabs, but are as unlike that race as a Scotchman is unlike an Italian. Berber is of course their common origin, and they are identical with the Kabyles of Algeria, the Touariks of the Sahara, and the Guanches of the Canary Isles. Shillah, the Berber dialect which they speak—one of the many dialects belonging to that race—is not a written language; but an educated Riffi learns to write and read at his village *jama* (mosque school); he uses the Arabic character in writing, and he learns to read the Korān.

Yet in one great point, like the Arabs, the Riffi, in common with the Berber race, lacks the power of cohesion and the spirit of patriotism, which should have welded all Berbers into one powerful people. Internal strife, that curse of Africa, has split them up into isolated units, and they stand at the same point they stood at a thousand years ago.

Nor have the Riffis, in common with the Moors, reached the point of discarding "petticoats and drapery"—that is to say, they wear the brown, hooded, woollen jellab, and the white woollen haik—a sheet of material without seam, which they cast round themselves something like a Roman toga. Perhaps a cotton tunic is worn underneath.

Part of the sleeves, the hood, and front of the jellab are often beautifully embroidered in coloured silks. On the border of the cloth thin leaves of dried grass are laid, which are worked over and over with coloured silk, and make a thick, handsome edging. The coloured leather belts which they wear; the large embroidered leather pouches, with deep-cut leather fringes, which hold bullets and powder and money and hemp-tobacco; their shaved heads, with one long oiled and combed or plaited lock; their turbans, red or brown, of strings of wool,—all complete a Riffi, and a very fine-looking fellow he can be.

The labour element, which as a whole is antagonistic to the spirit of Morocco, crops up here and there, less in the casually farmed fields than in out-of-the-way corners. The Potters' Caves just outside Tetuan constitute one of those corners. There is always work going on in the caves, and smoke coming out of one or other of the many kilns, all the year round. Morocco and Moorish architecture would be nowhere without the potteries. Those infinitesimal little tiles which fit together and make such artistic colour-patterns, lining the *al-fresco* patios, facing the walls of the rooms, the pillars and doorways and flooring, the houses throughout, are every one of them kneaded and cut and baked there: crocks to wash in, pans for charcoal, immense water-pots, small water-pots, bowls and shallow basins, dishes of all sizes, and saucers down to the smallest, even ink-bottles, all come into being there.

Leaving the city by *Báb-el-Nooadtha* (the Gate of Sheaves), a little winding path leads to the caves, which lie among thickets of prickly pear, at the foot of the Anjera Hills, out of which they have been hollowed, probably by the action of water. Immense ramifications they are—great dark halls, roofed *au naturel* in corrugated rock with fissured sides, where maiden-hair fern hangs cool and green. Here in the dark shadows are a little company of workmen, chiefly in brown jellabs and leathern aprons, one cutting squares out of the soft clay with a penknife—he has a pattern to help him keep them exact; another cuts diamonds, another stars: piled up together, they look like little pastry shapes in brown, beside the workmen, who are all sitting cross-legged on the ground.

A little farther on two more men are dipping the top surfaces of the diamonds into an earthenware bowl full of yellow "cream," which will glaze and colour them, all in one. This sulphur-colour, and a blue, and a white, are generally used for the tiles—no other shades, as a rule. A boy in a corner is at work at one of the first processes, treading out a vast circle of yellowish clay into the consistency of stiff dough. A rather superior old Moor in a white turban, perhaps the master-workman, is deftly cutting out rosettes. In the front of the cave a little brown donkey, with pasterns as weak as a reed, is standing under the weight of four great earthenware pots full of water, two balanced on each side its pack. A boy empties them one by one of the water, pouring it into a natural basin scooped out in the ground, well puddled with clay, and therefore without a leak. The water is wanted to mix with the "dough." Then the donkey patters off for another load, the boy sitting sideways on its pack and shaking his heels—that makes it go.

To the left stands a kiln in process of being packed with millions of the clay dice, which, baked hard, dovetailed together, and forming a smooth, polished surface, will keep many a room cool. The kiln next door to it, is full of pots and pans of all shapes and sizes, but its opening is plastered up with clay, and they are not to be seen. Into the great fiery furnace underneath, a man is thrusting dry brown bushes, and dried prickly pear, and whatever rubbish will burn. Much of it has been hacked off the hillside by women, and has come on their backs many a mile. There is a crackling sound, smoke comes out, and a pink flame glows behind the man's body. The tiles ought to bake all right.

Meanwhile, the same boy inside the cave has got his clay into good order—it is about two inches thick, and something the size of a big round table; then he stoops down, and, with a knife held in both hands, scores the clay across, much as toffee is scored ; which done, each square, about a foot in diameter, is carried off to be cut up into little shapes or to go upon the potter's wheel.

The potter sat in his little pit, working the wheel with his foot—as Carlyle says, " one of the venerablest objects, old as the Prophet Ezekiel and far older. Rude lumps of clay, how they spin themselves up, by mere quick whirling, into beautiful circular dishes."

The potter thumped his wet clay ; then, as the wheel turned, pressed and moulded it with clever clay-encrusted hands : the sleeves were turned back from his bony chocolate-coloured arms. He had a grey goatee and a quiet smile, a dirty turban round his head, a white tunic mostly clay, and underneath a claret-coloured garment showed at the neck.

He was a spare, wizened old man : perhaps his work, like Dante's, had made him " lean for many years." The faster his wheel revolved, the truer apparently was the shape of the vessel he turned out. His country might accept the lesson—that labour, like the wheel, conduces towards a good end. I fancy that a decadent people, who will neither work nor spin, but choose to rest and lie at ease, give the potter Destiny no chance. He has no wheel, this potter—for Morocco will not labour, nor be broken, nor disciplined ; and so he is reduced to a mere kneading and baking, without the means he fain would employ; and he turns out a mere makeshift—his production at best is " not a dish ; no, a bulging, kneaded, crooked, shambling, squint-cornered, amorphous botch—a mere enamelled vessel of dishonour."

The great pot which the potter slowly evolved out of the soft brown clay under our eyes was not perfect : he made it entirely by eye, and it matched the rest of the

SELLING EARTHENWARE POTS.

[*To face p.* 178.

group to the ordinary observer; yet it had a distinct "lean." Did it grumble to itself, that

> vessel of the more ungainly make?

as human vessels complain sometimes :—

> They sneer at me for leaning all awry;
> What! did the Hand then of the Potter shake?

Beyond the potter the ground was covered with an army of his soft mud-coloured vessels, all sorted and arranged in groups which matched, dozen after dozen, far back into the inner shadows of the cave, like some weird and interminable china shop. I gave the old man a cigarette, which he puffed at over his wheel.

In the next cave a white-bearded Aaron was solemnly dipping dishes into a bowl of blue colour and glaze, and placing each with his finger and thumb on a board by him among countless fellows, while with his other hand he gravely swirled the liquid to prevent its setting. Others next him were again cutting out shapes; and three potters were hard at work, one moulding the bodies of pots, another the necks, another the lids, while a fourth put all three together.

And thus they laboured on. Their slippers lay in the mouths of the caves beside their brown jellabs; and the smell of the moist clay and the drip of water up amongst the green fern mixed with the cool air.

> Almighty Potter, on whose wheel of blue
> The world is fashioned, and is broken too,
> Why to the race of men is heaven so dire?
> In what, O wheel, have I offended you?

CHAPTER VII

COUNTRY PEOPLE FORDING THE RIVER—WE CALL ON CI HAMED GHRALMIA—AN EXPEDITION ACROSS THE RIVER IN SEARCH OF THE BLUE POOL—MOORISH BELIEF IN GINNS—THE BASHA—POWDER PLAY—TETUAN PRISON.

CHAPTER VII

> Set not thy heart on any good or gain—
> Life means but pleasure, or it means but pain;
> When Time lets slip a little perfect hour,
> Oh! take it—for it will not come again.

MANY walks began by degrees to tell upon our boots, for the cobble-stones of Tetuan and the rocks of Morocco in general are meant less for boots than for bare feet, which they do not seem to damage. In time, stress of circumstances drove us to a curly black-headed Jew bootmaker, whose most expensive pair of thick black boots cost nine shillings. Another Israelite made us suits of rough brown jellab material, for the sum of £1 each—stuff which wore for ever.

The mountains on the opposite side of the river were our El Dorado, but the river would not go down in January and allow of our fording it; rain followed rain, and it was higher than ever. One market day we walked down to watch the people from the other side come across, on their way into the sok, laden with country produce. Years ago a bridge had been built over the Wad-el-Martine, but, like other Moorish architecture, it was not built to last, and the immense floods which swing down the Wad-el-Martine in winter-time soon left only a broken pier or two, to point out that a bridge had been thought of. The money to build it was supplied by Government: half of it went into the pocket of the builder; a little went towards the bridge, which naturally could only be built of rubbish, without proper foundations. Now that there is no bridge, it is once more, as it had been for ages upon ages, a case of ferrying across by the big ferry-boat, or of fording. Since ferrying means money, and fording only a wetting, most of the market-goers ford.

It was a sight to see the countrywomen wading through, one after another like a string of ducks, trying to keep dry: the water came just about up to their bodies, and the white haik and piece of towelling for a skirt could be bundled up somehow—a very few wore short white cotton drawers. Their legs were remarkable for an enormous development of muscle in unusual places. Once across, they wrung out anything which had been wetted, shivering somewhat; then arranged their voluminous haiks afresh over the mysterious great bundles on their backs, and, padding off in single file, made for the city. What those bundles, which bent their backs half double, had inside them it was impossible to certify: often part of it was a baby, judging by a round shape like a head under the haik, and the fact that, when it had a knock, there was a cry: the rest might be chickens, oranges, vegetables, baskets of eggs, baskets of coos-coosoo, heads of brooms made of bamboo, honey, and so on. Some of the chickens dangled in front of the women by strings tied to their waists: the chickens were alive, of course.

On the tops of their heads the women wore enormous straw hats, with brims large enough to act as umbrellas and to keep the rain off their shoulders. The ferry-boat, packed with them *and* these straw hats, was worth seeing, like a grand-stand in a shower hidden by umbrellas. The weights which the women carry for hours at a time are almost incredible; but they begin as tiny girls, lopping along after their mothers at a half-run under

A FERRY-BOAT ON MARKET DAY.

[*To face p.* 184.

Fording the River

tiny bundles, with the same bent backs; and habit is second nature.

After the string of women came along a youth, with two small donkeys, laden with panniers full of green vegetables. The donkeys jibbed upon the brink; many "Arrahs" and curses and much cudgelling with a stick got them started; the panniers swayed horribly, and threatened to turn completely round, as the current pushed the donkeys over this side and that. Once in, they made pluckily for the opposite shore; but the stream carried them down; the water was well up their bodies; the distracted boy plunged and struggled behind first this one and then the other, whichever seemed in most danger—for the ford was none too wide. Urging them to keep up-stream, he clung on to one refractory pannier. The water rose higher and almost took them off their feet; but that was the worst place; now it was better. The leading donkey was in safety in shallower water, nearing dry land; but the other poor fellow seemed less strong, and was not able to make half such a good fight of it—its load may have been heavier. In spite of the boy it got lower and lower down-stream: suddenly there was an upheaval and a splash; its head went under altogether, pack and everything in a hole. Then the boy surpassed himself; for, deep as it was, he was there in a moment, got hold of the donkey behind, and pushed and half lifted, at no small risk to himself, and pulled, until the little fellow, after several relapses, found his feet. Finally, he waded out, and stood, like a drowned rat, on the bank, pack and all streaming; then he collected himself after a pause, and doddered off towards the sok. The boy shook himself and his soaked clothes, clutched his stick, and ran after his donkeys.

A well-to-do Moor, possibly a sheikh, was the next

to go for the ford. He probably farmed, and his sleek mule was full of green corn and " beans." They were things of colour, the pair of them: all the mule's appointments scarlet, himself a glossy brown; while his master, in dark blue, sat tight on his scarlet saddle, his bright chased stirrups flashing, so short as to bring his feet right up the mule's side—his turban, white as snow, with the red peak of the fez underneath, the deepest blot of colour, against the sky. A white garment waved out in the breeze under the blue jellab; he sat straight as a withy, feeling the mule's mouth with a hard hand, and bringing its nose into the air. There were some bravado and a great deal of assurance in the whole. The world used him well. Moors ride everywhere, if they possess anything with four legs. Why should they give themselves the fatigue of walking? But besides that, they are horsemen and most at home on a horse, while their country is not one to travel in on foot.

Having decided that the river was fordable, and that we ought to be able to ride across it, we walked back by way of the city, and went in to tea with a Moor, ordering a donkey to be sent out the next day to Jinan Dolero, which should take us across to our El Dorado. The Moor who entertained us was a certain Ci Hamed Ghralmia, the eldest son of a Government official who had fattened physically and financially on the Customs, and whose fine house represented so many perquisites and bribes, and so much pared off the lump sum which went annually up to the Sultan.

It was as luxurious a house as Eastern could wish: soft Rabat carpets, old Fez silk hangings, round the four-post beds, standing back in recesses in the room into which our host led us,—hangings such as even Fez can no longer produce; such silk is not made. One piece, which was quite as handsome in its way, was made years ago in Tetuan, from Tetuan silk-worms, reared on the slopes outside the Mulberry Gate—spun, dyed, and woven in Tetuan.

Couches and divans filled up the corners; glowing colours and fine snowy linen abounded. It was a house in which to spend a sleepy Sabbath afternoon on a hot day, if it must be spent indoors. Cool air blew through the high rooms; the splash and ripple of fountains rose and fell in the cool marble patio below, and echoed up the tiled staircase; while back, far in the shade of the secluded rooms, among avenues of pillars, vistas of light and shade, women like butterflies, in mauve and yellow and white, rose from some soft scented divan and flitted across. And in the centre of it all, a little king, Ci Hamed Ghralmia—a pale, café-au-lait complexioned man, who looked as if life had never shown him one of its angles. He was fat and lineless: soft white hands, fleshy ankles, no knots of muscle in so well-turned-out a mould of cream, not a spot, not a flush, no sign of liver; the lips slightly suggested sensuality, and there was a line of cruelty round the mouth, but no further indication of self-indulgence; he might have lived on sugar and chicken coos-coosoo all his life, and altered in nothing but size since he was a year old, except for a beard on the soft white chin, and his eyes, which were infinitely cunning. Brown and cold, like polished marbles, they had not reached that stage of cunning which veils its cunning, but would still gleam at the sight of money and express satisfaction over a well-made bargain. They were suspicious, as the ignorant generally are, and believed in little that they saw. The old Biblical characters who walk Morocoo to-day have most of them the same failing: they are sly.

Ci Hamed Ghralmia was an "advanced" Moor—that is to say, in the afternoons, lying on his divan, he read Arabic books. He had bought some French knick-knacks too. He told us that he rented a shop, in which he sat in the mornings and chatted to his friends, using it not in any way to dispose of any goods, of which it was devoid, but as a sort of "club" or meeting-place. Then in the afternoons he occasionally rode out on his mule. He had a garden, I think, outside the city. Or he played chess with a friend, or read. Perhaps he would use his *hummum* (Turkish bath); he would pray at his own particular mosque, regularly, so many times a day; and he would drink much green tea, and consume sugar, and sleep inordinately.

Thirty years of this life in Tetuan found Ci Hamed Ghralmia still a contented man—supremely so. Wrapped in the finest white wool and muslin clothes, he lay along a divan opposite to us upon one elbow, the picture of ease, and talked away. No Moor was ever anything but self-composed. Upon our camera's coming out, he was much interested; and to prove his progressive and enlightened state of mind, let us photograph him just as he lay there—a vast, voluminous white chrysalis. Then he took us to see his wives and slaves—a large party of them. They were allowed to come out on to the staircase and talk to us; but when the interview had lasted five minutes, Ci Hamed Ghralmia clapped his hands twice—we had seen enough—every wife and every slave vanished like magic.

The next morning we made one of many expeditions up into the hills on the opposite side of the river, towards the south, and in the direction, though somewhat west, of the Riff. We rode in turns, it being somewhat of a rest to scramble along on foot, to say nothing of exercise.

THE AUTHOR FORDING THE WAD-EL-MARTINE.

[*To face p.* 188.

Across the River

The big grey donkey had our lunch, a camera, some field-glasses, and a box for botanical specimens slung about him. We had a fairly intelligent boy—Mohammed, a Riffi—and managed to understand a word or two he said. It had been explained to him by S'lam that we wished to get to the Blue Pool if possible. Arrived at the river, we found nobody—not being market day, it was utterly deserted. The current was still swirling in a forbidding fashion, but Mohammed led the donkey straight in with R.; he tucked up his clothes, held his yellow slippers high in one hand, and after some goading they landed on the opposite bank. Mohammed left his slippers, rode back through the river for me, and in due time I was deposited on the shingle. Off we set—first by a narrow path, thick on each side with scented violets, and closed in with the usual ten-foot-high cane fence. More streams had to be forded, but they were small and the donkey strong; so, to save time, I sat above his tail, behind R., and he carried us across in one journey.

So far we were still down on the flats; the hills towered in front of us; and among the streams, and where the river in its vagaries had often flowed, there was deposited many a rich bed of fruitful mud, turned into valuable land, the very soil *par excellence* for oranges. And they were all around us—garden after garden, acre after acre, foliage studded with gold knobs by the million. And among them, and as far as the eye could reach, up into the gorge between the hills, picturesque white garden-houses showed through rifts in the half-tropical foliage, or over hedges of prickly pear and oleander. Fig-trees, a hundred years old, made faded grey blotches amongst the vivid greenery; the pink bloom of apricot was stainless against stained-yellow walls. In such a place, the inexorable realism of the age in which we live, was shaken—spirits there surely were which should appear.

We passed an old countrywoman with a tiny donkey carrying two great panniers full of green-stuffs: she was in difficulties, having a wrestle to make it cross a little stream. Mohammed went to her assistance. Once over, she climbed on its small back with the help of a stone, putting her foot on its neck to get into her place.

And now, leaving the orange gardens and their wealth, our path took an upward turn into a more rugged country, a less fruitful soil. We left a field of pale blue flax on the left—a "blue pool" indeed; and about this point the donkey's pack, which had no breastplate, slipped over its tail; but Mohammed's knife, and some string, and the britching, put all to rights for the time being. Later on a stirrup-leather broke.

Following our winding path, we reached at last a white saint-house, which dominated a little hill overgrown with gnarled grey olives, and acted guardian over a large and flourishing village which lay below,—at least it was a collection of mud huts, and more of them than usual, but, like so many of these "villages," seemed to all intents and purposes deserted—a city of the dead. Many of the inhabitants were out no doubt, but those who were in were not tempted by curiosity to stare at us: without windows there can be no signs of the rites which are carried on inside the houses. All we saw were dogs, fierce brutes, which stones alone kept at a distance, where they sat showing their teeth and bristling their crests ominously.

The saint-house, of course, was forbidden ground: we went as close as common sense permitted, and from under the shady olives looked back at Tetuan down below us, a snow-white streak in the valley.

Rag-Trees

Some rags were hanging upon a bush near us. It is an interesting and curious practice, that of hanging votive rags upon the bushes around chapels and holy shrines: no less venerable is the performance of pilgrimages to the same. Both practices go back into the dim ages. They are in use to this day amongst the Shintoists of Japan, and the inhabitants of Northern Asia, India, the Orkneys, and remote corners of Ireland, where sickly children are dipped in streams, or passed through holes in stones or trees so many times running, going against the way of the sun, in order to produce the effect of making the sick child as strong as a lion. Then an offering must be made to the saint, and a rag is torn off somebody's garment, and tied to a bush near his grave, to show that they would have done more for the good saint if they had had the power.

Rag-trees, burdened with the tattered offerings of the devout and impecunious tribes-people, flourish throughout Morocco,—signs hanging out, and blown by the wind, in the face of travellers; warnings of the deep-rooted superstition entangled in the innermost heart-cells of its people, to be disturbed at imminent peril.

Leaving the saint-house and village, we struck a path upwards into a wild gorge, at the bottom of which a brawling torrent was tumbling. It turned many rude mills, and there were lush fields of corn on its banks. Far away in the grey distance now, to the north, we could see a dark wedge of rock, almost on the sky-line beyond the Anjera and other hills of Morocco: *the* Rock—Gibraltar.

At this point we lunched. Mohammed was provided, and dropped behind a rock: the donkey grazed. A little boy, minding goats, came up with a fascinating pocket-knife, but would not let it go out of his hand.

A clear stream gave us drink—it was warm ; bees hummed in the balmy air ; there was an aromatic scent ; clouds hung round the hills ; the panorama below was essentially peaceful and " Christian."

And then we went on in search of the far-famed Blue Pool. But though we reached where the river lay in still pools, blue beyond all known blues, we found no more—only traces of a great flood and landslips, which, I suspect, had washed away the lake people had talked of. We found enough to bring us back on other days, and to understand why the missionaries take up their tents and camp in the mountains in the summer.

We returned by a path farther west, and passed a great olive wood full of black shadows. The scrub on the hillsides holds pig—there are plenty of them ; and the boars become more or less antagonistic at certain times in the year. We were told tales of people who had met with terrifying adventures, but personally our expeditions had no such thrilling incidents connected with them.

It would have been unwise to stay out after sunset, and that time always saw us back at Jinan Dolero. It is said to be the most unsafe hour ; for men are coming into Tetuan, and if they can waylay and rob or murder a traveller, and make their way into the city before the gates shut, half an hour after sunset, and sleep there, who shall suspect them of dark deeds done outside in the evening? Besides, Mohammed would never have consented to be out late, on account of the firm belief which Moors have in evil spirits. There is a special race of beings, they hold, in many respects like men, in others like spirits, called *ginns*. Their principal abode is the under-world, but they come up on to the earth, and are fond of lurking in wells and in dark corners, even in houses. Rooms are often haunted by ginns : men are

Ginns

surrounded by ginns. Some of the more enlightened Moors are inclined to represent ginns as merely superstitious imaginations and hallucinations on the part of the ignorant; but probably in his heart of hearts, no Moor but has a secret desire to propitiate ginns, and a secret dread of falling in with them.

Ginns eat and drink and propagate their species, and even form sexual connections with men. A man whose wife is any way odd or mysterious has married of course a ginn. Ginns are fond of inhabiting rivers, woods, the sea, ruins, springs, drains, and caves; they come out at night more than by day, and in certain streets no Moor will walk at night. Nor will a Moor sleep alone in a room. Ginns, when they appear, take the forms of men, goats, cats, dogs, almost any animal in fact, and also monsters.

Whirlwinds, and shooting stars, and dear times, and famine, and epidemics, are all caused by ginns. It is the ginns who have eaten all the food in the city when prices are exorbitant. If a man falls down in the dark, it is a ginn: a sudden illness or an accident is the work of a ginn. There are good ginns, but bad ginns are more common. The worst of them all is *Iblis* (the devil). Iblis tempts men to wickedness. All iniquity is the fault of Iblis.

In order to keep the bad ginns at a distance, certain precautions may be taken. Salt and steel are antidotes. Salt in the hand when going out at night, salt in the pillow when sleeping, are measures which should be used. In building a house some people put salt and wheat and an egg into the ground, and kill a goat on the threshold. On sinking a well (the stronghold of ginns) a goat or sheep must always be killed.

The best talisman against ginns is the repetition of

certain passages in the Korān : when passing a dark spot, say the " Ajatu-l-kursi " : as for neglecting to say " B·ism Allah " (In the name of God) before going for a ride, or before doing any sort or kind of action, why, that is to have a ginn as your companion on your horse, and at your elbow, whatever you may be doing. As every place has its "owners," its good or bad ginns, on striking a light and going into a room Moors say, "Good-evening to you, O ye owners of the place." And if a tent is to be pitched, first of all the protection of good ginns must be solicited in that spot.

Supposing a ginn gets hold of a man, and he is ill, there are certain doctors, magicians, among the Moors who can cast the ginn out. They practice a regular "ginn-cult," and celebrate annual feasts, going outside Tetuan to a certain spring near the Moorish cemetery, and killing a bullock, a black goat, a black donkey, and some chickens.

The word *ginn* originally meant "the secret," "the mysterious," "the hidden"; and the belief in ginns is part of the actual creed of Mohammedans, Arabs, and Berbers alike. But Moors have a hundred superstitions. They believe that all animals had a language once upon a time,—that the horse prays to Allah when he stretches out his leg; that the donkey which falls down, asks Allah that the same may happen to his master. They say that the donkey was once a man whom Allah changed into his present shape because he washed himself with milk; that the stork was a *kadi*, or judge, who was made a stork because he passed unjust sentences upon his fellow-men. It is therefore a sin to kill a stork, or a crow, or a toad, or a white spider, or a white chicken. A white spider once spun its web over a cave where Mohammed hid : his enemies saw it, thought there-

A Moorish Funeral

fore that no one could have recently entered the cave, and passed on.

It is hardly necessary to say, that about Death—the Great Secret—there are numerous superstitions. There were too many funerals in Tetuan: early in the afternoon one was often encountered at the Gate of the Tombs; death would only have taken place that morning, without much inquiry as to its cause, and whether by fair means or foul nobody knew and few cared. The procession came swinging along, stately men in flowing garments, white and dark, chanting the weird funeral hymn or "lament"—always the same mournful, monotonous cadence, rising and falling in the narrow streets, and at last out into the air. And then once through the Báb-el-M'kabar, the great company in white turn into the Moorish burial-ground, and arrange themselves in a long line against the hillside, and the chant becomes general, almost a great cry, full of the strange fascination of certain Eastern music, withal so unintelligible to Europeans.

The body, loosely wrapped in white, lies on an open bier. After a sort of service on that rough hillside against the walls of the city, the procession winds on again to the shallow grave: a last chant, and the body goes into the earth, and is quickly covered. A scribe, or reader, is left behind when every one has gone: he reads pieces out of the Korān over the grave, and chants. Friends, mourners perhaps, will come out on other days, and sit round the tomb, reading the Korān together, and singing the weird, sad melodies. You may see them. But I have never seen a Moor give way to the slightest outward expression of grief.

Mohammedans firmly believe, of course, in a Paradise to which the good are admitted: their conception as to this land of the hereafter, largely consisting of gardens and shade, adds a bridge, by which means alone access to Paradise is gained. The bridge (*Al Sirat*) is finer than a hair and sharper than a sword: the wicked invariably turn giddy and fall off into the pit of Hell, while the righteous negotiate it in safety.

A rich man, when he is buried, is provided with a vault. The body is laid on its right side, its sightless eyes turned to Mecca. During the first night, Mohammedans hold that the soul remains in the body for the purpose of being interrogated by two angels before it can be admitted into Paradise. They appear, and the body is roused to a sitting posture and to temporary life. It replies to the dread examination. If this ends unsatisfactorily, the angels torture and beat the body, until the sepulchre closes in upon it. But if they approve the soul's replies, they bid the man sleep on in peace in the protection of God.

Travellers complain of a want of " pageant " in Morocco. Ostentatious funerals and processions of all sorts, public demonstrations over trifles, the worship of gilt and glitter, and the emotional spirit called *loyalty*, of the present day, do not exist in El Moghreb. There is a spirit of simplicity about its shows; they do not breathe of money: old as their customs are, there is vigour in them and a certain amount of use, for the people have not outgrown them, do not make of them so many lay figures on which to display signs of their own great wealth.

The Day of the Great Feast up at Court with the Sultan, that is *the pageant* in all Morocco. We missed it.

Connected with the bashas and kaids, who are the only great men in the country or in the cities, there is little or no respect or formality. Only on Sundays a sort of "flash in the pan" reminds the Moor that he has a little despot in his midst, who is more or less lord of his life;

The Basha Prays

and the drums are heard all over the city, the soldiers turn out, for the basha goes to pray at *El Aoli* (noon) in his own particular mosque opposite his house.

On Friday, the Sabbath, the biggest *sok* (market) in all the week, a little black flag was flown from the mosque-tops early in the morning to remind Tetuan of the holy day. The basha was inside the cool mosque, praying, at the hottest time of the day; outside a few people collected, though the same event happened every Friday. No Moor is ever busy, ever hurries, but can always wait. At a quarter to one a bugler on the east side of the street, who had been sitting in the sun with his bugle, got up and blew a call to fall in. About sixty soldiers, who had all strolled off after the great man had disappeared into the mosque, sauntered up from different directions. If they were a ragged and indifferently drilled company, there was colour in the ranks at least. Every man wore a short scarlet flannel tunic, a pair of white cotton drawers, and a red fez: one drummer had a tunic of beetle-green. As they lined the street, short sturdy men, with hairy legs and coffee-coloured faces, their bright bayonets flashing in the sun, the drums thumping and the trumpeter running up and down the scale, the dazzling sunlight gave a trace of splendour to the medley of scarlet and steel against the whitewashed walls.

Everybody waited expectant. A stout man in white came out of the mosque, ordered the small boys away, and saw that there was ample room for the basha to pass across the street and into his own house. Then the ordinary crowd of worshippers began to file out of the building—prayers over: green-blue kaftans lined with crimson silk, filmy white robes, snowy turbans, moved slowly along—a dignified, impressive crowd. There was a pause before the basha appeared, a man arranging his two yellow slippers side by side upon the doorstep of the mosque. Another moment and the great, voluminous, expected figure filled the doorway. A twist of his ankles and he was in his slippers, the bugle sounded, the ragged squad presented arms somewhat untidily, a line of servants bowed themselves low and respectfully before him, and the basha moved slowly across the street.

Leading his own troops, dispensing justice, an after-type of those great Arabs who sprang from the sands of Arabia and Africa, shook Europe, and flourished in Spain, a basha should be no tyrant, but a courteous gentleman, a noble of " The Arabian Nights." But there was no aristocratic trace about Asydaibdalkdar. Carrying his rosary in his hand, clothed entirely in white, his features bore traces of servility and sensuality, the result of poisoning the Arab and Berber blood with the strain from Central Africa. Slavery is proving fatal to the Moorish race. Unlike the well-bred Moor, the basha's face was deeply lined: cruelty, cunning, pigheadedness, all fought for the upper hand in his swarthy countenance. He walked in under his own gateway into a courtyard beyond: there he sat down in a corner upon a seat—a great figure, much like some Indian god—while his underlings came forward, stood in a semicircle, bowed low, and saluted him; followed by his soldiers, who marched in single file into the courtyard, round it, past their chief, and out again—this three times, to the sound of drums; then, headed by the officer in command, they trooped off to the barracks, the basha's gateway was locked, and Church Parade was over.

For half an hour all the gates of the city had been barred and bolted, while prayers were going on—there being a superstition among the Moors, arising from an

THE BASHA GOING TO PRAY.

[*To face p.* 198.

Lab-el-Barod

old prophecy, that on a certain morning of a Mohammedan Sabbath, Christians will gain possession of the cities while the kaids and bashas are in the mosques.

Two hundred soldiers are allowed by Government to the governor of Tetuan, by means of which he is to maintain law and order. However, a hundred only were maintained, and the pay of the remaining half went into somebody's pocket. There was apparently little for them to do; drill was a thing unheard of, and they spent most of the day hanging round the basha's house or doing errands for him.

On the feast days there was *Lab-el-Barod*—the famous "Powder Play" of Morocco; and then the soldiers all turned out into the *feddan* (the great market-square), and showed what Lab-el-Barod meant: to me rather a foolish game, with but one interesting point—that it is the imitation of the old Arab tribal battle. To-day the Moors gallop forward, stand up in their saddles, fire their guns under their horses' necks, over their tails— all this at full gallop—throw their guns into the air and catch them, and last of all pull up in an incredibly short space, dragging their horses right on to their haunches, which evolutions are imitations of what their ancestors did with spear and javelin. Lab-el-Barod prevailed in Spain till the middle of the eighteenth century, and it is still played in the East with reeds. There is of course a picturesque element in it—white turbans, white garments streaming in the wind, scarlet saddles, flashing steel, hard-held horses with yards of tail, and above all, the lithe figures in perfect balance whatever their positions; but the performance is often too "ragged" to be impressive, and it strenuously demands flats of desert as a background.

The basha would always come out and look on when

there was one of these "field days" at Tetuan: his figure was not adapted to his participation therein, being perfectly in keeping with his walk in life, and that walk consisted in his sitting from six o'clock to ten o'clock in the morning, and from three o'clock to six o'clock in the afternoon, in a small open room off the street opposite his house, in a reclining position upon cushions, before him an excited group (as often as not), contradicting, swearing, gesticulating, abusing, all at the same moment—one of whom is carried off by the soldiers to be flogged, another is sent to prison, or, if the seekers after justice wax more troublesome than ordinary, they may all be thrown into prison by the heels together to calm them. At the same time the basha absorbs bribes, and sweeps loaves of sugar, packets of candles, and pounds of tea into his net. These are the ordinary bribes.

When he was appointed basha, a royal letter from the Sultan was sent to Tetuan and read aloud in the mosque: then he entered upon his duties. He must needs go warily from day to day; and even then luck may desert him at any moment, and a summons may arrive from the Sultan—he is to go to Court at once. I recollect in what abject terror, one basha, who was sent for at a day's notice, set out upon his journey, only to find, when he got to Court, that he was to have a more lucrative billet and a higher post of honour. Many who have departed in terror, all unknowing of the future, have found, when they reached Fez or Morocco City, wherever the Sultan might be, that their worst fears were realized. Either placed under arrest, tortured, imprisoned, or bastinadoed, the little wealth they had accumulated is extorted from them, under the pretext of there being arrears in taxes or other dues, which must be made good. The wooden jellab is used for the purpose of extorting confession in the case of imaginary wealth supposed to be hidden (and much often is hidden): it is made of wood, resembling in shape a long cloak, and placed in an upright position; the inside is lined with iron points, which prevent the body from resting against it without suffering. Inside this "jellab" the basha is squeezed, standing up, and he remains there on a sparse diet of bread and water till he divulges.

Both the Prime Minister and the Minister of War were sent to the prison in Tetuan soon after the accession of the present Sultan; but that was for plotting against his life. In the common gaol, heavily chained, under the same roof with the herd of common prisoners, all they were allowed was a curtain across one corner, behind which they sat. The Prime Minister died there. The Minister of War is there to-day, March 1902, and, after over seven years' confinement, getting fat. Some members of the Rahamna tribe are there also. This tribe, which belongs to the far south, near Morocco City, about eight years ago was in a state of rebellion, to quell which the Sultan sent his army with orders to *eat them up*. Their fat lands and fine gardens were ruined; men, women, and children killed and taken prisoners; while six hundred of them were sent to the Tetuan prison, and a great number—I do not know exactly—went to Rabat. That was eight years ago. Sixty of them are in Tetuan prison now, the remnant of six hundred. There is a kaid among them who is very ill, dying: the eight years have done for him.

Since this was written, an order has come from the Sultan for the release of the Rahamna tribesmen. In Rabat, unfortunately, almost all who were in the Kasbah prison died long ago. Its insanitary condition has earned for it the name of *Dar-el-Mout* (the House of Death).

But in the other prison there were survivors. These came out with traces of the late governor's butchery.

For trying to send a written petition to the Sultan three years ago, which set forth their condition, and prayed that after five years' confinement they might be considered to have paid for their rebellious deeds, and be allowed to return to their own land for the last years of their lives, the late governor, Ba Hamed, gave orders that their hands should be mutilated. A knife was drawn across the back of the wrist, cutting the extensor tendons of the hand: the hand was packed with salt, and sewn up in wet cow-hide. When this was taken off or wore off, it was not recognizable as a hand.

Miss Hanbury, who did her best to institute reforms in Moorish prisons, and succeeded in Tangier, left at her death a sum of money, out of which £5 came to Tetuan to be spent on their behalf. It fell into the hands of the lady missionaries, and they spent it in making jellabs for the prisoners to wear, whose garments are worse than filthy. Unfortunately £5 was not nearly enough to clothe all; it only provided a jellab for one out of every three of the prisoners, and the poor wretches fought like dogs for them.

"They will wear them in turns," the gaoler said. He and another Moor had superintended the distribution of them; and to their lasting disgrace, deaf to argument and remonstrance on the part of the missionaries, they each appropriated a jellab to himself, saying, "This is my share; this goes to me." They were of coarse material, such as neither gaoler nor under-gaoler would ever wear themselves: all they would do would be to take them into market and convert them into money.

"Moors have *no* feelings," people say, and say wrongly; but that, to a great extent, it is true take just one instance

—the state of the prisons and prisoners. It was enough in the distance to "wind" the Tetuan prison. There remains the reflection—call it comforting if you like—that a people who consent to endure such filth, and misery, and harsh treatment, are not affected by them in the same way in which a highly civilized people would be affected.

It is absurd to blame the Moorish Government; it is absurd to say, "The people are obliged to endure." No people can be forced to endure: a point comes beyond endurance, and they rebel, choosing death rather. The vigorous and progressive race endures least. Therefore on the Moors' own heads be the state of their prisons, the treatment of their prisoners: to that cursed spirit of *laissez-faire* half the blame is due; the rest comes of their indifference to suffering, to bad smells and dirt and a sedentary existence. It is manifestly unfair to blame certain ministers and officials. Taking into consideration the manners and customs, hopes and fears, of the Moorish people, their prisons probably suit them right well, and they need no pity.

It was not always easy to get provisions, except life's bare necessities, in Tetuan. Provision Stores, which were long out of their goods, always had the same answer when asked for them—"Mānana" (To-morrow); and to-morrow never came. But it is unwise to "hustle the East": men have died trying to find a way of doing so. Therefore we chewed with philosophy the cud of the Moorish proverb:—

"*Manage with bread and butter till God brings the jam.*"

On the whole we fared not amiss, while our establishment, with its two Riffi servants, man and wife, worked well, until an occurrence took place which shook it to its very foundations, and left us to the end with a question which will never be solved.

One evening, about half-past five, just as we had settled ourselves down after tea to read, there was an unusual stir on the stairs. A minute later and the door burst open. Tahara staggered in, followed by S'lam, who seemed very much excited and alarmed. The woman was deathly pale; her eyes were ringed with black. R. and I, seeing she was ill, jumped to the conclusion that something or other was very wrong with her, and tried to make her sit down, or lie down, at once, on our divan. In a confused scene which followed, the only words we grasped were, "Tabiba, tabiba" (Doctor), and S'lam, at our instigation, rushed downstairs to go off to Tetuan, and to bring back with him Miss Z——, one of the lady missionaries. Tahara was almost beside herself, apparently with terror, and for a few moments one was inclined to doubt her sanity. We tried vainly to quiet her, almost holding her on the divan; but there was evidently something on her mind which every moment threw her into fresh agitations, and—*ah! what would we not have given to have understood Arabic!* for Tahara knew no French, like S'lam, and could barely say half a dozen words in English; her Spanish, of which she knew a few words, was Greek to us too.

"Signorita! signorita! tabiba!" she kept repeating, wailing, and then a torrent of Shillah and Arabic and Spanish would follow, and we were at our wits' end. At last R. managed to quiet her a little, and by-and-by to make her try to help us to understand, by saying slowly in Arabic two or three words which would be intelligible to us, together with the word or so of English which she herself knew. Then we gathered that her one desire was that I should go to the tabiba's. But why? We told her that S'lam had gone. She burst out into fresh agonies and shrieks: "S'lam not go! S'lam not go!"

Tahara says S'lam has Poisoned Her

Then she got up, and apparently wished to go downstairs—the last thing we thought she ought to do; but all our efforts to keep her still seemed rather futile; and from what she was trying to make us understand, there was more behind than we had an idea of. She went, almost ran, down into her and S'lam's bedroom, we following hard behind. Inside the room she tip-toed up to a recess high in the wall, almost out of her reach, and with difficulty lifted down a small bundle of rags. This she unrolled, fold after fold, before our eyes, while a thousand guesses as to what was coming rushed through the brain; the last rag came off, and a small blue bottle, about four inches high, lay in her hand. She held it up to the light It was half full of a colourless liquid like water. We read the label—" Prussic Acid. Poison"; and an ugly fear took the place of vague conjecture.

" Who has eaten this? " R. asked in scanty Arabic.

" Anna " (I), replied Tahara.

The remedy of hot boiled milk rushed into both our heads at once, but Tahara was again beginning in a fresh agony, which was now more persistent than only terrified; and choking off her stream of words, we managed to gather, that what she wanted was to go herself with me into the city, at once, to Miss Z——. Now a few drops of prussic acid of course meant that she had not long to live, and yet there were no symptoms of poisoning so far as we could gather at present. She might have taken it in a diluted form certainly. The whole thing was possibly wild imagination on her part. At any rate Miss Z—— would understand her, and that we could not do.

I hurried on my boots, questioning as to whether the woman really meant that S'lam had poisoned her. R. helped Tahara wind her long white woollen haik round her. In two minutes I was ready. Tahara slipped into her slippers, and, with the white shrouded figure clinging to me, in the fast-deepening dusk we started.

It took fully twenty minutes to walk from Jinan Dolero to the house in the middle of the city where the lady missionaries lived and had a dispensary. Miss Z—— had had some medical experience, and was a clever woman. She understood, probably as far as any European can understand, the Moorish character; and it was with some confidence—possibly on the part of us both—that we set out. But the way seemed lengthy; I knew that S'lam would be there long before we could arrive: through the city there are at least three intricate ways by which the house is reached, and my heart sank as I reflected that there was every chance of Miss Z—— and S'lam's taking another way than our own, and thus missing us. Meanwhile, it was growing darker every moment. Would the city gate still be open when we reached it? Was it not certain to be shut when we wanted to return?

Tahara hung on to my arm and hand. There had been rain, and we both slipped about in the dark, and splashed into unseen pools; she took off her pink slippers and carried them in one hand, and paddled along on her bare feet at a Moorish woman's top speed, still shaking with terror. Three or four times, dark as it was, she stopped and put out her tongue for me to look at it. It seemed very pink, and I did my utmost to reassure her, having disturbing visions of her collapsing altogether on the grass; for if she was to be understood rightly and believed, she had pains in her body, and breathing seemed an effort.

We were crossing the cemetery now by one of the intricate paths which intersect it. There seemed not a soul within sight or sound. Every Moor would be inside his house or hut. I hoped Tahara would pull herself together and last as far as Miss Z——'s.

She said she was *bueno*, meaning good, better, and spoke again of the bottle which she was carrying carefully hidden in her waistband. Then, as far as I could understand, she wished me to know that the poison had something to do with the signoritas—ourselves—and our food. This was a most unpleasant reflection: I devoutly hoped that R. would not begin dinner before I got back, and comforted myself with the assurance that it was unlikely, there being no one to get it ready. We had no outside man at that time sleeping in the house.

"S'lam *no* good; S'lam *no* good," Tahara kept repeating. And, to tell the truth, our long-legged ruffian rose before my eyes as no mean embodiment of a stage villain. The Riffis are notoriously treacherous and put no value whatever on life; at the same time I knew that they made good and faithful servants up to a certain point, and I shrank from distrusting a man who had so far served us well. And yet, how much does one know of them? Nothing. We had had suspicions that all was not going smoothly with the two servants: though they had been married so lately there was friction between them; Tahara had been heard crying at night, and had looked red-eyed. It was likely, therefore, that there had been a quarrel.

S'lam's old mother may have made mischief. She was madly jealous of Tahara, whom S'lam had married without letting her know. He had gone over to Tangier; had arranged the marriage with Tahara's brother, who was living at Tangier with her; had brought her off, hardly a happy or willing bride, for he told us that she cried the whole of the journey; and had sprung her upon his old mother at Tetuan. In his bachelor days S'lam's earnings had gone to the old woman. Now they were spent on his wife and himself. Therefore Maman saw nothing that was good in Tahara, and would have given much, no doubt, to see the last of her.

Meanwhile, the city gate drew near. Tahara was moving along firmly with her hand in mine. The gate was still open!—that was a relief. We hurried through, and, seeing a group of soldiers waiting outside, I judged that it was just about to be shut. We were none too soon: the bars behind us clanged into their places. I much wished that R. was not henceforth cut off from all communication with me, and left outside the city entirely by herself: there were the two guns and revolver; after all, the house was no more likely to be molested on this night than on any other.

The narrow streets were nearly pitch dark; shadowy figures passed us at first; and Tahara drew her haik all over her face, leaving only a slit for the eyes, and put on her slippers once more. Occasionally a little shop had its hard-working inmate, sewing at slippers by the light of an oil lamp; but for the most part all was black darkness. How long the intricate streets seemed! We stumbled on the rough cobbles and slid into the muddy gutter. Tahara's slippers again impeded her, and off they came. I wished devoutly I knew where Miss Z—— was, and could make straight for her, probably hurrying at that moment for Jinan Dolero, somewhere in the maze of streets and houses. We crossed the great open feddan, all deserted, and I strained my eyes for a glimpse of her tall figure beside that of S'lam's—in vain.

Late as it was, children were about; they collected gradually behind us and followed us, nor was it easy at that time of night to drive them off. Tahara, though

THE FEDDAN, TETUAN.

[*To face p.* 208.

Poisoned or Not Poisoned? 209

still struggling on, was leaning heavily on my arm. The sooner we get to the Mission House the better.

Two more narrow lanes, a last winding alley, and the welcome door of the tabiba's—never more welcome.

I called to Miss Z—— as I led Tahara into the courtyard. Her answering voice was all I would have prayed for at that moment. She was just starting with S'lam. Leading Tahara to the door, we found him on the threshold, with his old mother, whom he must have gone first to fetch—Maman, whom R. and I had ever distrusted: feeling that she was after no good the first time she came to the house, we had limited her visits.

I told S'lam to stay outside. He did not seem astonished at seeing his wife and myself, asking not a single question of either. Miss Z—— took Tahara upstairs into her bedroom, and I followed, explaining that Tahara did not want any one else to come in. For a moment or two, after we got her up into the room, all her old terror seemed to return; she was unable to speak, and collapsed upon the floor—a ghastly colour. Briefly explaining to Miss Z—— that Tahara believed herself to be poisoned, we knelt down on the floor and examined her. There were no apparent symptoms of poisoning—none; she was only cold and terrified beyond words. Miss Z—— did her best to calm her, and laughed away her fears, hoping to get rid of the state of panic which her condition suggested more than any poisoning.

The next thing to be done was to persuade Tahara to explain matters to Miss Z——. This might have been easy enough at Jinan Dolero with S'lam out of the way; but here, feeling that he and Maman were under the very windows, her terror was abject, and I almost gave up hope of getting a syllable out of her.

We shut every window, we shut the door, we pulled down the blinds, to satisfy her; we even stopped up the ventilation-holes; and then she still hesitated and trembled.

At last, crouched on the floor, Miss Z—— kneeling by her, Tahara, with her mouth at Miss Z——'s ear, murmured her tale in Arabic, while I wished I could understand. *S·lam had given her poison. People in the city had spoken against her and said evil things about her. S·lam was jealous. He had been very angry. They had quarrelled, and he had poisoned her. But he must never, never, on any account, know that she had been to the tabiba's to tell the tale. If S·lam suspected that Tahara knew he had tried to poison her, and had told us of it—well, her life was not worth a flus.* Even I knew that. Then in a fresh agony of terror she crouched on the floor. I told her to show Miss Z—— the bottle. Now to part with the bottle, or to run the faintest risk of S·lam's seeing it, was evidently a nightmare to the poor girl. If he ever found out that she had taken it and brought it to Miss Z—— ...

We wasted many precious moments in trying to persuade Tahara to take it out of her belt, where it lay concealed, and show it to Miss Z——. She looked at the curtains, at the door. Could S·lam possibly see? At last, more or less by force, I got possession of it, handed it to Miss Z—— with one hand, and kept Tahara still on the floor with the other.

The stopper of the bottle, Miss Z—— thought, had a suspicious smell, but she gave it as her verdict that the bottle itself contained nothing but water. She recognized it at once as having belonged to S·lam's late master, who always kept drugs in his house, and the name of whose English chemist was on the label.

Tahara is Reassured

Miss Z—— poured a teaspoonful into a tumbler, and returned the bottle to Tahara, who was getting rabid at the delay. The teaspoonful we decided should be given to one of Miss Z——'s little chickens which she was rearing. I said I would come in the morning and hear her report.

Meanwhile, Tahara had refolded and hidden the precious bottle as it was before, and Miss Z—— had managed more or less to reassure her, promising her that she was not poisoned this time, and laughing at her panic. The pain of which she had complained had no doubt a natural cause: giddiness might come on through bending over the charcoal fire cooking dinner, Miss Z—— told her. Now Tahara's only terror was that S'lam should ever find out what had happened. The bottle must be taken home—must be replaced exactly where it had been found.

Unsatisfactory as such a course was, there was some risk in pursuing any other. S'lam, if he found out that his wife had betrayed him or had suspected him and come to us, might shoot her like a dog, in a passion, and be inside the borders of the Riff in a few hours. And who would blame him, if he gave as his reason for his whole line of conduct that his wife had been unfaithful to him, false though such a statement might be?

A girl in Tetuan a few years ago was *suspected* of having been seduced. Her father took her and her mother out to the Mussulman cemetery, within sight and hearing of the city—the girl was sixteen: he shot her on the road, and he and the mother dug a grave and buried her by the roadside. They went home, and no one said a word. The man still lives in Tetuan.

Miss Z—— evidently shared Tahara's fears, and was anxious to allay any suspicions which S'lam might begin to entertain. First, however, she found out from Tahara that S·lam had no intention of poisoning the signoritas (*us*)—that was *quite* a mistake—at least so the girl assured her. Then, having once more reassured Tahara about her own health, Miss Z—— led her downstairs; there she explained to S·lam and to his old mother that the girl was very nervous, that she had not felt well, was to take a pill that night (one had been given her), and was to keep quiet to-morrow, in which case she ought soon to be quite right.

Miss Z—— wanted to walk out with me and to sleep at Jinan Dolero, evidently not liking our passing a night alone under such suspicious circumstances; but I was convinced there was no cause for fear, and I think we both knew that the less we made of what had happened the better; so, borrowing a lantern, I started back for Jinan Dolero, Tahara clinging to my arm, S·lam lighting the way, and the old mother following.

Arrived at the city gate, it was shut. I had a strange wait alone with Tahara and Maman, while S·lam fetched a soldier to unbar the gate. The basha's leave had to be got, and the basha sent to the English Vice-Consul to ask if it was his will that the gate should be opened for a British subject. Eventually we got through, all except Maman, who said good-night and went home.

It was a cheering sight to see at last a little light far away in the valley where our house lay—the only light visible. R. had left the curtains undrawn. In good time we reached the garden-house. I took Tahara straight into the bedroom, S·lam going to the kitchen to prepare dinner. The little bottle in its wrappings was immediately replaced in its niche, and Tahara ate some food which we brought her. S·lam, as usual, waited on us: he was oddly obsequious and deprecating in his manner, and I could not quite understand it.

Suspicions

The night passed quietly. Early next morning Maman appeared, which neither of us liked, but she had come ostensibly to ask after Tahara, who had quite recovered. I walked into the city, and went to the Mission House to see Miss Z——. The chicken was quite as well as Tahara, and the liquid which at least one of them had taken was probably water. Even so, the mystery was not cleared up. If it was water, why did S'lam keep it wrapped up, and why did Tahara think it was poison? It was half empty. If Tahara had ever seen it full, somebody must have drunk a dose. Of course S'lam's old master had not left a bottle of prussic acid about, and then not missed it. He probably emptied the bottle and then threw it away; it might have had a drop or two left in it, and the bottle may have been filled up with water; but that was pure conjecture.

The poisons Moors so easily get, and which S'lam or his mother could supply themselves with, are generally in a powder form. I do not know how they would mix with water: they are generally slow in working, sometimes weeks in taking effect. There was no reason why Tahara should not be poisoned by such a drug, and yet feel no ill effects for the present. Thus we argued. Poisoning in Morocco is such an every-day occurrence that it was a most ordinary suspicion on Tahara's part. After all, there might be nothing in it, but merely a fear grounded on all sorts of reasons and assumptions. It is only a matter of sitting down and thinking to conjure up plenty of fears in Morocco.

Feeling that it was not pleasant to have a bottle marked "Poison" in the house, and not to be positive as to its contents, I resolved to empty and wash it out, sending the so-called "water" to an analyst at Tangier, and refilling the bottle with *bonâ-fide* water before replacing it. The chicken test was not thoroughly satisfactory. As matters stood, Miss Z—— decided to come out that afternoon to our house, while S·lam should be sent away on an errand, in order that Tahara might be interrogated and the thing ended.

Arrived home, I found that S·lam had been dispatched to the city to market, and that Maman had gone with him. Alas! the little bottle had disappeared; it was no longer in the niche which could be seen every time the door was passed. Miss Z—— arrived in the afternoon. By that time some other occult influence had come to work in Tahara's mind, and directly Miss Z—— spoke to her it was evident that she was hedging. As long as she was terrified and had lost her head she blurted out the truth; but given time to think the matter over, a thousand side-issues weighed with her, and she was no more inclined to trust us than she would have been to trust a Moorish woman, who is brought up to lies, intrigue, and diplomacy, and fed upon such axioms as "When you have nothing else to tell, tell the truth." *The bottle*, she said, *had been taken away by S·lam and his mother. It belonged to his mother. It was poison to poison people in the Riff*. A little later on she said *it had nothing whatever to do with S·lam, and that it had only water in it—that S·lam had told her so. That she had never seen him put anything into her food. That he was "good." That she only had a bad pain last night. That she did not know why the bottle had been brought there.* And so on. Her one prayer was that the signoritas would forget all that had happened. But for days she would not let us: by creeping up when S·lam was out of the way and putting her finger on her lips, by anxious questionings and gesticulations, the thing was never allowed to rest. She felt, probably, that

CHARMING SNAKES.

[*To face p.* 214.

she was past one danger—there was no more to fear in that direction for the present; but that if her Riffi husband ever suspected she had "given him away," he would soon dispose of so troublesome an incubus.

And so we found the matter had come to a deadlock: more we shall not know. It was typical of the Moors and their ways. It was, I cannot help thinking, rather a shady business. Taking into consideration S'lam's manner towards us for days after, added to those intuitions which one has and cannot put into words, it struck us that S'lam himself did not think the bottle had only water in it.

Ask no questions in this strange land. Lies are the portion meted out to the inquirer: it is not well to know too much. "Knowledge and virtue and a horse's mouth should not pass through too many hands," and "If you question knowledge, it falls from its estate"—thus the Moors.

I shall hear from Miss Z—— of Tahara's future welfare, unless she is moved from Tetuan. If she comes to an untimely end within the next year or so, our suspicions were not groundless. For the present we "forget," of course. For the whole affair—

> Oh no, we never mention it;
> Its feet are never heard!

CHAPTER VIII

MISSIONARIES AT TETUAN—POISONING IN MOROCCO—
FATIMA'S RECEPTION—DIVORCE—AN EXPEDITION
INTO THE ANJERAS—AN EMERALD OASIS.

CHAPTER VIII

" The friendship of man is like the shade of the acacia. Yet while the friendship lives, it lives. When God wills it to die, it dies !" musedDicky, with a significant smile. " Friendship walks on thin ice in the East."

THREE times a week, from ten o'clock to twelve o'clock in the morning, the lady missionaries opened their dispensary, which, as there was no man missionary in Tetuan, was in women's hands alone, Miss Banks at the head. Though, unfortunately, she was not an M.D. nor a qualified surgeon, the good which she and her staff did was incalculable. The first day on which the dispensary was open after Rámadhan over sixty Moors came to be doctored. The day I went, there were forty-four; and the two rooms—one for men, one for women—were as full as they would hold, while a large surplus stood waiting their turn outside. Most of them were of the lower class of Moors: the better class of women would ask Miss Banks to visit them in their own houses; the better class of men would not go to lady missionaries.

The patients sat round the rooms in a circle. Miss Banks went to each in turn, and made a note of the case in a book. This over, she retired to an inner room; and, among scales, and glass measures, and drugs, and tins, and bottles by the score, proceeded to make up all the various medicines. Meanwhile, two others of the staff took up positions in the middle of the circles of men and women, and read the Bible to them in Arabic and talked to them. They seemed to listen attentively, and one or two nodded occasionally in agreement with what was said.

Thus, though everybody was doctored and provided with medicine gratis, they had to sit and listen for a certain time to Christian views, *nolens volens*; and this is the chief opportunity which missionaries have of preaching to the Mohammedan world.

Many of the patients who had been before brought medicine-bottles and ointment-boxes to be refilled. If not, the bottles had to be paid for. In the first instance they were given in with the medicine; but bottles are things of great value to the labouring Moor, and it was found that the people came purely for the sake of getting them—once outside the house, the medicine was thrown away.

One woman paid for her bottle in kind—four eggs. Some of the bottles were absurdly small; others the reverse, for one woman appeared carrying a great earthenware water-pot standing three feet high.

"My daughter," she said to Miss Banks, "I want medicine."

"Yes, but I cannot give you medicine in such a huge pot."

"My daughter, I have been three days on the road, and I want *much* medicine."

Another woman, who looked old and decrepit, begged and prayed that a bottle might be given her. Miss Banks was adamant. The woman whined and entreated from ten till half-past eleven: "I am too poor to buy one. Look at me; I am ill," and so on—until at last one of the other missionaries begged Miss Banks to give her a bottle and send her away. Still she refused to break her rule. The last patient got up to go. It was twelve o'clock. The old woman thrust her hand into the rag round her waist, pulled out a bottle, and handed it to Miss Banks to be filled.

The cases we saw were numerous. A mother with two little boys whose heads had to be examined: they were dispatched with a box of ointment (sulphur and oil) and a bottle of medicine. A boy with swelled glands had them painted. A woman had her chest painted, a man various parts of him. Pills, ointment, powders, etc., were distributed, with manifold instructions, repeated again and again, until the patient's clod-like brain had been penetrated and set in motion. Even then one would turn round at the door and say, " Then I am to eat this ointment ? "

A woman was given some salts wrapped in paper, to be mixed with water and taken the next morning fasting. She did not come again for a month, and she brought with her a large earthen pot half full of water and paper. She had mixed the salts in this with their wrapping, and had been drinking a mouthful daily, but felt no better.

Miss Banks gave a woman in good circumstances a bottle of medicine which was to last her eight days, and be taken after food; also some liniment for external use. An urgent summons came two days later: the woman was dying. " I thought it did me so much good that last night I took all the rest, and then I drank the liniment," she said. She recovered.

A man did the same with pills—was so much pleased with the effect of one that he devoured the rest all at once. They invariably ate the paper in which pills or powders were wrapped.

On one occasion Miss Banks went to see a girl whom she was attending, and who seemed worse. The answer, when asked if she was having her medicine regularly, was, "Oh no! she's so ill just now. When she's a little better, we shall give it to her."

Supposing that a patient dies, or a man who has once been a patient dies, the people have no hesitation in saying to the missionaries when they meet them in the street, "Oh! So-and-so's taken your medicine, and it's killed him."

It is impossible to trust Moors with medicines which could damage them; this seriously handicaps a doctor: in extreme cases the dose must be administered by the doctor personally.

Besides the dispensary, the missionaries had day schools for the children, night schools for boys, and mothers' meetings for women. Here, again, the mothers who attended the meetings were given the material of the clothes which they made for nothing; but they were obliged to sit down and listen to a Bible lesson first. It was one way, it was an opportunity, of bringing Christianity before Mohammedans.

Thus through the meetings and the schools and the dispensary the missionaries knew many of the women in Tetuan, and there were few houses into which they had not been at one time or another. Sometimes it was possible to read to the people in their homes, sometimes to talk. But with the men they seldom came in contact. Never with an educated Moor. He would despise women in general, despise Christianity past words, and decline to argue on such a point with a man.

People are apt to forget that Mohammedanism is a faith to which many millions of earnest and intelligent men

MOORS AT HOME.

Missionary Work

and women have pinned their salvation. To talk and argue with these—it is almost a truism to say—a missionary must be " up " in that subject which they have at their finger-tips—namely, their religion. This means that he or she must have a complete knowledge of the Korān; must know the traditions relating to Mohammed and his companions; must be able to converse about the divinity and the innumerable saints of Islam; must have read various religious treatises; and, above and beyond all, must understand to the smallest point the habits of the Mohammedan himself, know his life, be able to follow his thoughts, understand his actions, and be in sympathy with his recreations as well as with his work, otherwise the missionary treads on the Mohammedan's toes fifty times a day, and provokes amusement, mingled with contempt, of which resentment is born.

Needless to say, few missionaries in Morocco, except at the end of their life's work, possess these qualifications. Only a limited number know the Arabic language: they speak it colloquially of course, but the immense difficulties, which a thorough knowledge of it entails, debar most of them from satisfactory study. After years upon years of hard work, an Arabian scholar frankly avowed to me that he had but skimmed the surface of the depths of the Arabic language.

As far as the old idea of missionary work goes—of preaching to an attentive throng of Mohammedans and baptizing converts—Morocco ranks nowhere. The missionary who comes out to El Moghreb does incalculable good in curing the hereditary disease and taint with which an Eastern nation is rife, and many influence the surrounding people by the example of a good life and contact with a civilized mind: he or she is to be profoundly admired for the determination with which one end and one aim are held in view from first to last, and to the furtherance of which the whole of life is made subservient; and yet the shadows of disappointment must darken that missionary's path sometimes, unless he or she is a philosopher. For we met with none who could point us out a single convert, openly declaring himself to be one. In Tetuan, after twelve years' work, there was not one. Two women there were, who acknowledged to the missionaries, that they preferred Christianity to Mohammedanism, and who in private make use of Christian forms of prayer, but they would not " declare" their belief.

It is said, and no doubt truly, that there would be many converts to Christianity in Morocco among the lowest class, if it were not for the persecution of the Government, and the strong anti-Christian feeling which exists amongst those in authority. The religion and the Government are one; the Sultan is the religious head, a direct descendant from Mohammed; consequently Mohammedanism is *enforced*. A woman who declared herself a Christian would have her children taken from her; a man would be flogged round the city and boycotted, if he was not killed. Thus the prospects of the would-be convert are not happy: all which the missionaries have to offer him is, on the one hand martyrdom, on the other a miserable line of compromise—a life, that is to say, of concealment and deceit towards those nearest him, for though Christian at heart, he must yet remain Mohammedan to the world. This latter course of compromise is the line which is followed, and it is the course which is tacitly inculcated by the missionaries. I heard of no martyrs, nor Christian Moors openly declared, living in Morocco at peace with mankind.

There is a hitch somewhere. Christianity is in danger of being dragged in the dust. If it were possible for missionaries to make their doctrines appeal to the powerful and more enlightened class among the Moors, influencing the country to such an extent that it should adopt Christianity of its own accord, this could never be so. But it is not possible. In the present state of Morocco the idea is laughable. It is hardly to be expected that the most fanatical and conservative nation ever evolved, will cast its religion, like a snake its skin, at the bidding of a body of despised Europeans. Before such a revolution could take place, the character of such a nation must entirely change; the Moor must be broadened and given a scientific training, if he is ever to become of a "progressive" turn of mind, desiring other ideals than those of his forefathers.

At the same time the missionary must be adequately equipped for the fray, must be a "strong man," must possess some of the qualifications of a leader.

The first point is the all-important one: that more knowledge should be given to Mohammedans—scientific knowledge; that they should be fired to improve their own condition and that of their country, making themselves capable of mixing as equals with men who stand for the highest products of civilization the world so far knows.

Then, educated and self-educating, their creed, whatever it is, will be the outcome of their secular training. It matters little what the belief, so long as the individual is free as air to adopt it or not at his own discretion.

It would appear, then, that Morocco needs schools, colleges, and men of unusual calibre to deal with them. The doctor-missionaries do a vast amount of good; but it would seem that effort directed in fresh channels should meet with better results, and that so far there has been a tendency to "begin at the wrong end."

It is easy to sit down and criticise; it is easy to map out new paths, the difficulties connected with which, few critics can realize. While we see that many of the old by-ways are tortuous and lead to error, and that many of them only result in waste of energy, let us at the same time not forget to give all honour to those who set out to dig them, for even "defeat, is great."

One afternoon I walked round with Miss Banks, visiting patients. We started from the Mission House with a basket of medicines, ointment, thermometer, paint-brush, etc., and dived into the little, narrow, crowded streets of countless windowless houses. The first call we paid was at the house of a Moor in the capacity of "gentleman farmer": of course he was out. Miss Banks knocked; there was a movement on the other side, but no answer. She called through the keyhole, "Anna. Tabiba" (I. Doctor); and a discreet slave, trained by a jealous and distrustful master, opened at the sound of her voice. We walked into a three-cornered, tiled patio: the lady of the house came to meet us in a pink jellab, shook Miss Banks's hand and kissed her own, shook mine and again carried hers to her lips; then led us into a room opening on to the courtyard, with divans, in white, all round upon the tiled floor next the wall.

We all three sat down cross-legged on the cushions, and our hostess related her symptoms to Miss Banks. She had a bad cough, and seemed glad to have her chest painted with iodine. She was the daughter of her husband's cowman; and if, according to English ideas, somewhat below him in rank, was no worse educated than the first lady in the land. It is odd that, while Moors are gentlemen born, their woman-kind, narrowed and degraded, are in no sense aristocratic. They will stand upstairs and shout "Come!" to any one

Doctoring in Tetuan

who is calling upon them and waiting below. "Sit down," they will say imperatively: it is always the imperative. If they are asked to show anything, they will bring it and almost throw it at the visitor's head. They have no "breeding."

Our hostess was thin, and not at all typical of a Moorish wife; for a Moor likes a waist which he can barely clasp with both arms, and women, when they desire to attract, fatten themselves at once. A woman who is engaged, is crammed with sweet fattening pills and farinaceous food.

At one end of the room we sat in, was a gorgeous four-poster bed, hung with scarlet, and covered with embroideries, the posts painted bright green, and a great gilt crown on the top of all. When no furniture is bought except divans and a bed, all the dollars can be piled on the bed. We left a bottle of mixture out of the basket and a doll for the only child, which would be treasured, for a bunch of rags is the nearest Moorish approach to a doll.

From this house we went on to our hostess' old home, where her father, the cowman, lived. The patio there was cold and bare, and seemed the general living-room; some wood was stacked in one corner; there was a well in another; there was an overpowering smell of "drains" everywhere; while in the third corner a poor, miserable little girl sat huddled up, with frightened eyes. Several families lived together in this small house, and no fewer than six women crowded round the girl to explain her symptoms to Miss Banks. It was only too apparent what was wrong, when she uncovered her neck. Syphilis, hereditary—a terrible evil, to be found all over Morocco, the result of Mohammedan customs and bad food. Considering that women are divorced and remarried over and over again, and that the conditions under which they live are so unhealthy, it is small wonder if disease in some form or other does not show itself. Examples are to be met with in almost any street—the features of the face obliterated, and so on.

The poor child, whom Miss Banks was treating, had been married. Now that this disease had broken out, her husband would probably divorce her. If she were cured, she might marry again. Her friends had brought her all the way from Shesawān to Tetuan to be cured, and a Jew doctor had offered to put her right for the sum of £4.

"But," said her friends, "suppose she dies? What shall we get for our money then?"

So they sent to the English *tabiba*, who cures for nothing.

Miss Banks left ointment and medicine. Cases can be cured if the patient will persevere long enough with the medicine; but many of them are too far gone when they first come.

An old man upstairs in the same house, but of a different family, claimed her attention next. Three weeks ago he was perfectly well. He went to a café one evening, drank a cup of coffee, came home, was seized with pain, and became completely paralyzed. It pointed to poison, but he had no enemies.

Mercury is very largely used as a poison, and is given in different forms. Little is thought of ending life by this means, unless there happen to be influential relations who object to their relatives being in this summary manner "put out of the way."

There is a girl now in Tetuan who keeps a shop. Her father and mother kept it before her, but she said that they were both so old, had lived so long, and had had their day, that she felt something must be done to secure her own turn, and that speedily. Therefore she gave them both some poison. There was a funeral. She took over the shop.

Another woman was anxious to poison her husband because he was about to take a second wife. She prepared him the dish with the poisoned pieces. Suddenly she saw her child run into the house and join his father at the meal. Careless of betraying herself, she rushed to her Benjamin with cries of alarm,—too late; he had eaten, and he succumbed that night. The husband died at the end of a year from the effects of the same poison. Some of the drugs which Moors use take even longer to destroy life, but it is only a matter of time. The woman was put in prison, but she came out after twelve months, and another man has taken her to wife.

Some missionary and poisoning experiences are amusing. People often came and asked for poison to administer to somebody who happened to annoy them.

A slave appeared once and said, "I have a mistress: she's very old, isn't she?"

"Yes," said the missionary.

"She doesn't enjoy life now much, does she?"

"No, I don't think she does much."

"Would she enjoy being with the Lord much more than living on like this?"

"Yes," said the missionary, "she would be far happier with the Lord."

"Then," said the slave, "give me some poison to send her to Him."

Meanwhile, Miss Banks looked at her patient, who might or might not have had his life tampered with; but there was little she could do then. We left that house and walked on into the poorest part of the city, down a little alley which was hard to find, in search of a certain door which was still harder. After two or three mistakes, we hit upon the right one, and knocked at an old, battered, rat-eaten entrance falling to pieces.

"Anna. Tabiba," called Miss Banks; and the door was opened by a countryman, a Riffi, rough-looking, only a coarse jellab over him, but with a kind expression on his face. The space inside was something like a chicken-pen. We stooped under a very low doorway in the farther wall, and went into a little shed-like lean-to, where the inhabitants evidently lived entirely. A boy of thirteen was lying on the ground, covered with a piece of sacking. The father squatted down beside him. Two girls were grinding beans close to them in a hand-mill—the old mill of . . . "the one shall be taken, and the other left."

Miss Banks and I seated ourselves on a wooden rail, which was part of a manger or a sheep-pen. These Riffis had been forced by famine to abandon their home and come down into Tetuan, where at first they had lived in a cave, on roots principally. The father would go out and hoe when he could get work—every landowner has hoeing to be done; but lately he had had fever. The boy had an abscess, and could not move. In spite of it he smiled cheerfully, and was delighted with a new red jellab which Miss Banks brought him. Poor little chap! he did not live to wear it. I gave him a trifle to buy food. Beyond the dried beans in course of being ground, and half a lemon, there was no sign of anything to eat. Beans and lemons to fight an abscess!

After Miss Banks had attended to the child, we took our way to the house of a Moorish doctor, who had

STRAW FOR SALE.

[*To face p.* 230.

been unable to cure himself, and had sent in desperation for his European rival.

He was lying on a divan upstairs, himself the colour of oatmeal porridge, with his wife attending to him; and he had a terrible sore on his thigh. This was duly attended to. The long fast of Rámadhan might partly account for his state of health. In spite of his faith in Miss Banks, which he would sooner have died than acknowledged, he had unbounded confidence in his own skill as a doctor.

We asked him if he could read.

"Read? No. Why should he read? What was the use of reading? The thing you wanted to do was to *remember*. Now he, if he was doctoring any one, he would try first this herb and then that. This herb no good. Try another. Another no good. Another no good. He might try twelve herbs, and all no good. And the thirteenth herb would be good. And then he would *remember* that herb. Why! all his doctoring he taught himself . . ."

A rough sort of doctoring it is too, consisting of two remedies—a violent purge, or else burning with a hot iron. Every sore place is burnt; and for all sorts of illnesses, in cases of rheumatism, etc., etc., the patient is scored, perhaps all over his chest or back—"fired" like a horse. Sores are always cauterized. Bullets are never extracted. Wounds are bound up with earth and rags. A serious gunshot wound, means death. Certainly there is a wide field for women doctors in Morocco.

From this house we went on to one where the father, mother, and children were all having a meal—a poverty-stricken family again, where one of the children was wasting away with fever. The rest of the party were sitting round an earthenware pan, which was full of mallow leaves, stewed in native oil, with red pepper and garlic in huge quantities. They were dipping in their fingers, fishing out the greasy mallow and garlic, and laying it on their brown native bread and eating it. They insisted upon our joining them. It is no excuse to say " I have dined lately," for a Moor eats at any time, when there happens to be food. Miss Banks tasted the stew with a heroism worthy the noblest end.

We went on to the house of a man who has one of the best shops in Tetuan. It was consequently comfortable, and delightfully fresh-looking. The master of the house was in bed with fever—that is to say, we found him reclining on a divan on the floor, beside a gorgeous bed, with a lily-white turban fresh from the wash-tub wound round his head. We sat down on the divan running round the room, and Miss Banks was glad to hear that her patient had at last consented to take quinine. He was worn-looking, with small black beard and moustache. Moors, like every effete people, are unable to grow a great quantity of hair on their faces.

After visiting her cases Miss Banks suggested something of a change, and we turned into the best part of Tetuan, to pay a call upon one of the first families in Morocco, the head of which is now dead. B—— was probably the most wealthy and enlightened Moor in the city: he was once employed by Government, and he made his little pile; but he had never married—or, rather, his only marriage had ended in a speedy divorce; and most of his life he had been able to afford to keep a galaxy of slaves, whom he had freed in time, and whose offspring represent the family to-day.

The name of the chief of his slaves, and the mistress of the dead man's house at the present moment, is Fatima. Fatima has a history. B—— possessed twenty white slaves :

they were chiefly stolen from villages in the south, and they passed into his hands; but his treasures were two beautiful Circassian women from Turkey, one of whom he sent to the late Sultan (who is the mother of the present Sultan), the other he kept for himself—Fatima. Fatima early showed a disposition far from humble, and B—— spoilt her. At last he made her head of his house and all his slaves. One day she caused two of these women to be beaten in such a manner that one of them died. The other vowed revenge; went to B——, and told him that she had seen Fatina looking through a window at a man in the garden below. Considering that a woman of superior class must not look out of her window, though the prospect be an arid yard, the statement was calculated to rouse B——. Brought up on such proverbs as "When the bee hums and the buttermilk ferments, place, O brother, a halter on thy little daughter," and to consider women "the nearest roads to hell," B—— took prompt and drastic measures. He chained Fatima up to a pillar for three months, and fed her on bread and water. Her eldest daughter was to be married. Fatima was released and told she might attend the wedding, but only as the equal of the lowest slave, and dressed as such. She said that she had been accustomed to mixing with the first-born of Tetuan as an equal, and she would go among them as nothing else. To break Fatima's pride, B—— married a wife; but the wiles of his old favourite were too strong for him, and he gave her presents, including a gold bracelet. The indignant wife, furious at her husband's attentions to a mere slave, got a divorce and left B——; whereupon he fell into the arms of Fatima, and she graciously consented to become once more head of his house. She is now the proudest woman in Tetuan, inclined to look upon the missionaries and European women in general as dust under her feet. Her ignorance is unbounded. "India!" she said to Miss Hubbard. "You say all India belongs to you English. You may well wish it did. You've only got one port."

Meanwhile, we had reached the door of this famous lady's house, and were clanging the great knocker. It was superior to any door we had "wakened" that afternoon—made of pale, cinnamon-coloured wood, and immensely wide, carved up above and brightened with great fork-like hinges and nail-heads as large as pennies. A vastly stout slave, smart in proportion, opened the door, and said something in Arabic to Miss Banks, which, translated, intimated that a large tea party was going on within. She led us along far-reaching, wide passages, which at length opened out into an extensive patio, paved with great black and white marble tiles, like a giant chessboard. A double row of finely tiled pillars supported the roof, and a fountain shot up water in the centre of all. The style of the building suggested that the dead man had known how to spend some of his money, and to make for himself a place refined and romantic rather than gorgeous.

Stepping down the cool aisles between the pillars, the slave took us towards a room opening out of the patio; and such a room!—hung with embroideries, surrounded with luxurious divans worked in scarlet and white, carpeted with deep-piled carpets, and yet no more than a mere setting for the fantastic butterfly world which seemed let loose inside. Tetuan's most aristocratic women, scented favourites of Moorish society, kept in lavender and reared on sugar and orange-flower water, are not among those things which one easily forgets. About twelve of them or more—enough to dazzle and not

A Harem "At Home"   235

bewilder, furnish to perfection yet avoid a crush—were half reclining on the divans round the room. Fatima was on our immediate left as we entered; a holy Sharīfa on the right; the daughter of another Sharīf sat beyond her. The circle was one of Sanctity and Rank.

We shook hands with the mistress of the house, and were motioned to take our seats on the divan exactly opposite her.

Fatima was no disappointment. She suggested much, and more than fulfilled the promise of her history. She was pale and dark, with a little head like a snake's, thin sarcastic lips, and eyes full of smouldering devil. Two silver trays stood in front of her, covered with fragile porcelain cups and thin gilded cut-glass, with a silver-topped box full of fragrant mint, another quaint box containing fine green tea, an enormous cut-glass sugar-basin heaped with small rocks of white sugar, two silver embossed and steaming teapots, some scent-sprinklers and incense-burners of silver. At her elbow, on the floor, was the largest silver urn I ever saw, capable of supplying half a dozen school feasts; down the room, in a line, upon the carpets, stood round baskets, three feet in diameter, filled with palest cream-coloured bracelet-shaped loaves of bread, made of too fine and white a flour and too perfectly baked for any but the upper ten to indulge in. The centre basket contained perhaps fifty cakes—nothing on a small scale here—made of thin flaked pastry, iced over with sugar, filled with a confectionery of almonds, and quinces, and raisins, and orange-flower water, and an essence, one drop of which cost five shillings. These take a day to make, and are only met with in an elaborate *ménage*. Other tarts, lavishly coated with a snow of white sugar, contained jams and nuts and all the sweet things dear to the Moorish heart.

The movements of Fatima's small hands among the cups, covered with rings, each polished nail just touched with a half-moon of dark red henna, were born of *dolce far niente*, backed by a long line famous for their beauty : her restless black eyes alternately gleamed with cruelty and cunning ; flashed with passion ; grew sad as it is given to few eyes to grow.

Many embroidered buttons, as edgings in front, betokened garment within garment, which she wore, all of them at last confined by a broad, richly worked belt ; her kaftan was of lemon-yellow, shining with silver borderings ; the muslin "overall" was the thinnest atmosphere of white ; there were many necklaces, chiefly pearl, round her neck, and, most characteristic of all, a tiny yellow silk handkerchief was knotted once round her throat ; on her black head, colour ran riot in silks of all shades, tied and twisted and arranged as only a Moorish hand knows ; her feet were wrapped in a soft pale yellow shawl, embroidered. She did not get up when we came in.

Multiply Fatima twelve times, in colours more opulent and more bizarre than her own, instead of her lithe figure, picture stone upon stone of sleek flesh, and some idea of the epicureanism of the scene is arrived at. Sitting on each side of us were two of the fattest women I have ever seen.

Meanwhile, Fatima signed to a slave to carry across the cups of tea which she had poured out, together with thin china plates ; then we were supplied with the fine sweet bread. Miss Banks explained that I was not a *tabiba* (doctor). Fatima told her I was to ask about anything which I did not understand, and with interpretations we

A GROUP IN THE FEDDAN, TETUAN.

[*To face p.* 236.

carried on trifling conversation. It was like stepping into "The Arabian Nights" come to life. These women seldom go out of doors, or, if they do, nothing is to be seen of them except a figure in an immense creamy woollen haik from top to toe, heavily veiled: possibly a pair of haunting eyes and beautiful slippers suggest an attractive "beyond." But here were we "i' the centre of the labyrinth," where mere men can never go; in a maze of hot imperious colour; in a world of ivory-tinted faces, flowing lines, and stately gestures; among *abandon* such as one little dreams of in a Mohammedan double-locked world.

They lie at the ends of the pole, the women of Morocco: the countrywomen, beasts of burden; the wives of the rich, sumptuously fed and caparisoned lap-dogs.

Amidst such a show of silk and embroidery no Englishwoman, in the utilitarian coat and skirt best fitted for travel, could feel other than out of place, nor resist the weak desire that the imperious Fatima and her circle should have another impression of our countrywomen made upon their ignorant minds than that given by short skirts and nailed boots—say, Covent Garden one night when the opera has drawn all the diamonds in town.

I remember the Moorish French Consul, in the Tetuan post-office, saw R. writing a card in there once.

"What a great thing it is," he said to Mr. Bewicke, "that your women can write and can arrange things for themselves. I go away; my wife cannot write to me. Our women are just like animals."

As far as I could gather, a Moorish woman does not think for herself until she is divorced. Her father, mother, or brother marries her to whomsoever he or she chooses;

but when once she is divorced, she is free to marry after her own heart, and no one can interfere with her. Divorce was of course allowed by Mohammed. It is so common that no wife is surprised at being divorced a year after marriage, or six months, even a week. If she does not get up in time in the morning, her husband can divorce her, or if she becomes ill, or for a hundred petty reasons. Therefore upon the marriage-lines is always entered the sum of money which a wife brings her husband; a poor woman will bring from thirty shillings to three pounds, a rich woman from a hundred to three hundred pounds; and whatever the sum be, the husband must refund it to the wife when he divorces her. The actual getting of the divorce is simplicity itself. Man and wife go before the deputy of the governor of the city or province and state their case. The deputy will probably say, "Very well. Pay the woman such-and-such a sum mentioned in the agreement, and go your several ways."

A man, however, often changes his mind, and marries the woman whom he has divorced; and perhaps they are divorced a second time and married a third time. But he may not marry her the third time unless she has meanwhile been married by another man and divorced from him.

Many of the Moorish husbands leave their wives—the Riffis, for instance, going back into the Riff. If they are away over a year and send no money to the wife, she can claim a divorce: going before the deputy with a witness or two, it is soon arranged; she then probably marries a second husband. Were it not for this arrangement, Tetuan would be full of deserted wives.

It must be most difficult to try to "preach" either to

the men or women. The men would not have it. I knew one missionary who used to sit in their shops and talk to them, but directly he veered round within a point of "religion" that talk was over. The women were less difficult in that respect; they would discuss the point: one woman I heard say something as follows:—

"Why should I turn a Christian? See—I may steal, I may lie, I may commit murder; my sins may reach as high as from earth to heaven, and at the day of my death *God is merciful.* He will forgive me all, because I witness to Mohammed as his Prophet. Your religion is a narrow little religion; mine covers everything. You go home and go away by yourself and *witness to Mohammed* as his Prophet, and all your sins will be forgiven."

It is a sign of their being low down in the intellectual scale when the members of society talk for the most part of "persons," just as it is a sign of a higher tone when the conversation runs chiefly upon "ideas." Among the women at Fatima's tea party there was no sort or kind of exchange of thought of any description, nor was there general conversation. They talked in a desultory way to each other about their children, their clothes, their food, their money, and each other—sometimes they included Miss Banks, but never touched an interesting point.

If a woman unable to read or write only meets women also unable to read or write, and knows but one man, her husband, who feeds her and values her much like a tame doe-rabbit, it is unreasonable to expect to find in her much intelligence and energy. Wives, when asked if they did not wish to do more, would not like to read or write or work, only laughed derisively. The idea was absurd : they could not understand any one wishing to exert herself in a novel and unnecessary way.

On my left, still sat the stoutest woman in the room—the holy Sharīfa. She lost her snuff-box, and roused herself to hunt all over her enormous person for it—a work of time; but a friend had borrowed it, and it was passed back to her. She sat on the divan, cross-legged like some gigantic idol of ancient Egypt, many yards in circumference at the base, her fat little hands folded across the embroideries and gold-worked buttons and worked edges of the many gorgeous waistcoats and kaftans, which seemed piled one on top of each other on her immense frame. Her head, the size of two footballs rolled into one, was swathed in violet and scarlet silk : straight whiskers of hair, dyed jet-black, were combed a few inches down each cheek, and then cut short. The whole "idol" sat very still, speaking but rarely, and then in a harsh croak like some oracular and forbidding bird : " it " had the appearance of being comfortably gorged.

Meanwhile, Fatima signed or murmured to the slaves, and the sweetmeats were carried round, and the fragile cups refilled; and there went up a great aroma of sweet mint tea.

Through the wide doorway the patio and its colonnades of many pillars lay cool and shaded; cages of singing canary-birds hung from the ceiling; the fountain rippled in the middle; a tall girl in green and white sauntered across in her slippered feet, carrying a tray; a gaily dressed slave passed silently; and the whole thing might have been a dream. . . .

Past the patio lay the courtyard, all one large garden, with tiled walks and red-gold oranges and heavy foliage

We go up into the Anjeras

set against the blue sky. Broad date-palms, mimosa, and climbing creepers sometimes shook in a breath of wind. The clear tanks, full of ever-running water and lined with maiden-hair fern, moved with gold-fish, which matched the oranges; a pet monkey played amongst the lemons on a lemon-tree; a green parrot nodded to us from a bower of pink almond blossom.

We wandered round the sleepy, silent courtyard, and in and out the chequered greenery, hot with windless, sun-filled air, back through the black-and-white courts, until at last the great outside door shut upon Fatima, her tea party, and the eternal mysticism of the East:—we were without the gates of Paradise, and in an atmosphere of rude realism once more.

Soon after that afternoon of many calls with Miss Banks, a day up in the Anjera Hills, to the north of Tetuan, gave some idea of the strip of country which lay between us, and the sea, and Gibraltar. This country possessed the fascination of being little known. No one troubled to go up there, except its own wild inhabitants. Our own Consul had never been. The missionaries had not climbed so high, nor so far, this side the river.

Now the Tetuan *sok* (market) is greatly dependent upon the country people belonging to the Beni Salam tribe, who live up in the Anjeras; and from the flat white roof of our garden-house we had watched through a pair of glasses on market mornings, strings of women, winding by a precipitous path down the hillside, which is abrupt and mountainous, themselves dropping as it were from an upper world. They scrambled slowly down, one after the other, descending many hundreds upon hundreds of feet; then filed slantwise over the slopes, right into the rocky Mussulman cemetery, across that, and thence into the city by the Báb-el-M'kabar.

The relations of these tribesmen between themselves and the city are more or less friendly, and it is comparatively safe to wander about the mountains as long as the "enemy," as the Moors call the sun, has not set. We were most anxious to visit the country whence these market-goers came, appearing first upon the crest-line, then against the rough hillside, like a string of industrious white ants crawling down the wall of a house; therefore we engaged a youth with a downy beard and hairy legs and the big grey donkey—the most active of his race—and set off one morning at half-past nine, prepared to climb into a Top World, like Jack of the Beanstalk, by means of a path which was less smooth "going" than his supernatural ladder.

There was a strong north-west wind, and it was hardly an occasion for "aloft"; but there was no haze; the clouds were scudding away to South Australia; it was a day for a view.

Taking the broken road towards the city, we branched off to the right, crossed a stream, and began the ascent. No one could ride at this point. R. tried a tow by means of the donkey's tail, and met with a remonstrating kick. Certainly, if this could be called "one of the Sultan's highways," it was an odd specimen. We scrambled up the east side of the range of hills, sometimes by a succession of rocky staircases, sometimes sliding (backwards chiefly) on loose shale: how the donkey contrived to look after its four feet must remain a problem, but the Morocco ass is brought up from birth upon stony ground, with naïve and simple notions upon the subject of paths.

It was a long time before our heads showed up above the top of Jack's Beanstalk (so to speak), and we met with a gale, at which the donkey's hair stood on end,

Up Aloft

and which occupied all our attention for a minute. We had seen Tetuan disappear far below us behind the elbow of a hill; the topmost point of the Gib. Rock had loomed into sight; Ceuta looked as if one might have thrown a stone upon it; and the Riff Mountains were next door, clear and blue. We had passed some red fritillaries and the bee-orchid, a little wild mauve crocus, and some magnificent clumps of white heath, which smelt of almonds and honey; had seen several pairs of stone-chats with their white collars; had sat down for many "breathers"; and at last were at the top, in a wind which flattened every palmetto-bush plumb against the hillside. It was a breezy spot for riding (and here one *could* ride, for the grey donkey was on *terra firma* once more); therefore we cut short a survey of the country below us, hurried off the crest-line, and followed the path which led straight away into the heart of the Anjera country. It was a good track when once the top had been reached, exactly the right width for one individual, and used by thirty or forty every market day—three times a week. At the time when the cave-men lived in England, *single file* was a standing principle in Morocco, and the practice still holds good.

The path was beaten hard, by bare feet, in the rich dark red soil, and had taken a shiny polish; the wind was held off us by boulders and small hillocks; we got along at a steady pace. On each side mountains and only mountains were to be seen, peak beyond peak, slope after slope, covered with short wind-tossed scrub and sharp, hard rock, except at any great height or in the prevailing wind; there ledge after ledge lay peeled by the weather, blistering in the sun, the scarified faces of the cliffs worn at the summits into pinnacles of gaunt stone. No mark of humanity, except the single red path, suggested that civilization ever troubled these heights, and there was hardly anything worth the notice of a goat in the shape of fodder.

The path rose and fell, skirting now this shoulder and now a gully, but keeping for the most part on high ground, here and there winding upwards across the sharp spine of a ridge, and, by way of some awkward staircase, once more landing us on the level. More often than not, the donkey had only himself to carry; the boy probably thought us mad, but there was no understanding what the other would fain have said. Except for the wind—and even that dropped—a great silence lay on the proud heights; they defied man to interfere with their grizzled *débris*: the birds had forgotten to sing: all around was that certain awed solemnity, always to be found, in the companionship of the everlasting hills. But the air was champagne; the heather was mad in the breeze; the sky where it met the rocks, an intoxicating blue. And how the clouds "travelled"! Though, in spite of that, the hills never spoke: like the Sphinx, whose repose no dance of lizards nor flashes of sunlight can disturb, they are "too great to appease, too high to appal, too far to call." Occasionally a dip in the hollow back of a mountain showed the sea beyond: there are few seas bluer than the blue Mediterranean can be, and this was one of its days.

The polished track led us on: still no sign of a village, nor any evidences of civilization. At last from the top of a ridge we looked over and down into a calm green oasis, "a lodge in some vast wilderness," secluded, sheltered, where it would have been good to pitch a tent and camp for many moons. We swung along downwards, dropped under the lee of the hill, and our path skirted the fringe of the green oasis. It was not many acres in extent; it was covered with short scant grass; it would have made an ideal polo-ground.

Water lay over a small corner of it, and beyond a shadow of doubt it had once been the bottom of a lake; indeed, the Beni Salam tribe believe that water still lies underneath the turf. Here the first sign of humanity showed itself: two goatherds drove their flock down to the water, and one of them carried in the hood of his brown jellab a few hours' old kid; they soon passed on and disappeared among the boulders and heath.

The long level lines of the green oasis were broken at the edge by diminutive bones of rock protruding through the grass. Sunk in the hollow of the hills, there was little or no wind; the sun glowed indolently down on the green lawn, tempting us to stay; but the foot-prints in the red soil pointed forward, and we turned our backs upon the flat stretches of sunny turf and left the waveless tarn behind.

No more emerald oasis, but grey-green scrub and stones on the mountain-sides: we were up again in a stern and desolate defile, waste beyond waste strewn with rocks. The distances were oddly deceptive in the rare, clear air: a saddle between two peaks looked miles away—we were upon it in half an hour; again, a turret of rock apparently within a stone's-throw was a weary climb. And still the red trail snaked on before us. Even the big grey donkey began to lose its interest and to require "encouragement" from the Moorish boy.

We speculated as to whether we should ever reach a village before it was time to make tracks for the world below, while the sun was well up. At last, in front of us, a long low saddle intervened, with rising ground on each side: this we determined to scale, once mounted on top see all there was to be seen, and go no farther. And toil brought its unexpected and exceeding great reward. Standing on the crest-line, shading our eyes with our hands, mountain beyond mountain lay in the distance—the Anjeras, the hills of Spain, the Mediterranean, Gibraltar; while in the foreground clustered four villages, brown mud-coloured huts upon the brownish slopes, and only picked out of their surroundings by means of the one little whitewashed spot of a mosque. Below us a river had carved a gorge in the red soil and tumbled over worn boulders beside the nearest village, but it was more or less hidden from sight.

Much as we wanted to go on, it was impossible. First, there was not time. Secondly, the donkey would have had as much as was good for him by the time he got back. Therefore we chose a warm, sheltered spot, backed by sun-baked rocks and scented with cropped tussocks of yellow gorse; and there we lunched, the boy and donkey slipping out of sight, and leaving us alone, with the hills, and the sound of the wind.

It must be a long tramp into Tetuan, even for hill people born to the life of the open road,—four hours into the city with heavy loads of charcoal, faggots, chickens, eggs, butter, vegetables; four hours back again with oil, sugar, salt, tea, and every sort of necessary which is not home grown. And three times a week. And only women. We met a string of them as we set our faces homewards, like "toiling cattle straining across a thousand hills"; but they all had a word to say and a smile, as they sloped along at a steady swing.

The sun was setting when we left the good upper

world of silence and the winds; by-and-by the crest-line intervened between ourselves and the strong serene heights—they were seen no more; and we came "hand over hand down the Beanstalk" which led to the white city below.

CHAPTER IX

WE LEAVE TETUAN—A WET NIGHT UNDER THE STARS —S'LAM DESERTS US—WE SAIL FOR MOGADOR —PALM-TREE HOUSE—SUS AND WADNOON COUNTRIES—THE SAHARA—THE ATLAS MOUNTAINS.

CHAPTER IX

*The stream of life runs, ah! so swiftly by,
A gleaming race 'twixt bank and bank—we fly,
Faces alight and little trailing songs,
Then plunge into the gulf, and so good-bye.*

ABOUT the month of April, Morocco takes its head from under its wing; the bad weather turns its back on the country; the tracks dry up and are fit for travellers to take to once more. The time had come for the sake of which we had borne with the rains, and we longed to be off, to know something more of this strange and fascinating land.

May is a better month than April, up in the north, for travelling; April is often dashed with the tail-end of the rains; but our desire was to go down into the far south, and May and June in the south are both too hot to enjoy camping out. April is quite warm enough; indeed, Morocco City "stokes up" early in April; therefore we made it the middle of March when we said good-bye to Jinan Dolero and set our faces Tangierwards, there to await some steamer which should take us down the coast. The odds and ends which had furnished us at Tetuan and were not wanted had to be sold—a very simple matter. The day before we left our white garden-house, S'lam and some *mesdames*, as in his best French he always spoke to us of his ragged countrywomen, carried them into the sok, as they were, on their backs; and they were sold to the highest bidder among the market-goers.

To transport ourselves and our belongings over to Tangier, a Jew muleteer was requisitioned, who provided men and mules for the two days' journey. After long consultations we decided to take S'lam with us on our travels in the capacity of personal servant and head cook—partly because he could cook, partly because, in spite of the Tahara-and-bottle-of-water-or-poison episode, we liked him, and he had been a good servant according to his lights. After all, he was probably as trustworthy, and more so, than any man we could pick up in a hurry down south—at least, everybody warned us that they were a set of rascals there, of whom we were to beware. Finally, he was used to us and we were used to him. So S'lam set out with our cavalcade, and we proposed to keep him while we were at Tangier, take him by boat to Mogador, and after our march was over return him to Tetuan. But, while " man proposes———"

I was sorry for Tahara. She was left behind with her old enemy—S'lam's mother. He left the mother money, but Tahara not one flus. He said, too, that when he came back from Morocco City he should go straight off to the Riff and get work there; and Tahara would be left again. Such is the custom of the country: the husband may go off for a year, at intervals returning to his wife, whom he leaves generally under some sort of supervision. So poor little Tahara, who had no voice in her marriage, but had wept all the way to Tetuan under the escort of her bridegroom and brother, was left penniless in the old mother's clutches. She had no relatives near to help her, otherwise I have no doubt that she would have got a divorce. We could only ask Z—— to keep an eye on her, for interference in the Moorish domestic hearth on the part of a European would be a fool's work indeed.

It was March 19 when we began to wander once more, having handed the keys of Jinan Dolero back to its owner and cleared out the little white house. Unfortunately we pitched on the *Aid-el-Kebeer* (the Great Feast), starting the very day before it was due; and, in consequence of the Mohammedan-World being upside-down with joyful anticipation, could get no good mules, nor induce any one but a Jew to leave Tetuan at such a time. S'lam looked forward to feasting with his brother at Tangier, and started off with a good grace. A more serious miss than either Moorish servants or reliable mounts was perhaps a tent. There was none to be had in Tetuan at just that time, and a night had to be passed upon the way. However, there was no help for it: we set off as we were, and arrived towards sunset at the half-way caravanserai, the little white-walled fondâk on the top of the hills, where we passed such a windy night, on our way over from Tangier in December, under canvas.

It was a good ride, and our mules travelled badly: saddles and bridles were tumbling to pieces too. For the last mile or so we both walked and sent the baggage on ahead. From a bend round the crest of a hill we said farewell to an uneven white streak set at the foot of the distant hills—Tetuan—and saw it no more. The fondâk was in front of us, four lonely walls exposed to every change of weather, and no life stirring outside. We walked through the arched gateway into the square, which is surrounded with Norman arches, and found a company of mules and donkeys, of owners and drivers, taking shelter for the night: our own baggage animals were already hobbled in a line in front of the arches, under which the muleteers sit, and drink, and smoke, and sleep the hours away, till the first streak of dawn.

We scrambled up an uneven stone staircase at the corner of the square, and investigated the two little rooms at the disposal of travellers. One look: there were suggestions of the insect world in both. We recrossed the thresholds and sought further: the flat white roof above the arches round the square, if windswept, was too airy to be anything but fresh and wholesome,— it should meet all our demands. Here then, out in the open, under the sky, our two beds were arranged, in the lee of a few yards of parapet which had been built to shelter the west corner of the roof. S'lam had a small pan of charcoal also up on the roof in our corner, over which to get something hot for us to eat; and as soon as the odd little meal was finished we turned in.

The precipitous twilight had shadowed down sufficiently to undress in more or less privacy even upon a housetop; over our beds we spread a thin woollen carpet to keep off the dew; the moon, which was beginning its last quarter, faced us full, in a sky picked out with a few stars, against which the dark outline of the hills was cut clear; there was hardly a fleck of cloud in that best roof under which a man can sleep.

Below, down in the square, the picketed mules stamped and munched barley; the muleteers' voices, back under the arches in the colonnade, arose and fell, round a fire where green tea was brewing and much kif was in course of being smoked; occasionally an owl hooted. Waking from time to time, the moon was always staring down (I shall never forget that moon); but at

A BREEZY CAMPING-GROUND ON A ROOF-TOP.

[*To face p.* 254.

each interval it had moved farthur round overhead. At last it sank behind the field of vision, and up "in that inverted bowl we call the sky" the remote and passionless stars had it all to themselves.

About half-past three in the morning we were awakened suddenly by the patter of rain on our faces, great single drops, which quickened into a hurrying shower; while gusts of wind from the south-west rose and swept round the corner of the low parapet against which we had put the heads of the beds. One glance showed that the sky was overcast; it was very dark, most of the stars were hidden, and there was an ominous sound of rain in the wind. The fondâk is notably a wet resting-place, for it lies on the top of the watershed which divides the plains of Tetuan and Tangier, and it draws the clouds like a magnet.

One of us put up a sun-umbrella, which had been useful on the hot ride the day before; it kept an end of one bed more or less dry, and fortunately the shower did not last long, while underneath warm bedding it was possible to keep dry for a time. The wind rose, however, and forced itself in at every fold of the bedclothes. We had carefully arranged all our kit under the parapet close to the beds, partly to prevent its being stolen, which sometimes happens if left out of the owner's reach, partly to prevent its rolling or blowing off the unprotected edge of the roof.

The sunset of the night before had not foretold wind; but wind there began rapidly to be, and by-and-by the lid of one of our cooking-pots bowled along the roof, fell over the edge, and rattled on the stones in the square below: a cloth belonging to the cuisine took flight next over the outer wall, and was seen no more. We lay speculating on what might follow. Then another shower began; but the clouds were lifting a little, and it was short if it was sharp; while underneath the blankets there was not much to complain of.

At four o'clock a sound of life began down below; the muleteers were all up and stirring in the square. Lights were lit, for since the moon and stars had been obscured, the night had turned from brilliant light into one of shadows and blackness. Was there to be more rain? Nothing else mattered. In this fine interval—for the last shower was stopping—it seemed wise to get up and dress and have our bedding rolled together: neither of us was going to move into the rooms. Certainly dressing was a chilly opportunity. The evening before had been warm; but the rain freshened the air, and the wind made it still more brisk. It was darker than ever—too windy to have kept a light going; and clothes, discovered with some difficulty in the shadows in hiding-places under rugs and pillows where they had been stowed the evening before to escape the dew, were hurried into in the dark anyhow and any way, half blown inside-out in the wind.

At half-past four S'lam came up on to the roof-top with a light (which was promptly extinguished) and a pail of cold fresh water, in which we had an acceptable wash. He rolled up our bedding, and brought an earthenware pan of burning charcoal, which was stowed away in a corner of the stone stairway out of the wind, and on which the kettle soon began to boil. At this point two remaining stars were put out by the advancing dawn—a wan and shivering dawn. Sitting in the lee of the parapet, five o'clock saw us ready, and supplied with hot tea and eggs. Not long after, the rain-clouds blew over and the day broke clear.

Meanwhile, the muleteers had loaded up and vanished with the first streak of daylight, in order to be in Tetuan

In Sloughs of Despond

in time for the great feast that day; the inner square of the caravanserai was deserted; our own five mules were all that was left. It was not a long business loading them: the last rope was knotted, and the muleteers drove them off. We followed, riding out under the gateway, whereon is written in Arabic a sentence to the effect that Mulai Abdurrahman built the fondâk in 1256, according to Mohammedan reckoning of time.

The sky was grey and menacing: too many of the little single clouds called "wet dogs" drifted across it. Having started at half-past five, not till three o'clock that afternoon did we reach Tangier; halting once on the march, at ten o'clock, and that only for half an hour for lunch. A heavy storm cut that halt short, for the rest of the day the "wet dogs" were true to themselves, and we were deluged. Vivid lightning flashed and cracking peals of thunder rolled over the plain; it was one of those March days which make March no month for camping out in Northern Morocco. Added to that, the track was in a shocking state—up to the girths in mud and water and clay of a sticky and treacherous nature. The mules slipped back at every step. We had many small rivulets to cross, and were obliged to make great detours in order to circumvent them at all. Even then our baggage was in the greatest peril, for the mules could barely keep their feet; and once down in some of the deepest quagmires, there would have been the utmost difficulty in getting them up again, or in rescuing our unfortunate kit. And the rain came through everything, bedding and all being fairly drenched. The mules which carried the baggage were of course much the best of our beasts: R.'s and my mounts were indeed sorry for themselves. The last hour was the darkest, during which R.'s mule fell down for the sixth or seventh time—it was slippery and rough—and we had the worst piece of country of all to cross, where we found one unfortunate mule bogged in a sort of mud stream. Though a soaking does not greatly signify when dry clothes and a roof lie at the journey's end, nine hours at a foot's pace, through mud and water, wet and weary, will take the heart out of most people. We tailed into Tangier, a dilapidated, worn string of bedraggled vagrants, and rode to the Continental. An hour later, clean and dry, in comfortable chairs, with hot coffee, there was content.

Meanwhile, S'lam was not at all fulfilling our expectations; and since we left the fondâk, far from distinguishing himself on the march, he failed over and over again to rise to the occasion, excellent servant though he had been in the garden-house near his own city. While the muleteers walked all the way from Tetuan, driving the baggage-mules and urging on our own, S'lam by arrangement rode on the top of a light load; and there he sat, huddled up on the mule, wet and discontented, dawdling behind, last of all, in the cavalcade, and anything but living up to his character of soldier-servant and escort. By virtue of his late service in the Algerian army and his rifle, he should have been admirably adapted to fill that capacity; but less like a soldier, and more like a whimpering dog, man never looked. Nor did he look after our things, allowing them to be badly exposed to the rain, and taking no precautions for protecting anything. In the face of condemnation he sulked.

Arrived at Tangier, nearly a week elapsed before a Hungarian boat put in, by which we could sail for Mogador. S'lam was of course due daily at the hotel to report himself and to execute orders. It was on one

S'lam Deserts Us

of these occasions, upon the very morning before we were due to start for Mogador, that he sprung upon us his intention of going straight back to Tetuan. This announcement came rather like a bolt from the blue. We had congratulated ourselves upon taking down into the interior a more or less tried and faithful knave, where knaves of such a description were proverbially scarce; and now our henchman announced that he had no longer any wish or any intention of accompanying us to Morocco City.

The reasons or excuses which he gave were: first, that his wages were insufficient; and, secondly, that "a courier" had been sent over to him from Tetuan to tell him that his mother and his wife were quarrelling to such a degree that Tahara had threatened to go back to her native Riff country with her brother unless S'lam returned, and if she took that step it would mean a divorce.

His wages had been already raised considerably, because the post he was now to fill had more duties connected with it: they might have been further increased. The other excuse may or may not have been true; but as the two women had never done anything else except quarrel, the situation was a foregone conclusion. The old mother may have been trying to poison Tahara again. But would S'lam trouble to prevent that? Whatever his motive, it was more than annoying that at the last moment he should throw us over, leaving no time in which to look out for a new man, and a reliable man, without whom, in a country as lawless as Morocco, it would be a little rash, on the part of two people only, to travel.

But an unwilling servant is not to be endured. We gave S'lam his release, stipulating only that he should return the dollars advanced him for his wife and mother not many days before.

To this he protested that he had no money, not a peseta left—every coin had either been spent at the feast or had been left at Tetuan.

In this case, the best plan would be, we said, for S·lam to take with him a letter to the Consul at Tetuan explaining to him what had happened; then as S·lam earned money, he might pay it into the Consul's hands for us, until he had made good the sum advanced him. At this S·lam looked blank: he said such a letter would mean *prison* for him. We stood firm. It was a rude shock to our faith when his hand found its way into the leather bag at his side under his jellab, and he pulled out and threw on the table two-thirds of the money which had been given him.

It was suggested that he should pay the whole sum.

No! he was penniless.

Then in that case he could sell the new jellab he had just bought.

He scoffed at the idea.

In reply to our order to come to the hotel the first thing the following morning and see our baggage safely on board the steamer, he said that he should leave Tangier at daybreak, and that it was quite impossible for him to attend upon us, evidently expecting that his prepaid wages would be amicably allowed to slide. But not in the face of this final desertion. We reiterated the former course—a letter to the Consul at Tetuan; again he pleaded abject poverty; but meeting only with inclemency, once more plunged his hand into his bag, and pulled out dollars amounting exactly to the sum which he had been advanced.

So much for his poverty. We were now, he explained,

"quits." "All was right between us." He "would not like to leave us with a trace of ill feeling remaining between us and himself."

He *did* leave us, however, with his tail fairly between his legs, and, if he had been kicked out of the hotel, could not have gone forth more sadly.

What motive he had for going back to Tetuan, or what whim seized him in Tangier, remained a mystery. Impulsive as a child, he had been at first madly keen, so he said, to go with us to the world's end; then, as the time approached, in the same ratio his ardour evaporated; until, finally, he had no more desire left, and on the march over to Tangier grew more indifferent and morose at every step. While we were in Tangier he was like a fish out of water. And yet he had been once to Fez and to Morocco City: he was a travelled man. Possibly he had a more remunerative billet in view, or was homesick, or jealous about Tahara. After all, whatever the reason, his line of conduct was only distinctly Moorish, and characteristic of a race in which, as a whole, no wise man places great reliance. A Moorish servant will not rob his European master: perquisites are a *sine qua non*, of course. Probably his lies are no blacker than those of European servants; but the Moor, in place of that quality of faithfulness which can ennoble an English rascal, has a cold-blooded current in his veins. His manners may be charming—he is a plausible devil; but lean upon him, and he turns out to be as jerry-built as his own crumbling whitewashed walls.

It is with somewhat of a feeling of banishment into the unknown, that the passenger by the little coast-steamer takes his departure from Tangier, and sees first its white houses and yellow sands, and last of all Spartel lighthouse, disappear as the boat ploughs southwards. Once upon a time Gibraltar had constituted in our minds the outposts, so to speak, of civilization; but since we had spent three months in such an unexplored spot as the Tetuan vale and mountains, without society of the conventional type, or library, or church, or any other adjuncts, Tangier, when we came back to it, appeared in the light of a Paris. And now Tangier was again to be left behind; and on one of the little coasting-steamers, which deliver cargo at ports on the way, we meant to travel down to Mogador. To have marched the same distance would have meant perhaps a month on the road, going by Fez and taking it easily; therefore we saved much time by taking the steamer. Though by all report it was not likely to be at all a comfortable journey, it could only last four days at most; and few travellers but can stand four days' discomfort.

We did not start without a few warnings and cautions from various friends, who seemed inclined to think that we were doing an unprecedented thing in thus setting off alone into the interior without even a reliable servant, which since the desertion of S'lam was the case. That could not be helped. We hoped for the best as regarded finding men in Mogador.

Sir Arthur Nicolson had provided us with letters of introduction to the British Consul in Mogador, and to a Moor in Morocco City, where it is unnecessary to say there are no representatives of the English Government. I had written to him on the subject of getting up to Glaouia, in the Atlas Mountains, and had received the following reply:—

"Dear Miss Savory,—

"As the Court is away from Morocco City, I hardly think it would be wise for you to attempt a visit to Glaouia. Matters are never very staple when the seat of Government is away, and I do not think the Government would be

ILLUSTRATIVE OF THE WAY WE RODE IN MOROCCO.

[*To face p.* 262.

disposed to give you a permit at present. There would, however, be no objection whatever to your going to Morocco City, and I think you will find the journey interesting.

"Yours very truly,
"A. NICOLSON."

This letter was a blow. But when we finally reached Morocco City we found that the thing could be done—that we could get up to Glaouia either under the protection of the English missionaries or with a certain Jewish trader who lives in Morocco City. The fact of the matter is, that to travel "officially," as it were, in Morocco is a fatal mistake. It means a written permission from the Sultan, an army of followers, a commotion wherever a halt is made, and a great deal of hospitality. The Sultan does not encourage Europeans to travel out of the ordinary line of route, on account of the superstitious and fanatical spirit of his people, which would be roused to wrath against him, were he to countenance the invasion of their sacred land by infidels. Consequently, when he gives a permit, he writes upon the document to the effect that the Christian is committed to the care of Kaid So-and-so, and Kaid So-and-so is to see that no ill happens to him.

When the Christian traveller arrives at the district belonging to this kaid, through which he wishes to pass, he goes to the castle and delivers the permit. The kaid reads it, and knows what it means: the Sultan only wishes the Christian to be kept to frequented roads. Therefore the Christian is offered every hospitality, and the kaid almost weeps as he explains that it is impossible for the traveller to proceed—the tribesmen are dangerous, are in revolt along the line the Christian wishes to go. The traveller says he will take his chance. His servants, primed by the kaid, refuse to go with him on the score of the danger. If he manages to get away with one trusty follower, the kaid sends soldiers after them, fetches them back to the castle—to save their lives, he says, and his own life, which would be forfeited if a hair of their heads was injured. The Christian, after his rebellious conduct, may be forced to return discomforted to the coast towns, or he may be allowed to march on in another direction, keeping on the beaten track. Thus the Moorish Government will politely frustrate enterprising spirit on the part of the infidel. But if the traveller is content with other than a royal progression through the country, if he will travel quietly and without ostentation, dressed according to the habits of the people, and be prepared to "rough it," the chances are, that he may get to places which he could never have reached while impeded by a Government escort.

But the way above all others to travel in Morocco is to secure the help of a missionary and to go with him. Medicine is the golden key which opens every gate; and a Moor will do anything for a *tabiba* (doctor), which is what a missionary practically is to him. The missionary arrives at a remote village, and the countryside flocks to him to have its teeth pulled out, its sores doctored, its fevers cured; and if the tabiba wishes to go on farther, by whatever path, who shall gainsay him, while he carries life and health in his hands? He understands their dialect a little, he dresses as they do, and he brings no overbearing servants to eat up their substance. Nor is he a spy, but only some harmless fanatic, some quaint Nazarene, who thinks to win heaven by thus walking the earth and doing good.

Thus several missionaries have penetrated to places in Morocco, from entering which, Europeans are debarred:

they have not "advertised" themselves nor written books upon what they have seen. But the thing has been done, and not only by men. Women missionaries have been where no Christian is supposed to be allowed. Indeed, it should be easier for women, in one way, to travel in forbidden territory than men, because their sex is not credited with the sense which could do harm; and the idea of a woman spying, or thinking to exploit the country, discover mines, and so on, would be absolutely laughable to a Moor. Probably women, with a large stock of medicines and a knowledge of the country dialect, could travel in the unknown "Beyond" with comparatively little risk.

There is one other way for the Englishman to see something of the less-known districts of Morocco, and that is to travel under the protection of a holy Sharīf. Sharīfs are, like the Sultan, descendants of Mohammed, and they possess the holy *baraka*—that is, the birthright of the Sharīfian line. They are little gods, and they have immunity from the laws of God and man. Their advice is sought for and followed by the ordinary country people on every question, and their decision is invariably accepted as final. There is no such thing as an aristocratic class or nobility in Morocco; and yet the Sharīfs answer in a way to the same idea, for they possess a religious authority which sets them far above their countrymen, and constitutes them, in a sense, lords over the people. Besides, they act greatly as mediums between the secular governors and the tribes, and judge upon various matters. It is possible for a holy Sharīf to sin, but quite impossible for him to be punished, the obvious argument being that "the fire of hell cannot touch a saint in whose veins runs the blood of the holy Prophet."

The Sharīfian families form an entire class by themselves. They are fed and clothed and housed by a convenient system of religious taxation, and large presents are made them, while after death their tombs become objects of visit to all devout Mohammedans.

A holy Sharīf generally rides a horse, and he dresses in white, with a blue cloth cloak, or else a white woollen over-garment. He wears a pair of yellow slippers, or perhaps riding-boots, called *temag*, buttoned all up the back with green silk buttons, and embroidered down the side with silk and silver thread. A scarlet fez and a white turban complete him.

Sharīfs never shave under the chin, since the days when a certain sultan was being shaved thus by a barber who had it in his mind to cut the royal throat. But a little boy passing saw the evil design in the barber's eye. With great presence of mind he rushed into the shop, crying to the Sultan, "O Most Holy One! the Great Mosque has fallen down!" Both sultan and barber leapt up and rushed out: the boy explained matters to the sultan, and the barber was killed.

But neither Sharīf nor missionary-doctor had we any hope of meeting at Mogador, able and willing to travel into the Atlas Mountains with us. We started with plenty of chances open in front, but with nothing certain whereon to rely. Telegraph station and all such vanities were left behind us at Tangier: letters could not reach us till we ourselves reached Morocco City, ten or twelve days being the time they would take to arrive there from Tangier. Our agents—Cook & Son—in the latter place, had instructions to open all wires, and in an urgent case to forward to us by a *rekass* (a runner), who might do the distance in as short a time as seven or eight days. A wire sent thus, by a rekass, might cost three or four pounds, according to the time the man took: the faster he did the journey, the more he should be paid.

In spite of its hotels Tangier does not possess a single shop where English newspapers or books can be bought. Our literature had by this time reached a low ebb; and on board the Hungarian boat, at a time when one generally reads omnivorously because there is nothing else to do, we had but a couple of standard books to fall back upon—a history of the country was one, the other a volume of Lecky. The history was fairly committed to heart before travelling days were done.

On the whole, when at last we got off in the little Hungarian steamer, she did not leave much to be desired. For three days we had hung on at the Continental Hotel, waiting for the hourly expected arrival of the boat, beginning almost to despair of her ever coming in.

Finally, patience was rewarded, and one afternoon, with all our baggage, we went on board. We had everything wanted for camping out except tents, and these were to be hired at Mogador. A great wooden kitchen-box held pots, pans, knives, etc., and a case contained potted meats, soups, biscuits, and so forth.

R. and myself were the only women on board when we left Tangier: eight men joined us at dinner that night, at one long table in the small saloon, and we were said to fill the boat. She was very small, only eighteen hundred tons, and there was not much room for walking about on her; but we never went out of sight of the coast, and, sitting on a couple of chairs, could see through the glasses whatever was going on on the beach—which, I must add, was little enough, at a time when the smallest incidents become of importance. The greater part of the *Arpad* was given up to cargo. We landed green tea in quantities at Mazagan, and black-wood, cane-seated chairs for the Jews and Spaniards living there, as well as bales of goods and casks; but we took nothing on board, and the *Arpad* became more and more like an empty egg-shell, with a decided inclination to roll, on the swell which invariably sets down that coast.

The captain, a small dark Hungarian, when we left Tangier, changed into a thin tweed suit and straw hat: he did not understand English. There was no stewardess; but the steward, who did all the waiting at table, spoke a little German. One of our fellow-passengers was an Englishman, born in Morocco, without any desire to leave it—his horizon Gibraltar: he was Dutch Consul at Mazagan. Another man was a grain merchant in Mazagan. All were interesting, and could tell us a great deal about the country. Certainly the coast-line, as seen from the deck of the *Arpad*, was monotonous, desolate, uninviting to a degree: a long low shore, khāki-coloured, treeless, without sign of life, did not raise in us regrets that we had come by sea, especially when told that what we saw, was a fairly correct sample of most of the country we should have ridden through.

On the entire six hundred miles' length of coast south of Cape Spartel, and down which we were steaming, there is not a single lighthouse, bell, beacon, or buoy to mark a reef or shoal, nor is there any harbour, and no steamer dares to lie close in-shore off a port at night. Therefore, as there are several ports at which cargo has generally to be landed or taken on board, steamers go on the line of steaming all night, and lying outside a port in the daytime, while boats carry cargo between them and the shore. Rabat, Casablanca, Mazagan—we stopped at them all, and got accustomed to the eternal clank of the crane hoisting bales in and out of

LIGHTERS LOADING.

[*To face p.* 268.

the boats; to rolling on to the backs and down into the troughs of the Atlantic combers.

Finally, we reached Mogador early on the morning of Good Friday, 1902, and said good-bye to the uneasy *Arpad* and its primitive *ménage* without regret: irregular, white-walled Mogador, set in its rock-locked harbour, lay in front of us. It was the hot south—there was no doubt about that. The Riviera is called "the sunny south," and Tangier is warmer than the Riviera; but penetrate inland into Africa, go down as far as Mogador, and it is another thing altogether. Here there is no *trace* of Europe, but a great sense of being far away in letter and spirit from England—farther away than Bombay, and many another place, which out-distances it in miles again and again.

We saw Mogador first in a grey light: heavy thunder-clouds hung above; dim and visionary hills lay behind; a regiment of camels paraded the wet sands in front, and lay in the sun underneath the battlemented walls; black flags floated from the mosque-tops, for it was the Mussulman Sunday. For the rest Mogador is a city of sea and sand—sand, sand, and yet more sand: it takes two hours' riding to get to anything else except sand.

With the grey waves washing round two sides of it, and two sides blown and sanded by desert wastes, white-walled Mogador has a somewhat saddened aspect, as of lifeless bleached bones, apart from the fact that it is so far removed from the outer world.

And infinitely remote, it certainly is. A telegram takes about a fortnight to reach England; so that an answer by wire to a wire can be expected in about a month. A letter sent by a special courier to Tangier takes eight days—a distance of four hundred miles: by this means a wire could be sent to England in nine days. The steamers to Mogador are most irregular, because, in view of there being no safe anchorage, a boat will not put in in bad weather. Cargo, passengers, and mails are often and often enough not landed at all, and the inhabitants of the city see but the stern of the vanished steamer with all their letters on board, not to return perhaps for a week. When the English Consul married, and his furniture was sent out from England, the *Forward* boat, which brought it, came in sight of Mogador, and, being a rough day, went off to Madeira and on its round by the Canary Isles, back to London again, without touching at the sad white city at all. In this way things are apt to be lost: it has happened with passengers.

A rowing-boat landed us on green seaweedy rocks, and we walked up the old shell-encrusted water-stairs, and under the arch of the Water-port Gate, above which is carved in Arabic, "The glorious King, my lord Mohammed, ordered the building of this gate by his servant Hamed, son of Hammoo, 1184."

Once on a time, Agadir, a city on the coast, much farther south, was the great port and commercial centre of Southern Morocco; but it was far removed from the Sultan's grasp, the tax-gatherer could pursue the even tenor of his ways without interruption, and the kaid afford to be dictatorial and troublesome. Then the heavy hand fell, and the Sultan's armies closed the seaport, offering its throng of prosperous merchants the alternative of going to prison or of taking up their abode in Mogador. This they did, and Mogador arose; while to work the lighters (the cargo-boats), and to generally serve the merchants, a company of Berbers was transported with them from the Sus and Agadir to the new seaport.

Mogador

Beyond the Water-port Gate we met a line of heavily laden camels, with a company of athletic Berber drivers from the Sus, in quaint long tunics of butcher-blue, and lank black hair: many of the men veiled themselves; they all looked as wild as hawks, different from any type hitherto seen.

The familiar Hebrew broker, in dark blue or black gabardine and greasy skull-cap, was strongly *en evidence*; while as to the state of the dogs we met, of them must the Moorish proverb be written, "If fasting be a title to Paradise, let the dog walk in first."

Our baggage had all to pass through the Customs House inside the Water-port Gate; and there we walked, through great white-walled courtyards, whose vistas, of arch beyond arch, suggested Temple courts. Donkeys laden with skins were hurrying across them. Now and then a train of camels swung along, carrying gum or wax or argan oil or almonds. In a good almond year as many as a thousand camels have sometimes come into Mogador in one day. The Customs House officer was at breakfast, and we awaited his coming by our baggage. At last there was a stir among the many hands who had carried our things up from the boat, and the most solemn and dignified individual conceivable slowly sailed upon the scene, way being made for his flowing robes, which were white as a sheet of best glazed "cream-laid" before the pen marks it. I handed him our pass-paper from the Customs House officer at Tangier, feeling like a humble subject laying a petition before a monarch: he slowly unfolded it, and more slowly searched for and produced a pair of spectacles in a silver case. Lastly, having read the document and reviewed our pile, he "passed" it with an impressive wave of his hand. He then took a seat, a Moor minion on each side: we filed solemnly past him, shaking him by the hand. A new-born infant has not such a guileless face as that bland Arab.

We took up quarters in the Suera Hotel, managed by a capable Scotchwoman and her husband, who had once farmed on the veldt. Early next day I rode to Palm-tree House on a little horse belonging to the hotel: out by the Beach Gate, we cantered along the sands close to the sea, crossed the river, left the patron saint-house of Mogador' on our left hand, bore upwards across the sandy dunes, and struck inland over hard calcareous rock, where, in the teeth of the wind, the sand never lies. It was blowing, that day, a hot desert wind, which in a naturally hot place only makes one the hotter: with the wind, came a good deal of fine sand, on a really windy day making riding almost impossible.

Palm-tree House is a hotel four miles south-east of Mogador, in the loneliest of situations, with the advantage of a view and an open, wild country all round: it has none of the drawbacks of the city; it is breezy, wild, and bare. Having reached the top of the dunes, we struck off in more or less of a bee-line for Palm-tree House, still riding over soft sand, where nothing but miles upon miles of *r·tam* (white broom) grew, lovely when in flower, of which we were destined to see almost more than enough before we left Southern Morocco.

The horses ploughed their way through the white track; two or three butterflies hovered about the r·tam; chameleons scuttled occasionally over the path; a tortoise crept along. There were not a few locusts about either, looking like handsome little dragon-flies on the wing.

A last canter along one of the rough rides through the scrub led us up to the house, planted well on a rising sand-hill, a view of the sea in front, the hills behind.

There are no palm-trees, and there is no garden, nor is there any water, I was told, on the spot; but for all that, Palm-tree House might have been a satisfactory lodge wherein to put up. The stunted bush and the sand fringed the very walls. It had the country to itself, and there was nothing *but* itself which could spoil that country. It was cool and airy and oddly quiet. Inside, tiles and open patios and big panelled rooms gave all that could be desired : outside, there was an impression of simplicity and freedom.

The stables were a great point, and the bobbery pack, which hunt pig for five months all through the winter, accounted in one season for something like nineteen full-grown boar, ten tuskers, and nine sows.

Palm-tree House belonged for more than twenty years to a British merchant, who simply provided accommodation for any sportsman liking to come out and put up for a week or so outside Mogador: it has still the air of a shooting-box. The host, in breeches and gaiters and a great felt wideawake, rode up while we were there, and offered us every hospitality—a tall wiry man, with good hands and seat.

Had time been of no object, we should have moved on into Palm-tree House. It would be a spot to visit at any season, for the climate scarcely varies all the year round : the difference between summer and winter is not more than five degrees.

Back again in the city and strolling round it that same afternoon, the conviction was borne in upon us that of all saddening spots Mogador was possibly the saddest—that is, to the traveller, from an outside point of view: residents may have another tale to tell. But without vegetation or cultivation within sight, suggestive of life and change and labour, with the monotonous roar of the grey breakers beating its seaward walls, and wastes of blown white sand to landward, Mogador is the picture of a city which has lost all heart, and settled down into grim apathy, without a vestige of joy or activity outside its walls. The overcrowding of the Jews in the Mellah is a shocking evil, already stamping the rising generation with disease.

Earlier by three-quarters of an hour than Tetuan at the same time of year, the city gates at Mogador were shut at six o'clock, and picnic parties of Moorish or European traders were hurried back in broad daylight. We met the basha gravely pacing the sands on a white mule with scarlet trappings—of all stout officials, in a country where it is a sin and a shame on the part of one in office to be thin, the stoutest. His broad body overshadowed the big mule, and his two little legs might have been a pair of ninepins below a vast cask draped in white.

To the south of Mogador lies first the Sus country and then Wadnoon, dividing the Morocco which is partly known to Europeans, from the Sahara, which nobody knows. The Sus may be said to be practically unknown, and it is distinctly "forbidden" land, through which only two or three travellers have ever passed—Oskar Lenz, Gatell, Gerhard Rohlfs, and possibly a missionary; but they were all disguised and went in terror of their lives; nor have they left satisfactory records of their experiences.

And yet the Sus is comparatively close to Mogador,

AFTER RAIN IN MOGADOR.

[*To face p.* 274.

The Sus

with which it trades; mules from the Sus were always in the Mogador market; camels were coming in every week with wool, camels' hair, goat-skins, hides, beeswax a little gold dust, ostrich feathers, gum-arabic, cattle, and all the produce of the Sahara; while the Berbers from the Sus were interesting above any Riffis or tribesmen with whom we had hitherto met.

Their country is supposed to contain rich mines: it is said to be fertile and thickly populated; it is not loyal—on the contrary, it is ill-affected to its liege lord, the Sultan; it is fanatical to a degree, and largely swayed by a form of government best expressed by its title—Council of Forty. In return for their own goods the Berbers from the Sus carry back into their country all sorts of Manchester goods, powder, tea, sugar, cheap German cutlery, and the like.

These same Berbers, of unknown origin, were, so the Korān tells us, packed up by King David, in olden times, in sacks, and carried out of Syria on camels, since he wished to see them no more. Arrived somewhere near the Atlas Mountains, their leader called out in the Berber tongue " Sus! " which means " Let down ! " " Empty out ! " So the exiles were turned out of their sacks, and the country in which they settled is called Sus to this day.

Wadnoon trades to a great extent with the Soudan, and Mogador receives an immense amount of its ostrich feathers: slaves are the most important article of commerce in Wadnoon, and Morocco is the chief market for this traffic in humanity, the slaves being brought chiefly to Morocco City.

But if a fever lays hold of the traveller for penetrating into the unknown Sus, what must be felt of the great Sahara, that waveless inland sea of sand, with its eternal stretches of depressionless wastes reaching on, past horizon after horizon? Perhaps an occasional oasis, green as young corn; a well; a feathery date-palm; a melon-patch. But rare are these things, and for the most part the Sahara is an endless desert which few Europeans could cross and live. Its ancient lore, its mystic traditions, give it a fascination all its own. Imagine the ostrich-hunting on its borders; picture the natives riding their unequalled breed of horses, the *wind-drinkers*, which carry their masters a hundred miles a day, and which, ridden after the birds up-wind, gradually tire them down, until they can be knocked on the head with a bludgeon; the Arabs too, themselves, with the unforgettable manners possessed by such as Abraham, and handed down from time immemorial; last of all, Timbuctoo, the Queen of the Desert, the fabled home of the voracious cassowary,—does not the picture imperiously summon the traveller "over the hills and far away"? Very far away; for Timbuctoo is twelve hundred miles from Mogador, and a journey there would mean at least forty days across the Sahara, through a country belonging to peoples in no way friendly towards "infidels," where oases are few and far between.

Some day we may know the Sahara under other conditions, for a scheme was started years ago with the intention of flooding the great desert by means of a canal from the Atlantic Ocean, which should carry water on to El Joof, an immense depression well below sea-level somewhere in the centre. Thus, where all is now sand, would lie a vast sea: we should "boat" to Timbuctoo. So far, however, the scheme has begun and ended in words.

But though the great Sahara is desert pure and

The Sahara

simple, it is a mistake to imagine it devoid of life. Even as there has never yet been found a collection of aborigines without its totem, neither are there any extensive parts of the globe where life of some sort does not exist. The Sahara is little known, chiefly because the oases in the centre are occupied by intensely hostile and warlike tribes, whose animosity is chiefly directed towards the French, whom they hate with a deadly hatred. But the edges of the great desert have been visited, and on the northern limits two animals are found—the addax antelope, and Loder's gazelle. The wide-spread hoofs of the addax antelope enable it to travel over sand at a great pace. It is a large and ungainly beast with spiral horns. Probably it follows in the wake of the rains wherever they go; but what happens to it in the dry season is unknown. Similarly with Loder's gazelle: though more or less a desert animal, it is a mystery how it remains alive through the long rainless months, in places apparently without water, and on wastes of rolling, wind-drifted sand.

Of the natural inhabitants of desert country, the Sahara is by no means devoid: sand-lizards, jumping-mice, sand-grouse, sand-vipers, desert-larks, and even a family of snakes belonging to the boas, are to be found. The khaki-coloured sand-grouse are most difficult to see on the yellow face of the country: the sand-rats and sand-moles all take on the colour of their surroundings, and thus hide and protect themselves: one and all exist in some marvellous manner where it would seem that existence could only be miraculous. The skink is met with, beloved of the Romans, who imported desert-skinks into Rome in Pliny's day, and held them a valuable remedy for consumption, chopped up into a sort of white wine: the trade was brisk in 1581. To-day the Arabs consider it a remedy, and eat it as a food. It acts very much in the same way as do flat-fish in the bottom of the sea, sinking itself under the sand, allowing the sand to lie over its back and cover it, like a flounder, only leaving its sharp eyes out of cover, and sometimes the spines on its back.

For the maintenance of all this animal life, it is quite possible that rain may occasionally fall even upon desert, and disappear with lightning-like rapidity; for on the borders of certain African deserts in the north a phenomenon very much like the description of the Mosaic manna occurs when the plains have been wetted with rain. The surface is seen next morning " covered with little white globes like tiny puff-balls, the size of a bird-cherry, or spilled globes of some large grain." It is gathered and eaten by the Arabs, but, like an unsubstantial fungus growth, melts or rots in the course of a day or two.

Enough of the Sahara. Meeting with men in Mogador who had come straight from the mysterious country, veiled, untamed, and remotely removed from European touch, our interest was naturally kindled in that Back of the Beyond. There is no need for the traveller to penetrate so far as either the Sahara or the Sus. Long before he reaches them, and in order to do so, he must cross the Atlas Mountains by one of the wild passes, and the great chain of the Atlas is still unsurveyed and practically unknown. Sir Joseph Hooker and Dr. Ball explored a part of its valleys many years ago: no one since then has made a satisfactory attempt to learn details. The chain is supposed to be about thirteen thousand feet high, and it is about twenty miles from Morocco City; but the character of the lawless chiefs and tribesmen who inhabit it, so far prevents intrusion and exploration.

The Atlas

In a few days we were to see it—the mighty, solitary wall, on which the ancients believed the world to rest, described by Pliny, rising abruptly out of the plains, snowclad, one of the world's finest sights: the Atlas had largely brought us to Southern Morocco.

CHAPTER X

ON THE MARCH ONCE MORE—BUYING MULES—A BAD ROAD—FIRST CAMP—ARGAN-TREES—COOS-COOSOO—A TERRIBLE NIGHT—DOCTORING THE KHAYLIFA—ROUGHING IT UNDER CANVAS.

CHAPTER X

> And all this time you (at home) are drinking champagne (well, most of it, anyway), and sleeping in soft beds with delicious white sheets, and smoking Turkish cigarettes, and wearing clean clothes, with nice stiff collars and shirt-cuffs, and having great warm baths in marble bath-rooms and sweet-smelling soap . . . and sitting side by side at table, first a man and then a woman—the same old arrangement, I suppose—knives to the right and forks to the left, as usual.

THE hot desert wind in Mogador showed no signs of changing: there was no enlivening sun, and the sad white seaport could only charm in a morbid manner: to be out under the skies, in the open, away from the city and sealed houses and the *eyes*, was a thing to be sought after, and that quickly. Southern Morocco is like the East in that it is all eyes. The watchful East—it may be lazy, but nothing escapes its eyes. They gleam between the folds of the veil; they look from out of a smooth face, mild and yet as little to be read as the deep sea. And who knows what lies at the bottom of those quiet pools?

There need be no waste of time in Morocco, even as there is no convention: having decided to start—*start*. The 31st of March saw us away, leaving Mogador with the intention of marching to *Marrakesh*, which is the Moorish name for Morocco City, the southern capital of the empire. In order to see more of the country we marched by a zigzag route, crossing, but not following, the beaten track ; thus we were once or twice in villages where European women had not been seen : we met no one, and we camped in odd, out-of-the way corners, objects of huge interest to the wandering Arabs with whom we fell in.

Mr. Maddon, the British Consul at Mogador, to whom we brought letters of introduction from Sir Arthur Nicolson, helped us in several ways, and in his turn provided us with letters to an Arab in Marrakesh. We managed to buy two mules : one was from the Sus, with a backbone like a sword-fish and every rib showing, but he was as hard as nails, and would pace along all day without any trouble ; the other was a lazy beast, fat and older ; but they both of them proved useful animals, answering our purpose for the time being. We meant to sell, when we left the country : hiring is expensive work. Of course it was "just a dear time to buy" : it always is. The Jew broker, through whom we bought the mules from the Susi to whom they belonged, asked seven pounds ten for each of them, but came down to six pounds fifteen. We sold them some weeks later for five guineas each : hiring would have cost a great deal more. Ordinarily they are to be bought for five pounds and less in Mogador. No Susi will trade direct with a European, and every bargain goes through Israel's hands, which means a big percentage pocketed by the Jew.

Our hotel-keeper, the Scotch lady, provided us with reliable servants, one of whom turned out to be invaluable. Mulai Omar was, as his name indicates, a saint by heredity. Algeria was his birthplace. He was twenty-four years old ; and having lived in a French possession, spoke French, not like S'lam, but perfectly. He was a well-educated little fellow, enterprising, ener-

WHERE MANCHESTER GOODS ARE SOLD, MOGADOR.

[*To face p.* 284.

Mulai Omar

getic; interpreted Arabic and Shillah for us; acted as cook, in which capacity he was first-rate; generally organized the camp; and was our personal servant. Mulai Omar was quite a man to know, and a friend to trust. He was unattractive-looking—small, dark, and dirty; wore a red fez, a short black monkey-jacket, and immense, full, white cotton drawers. Saïd, our second servant, intended to look after the mules, was a lazy Arab, who acted the fine gentleman, and was never without a cigarette in his mouth. He helped Omar more or less, and was responsible for much loss of temper on our parts, before we parted. Another saint by heredity, Mulai Ombach, looked after our camel, which carried the heavy baggage. Our fourth and last man, Mohammed, drove a donkey, nominally for the purpose of carrying provender for the mules and camel, but which often as not bore either Mulai Ombach or Mohammed himself. The two principal servants, Omar and Saïd, rode two mules, which carried light loads as well.

We hired a couple of Moorish men's saddles for our own use, red-clothed, high-peaked, and well stuffed; also two big tents—one for the servants, one for ourselves. Our commissariat was not hard to manage, helped out with stores we had brought from Tangier; for bearing in mind Napoleon's truism that "the army marches on its stomach," we had laid in an ample supply.

Eleven o'clock saw us finally under way on the morning of the 31st. We had intended to start at nine; but any one who has ever travelled and camped out knows the difficulty of getting away upon that first morning—the final wrench between the servants and their old surroundings, the dozen petty obstacles. In this case one of the mules hired for baggage turned out to be in a wretched condition when it came to the hotel, and another had to be found in its place—no easy matter. The camel was started off at half-past ten with our beds, bedding, cuisine necessaries, part of the tents, and chairs and table; but, to our disgust, Mulai Ombach, its driver, stopped short at the bazaar, and there we found them both when we rode through the city. They were hurried up, and the whole party seen safely through the city gates; but once outside, the camel was so slow that we left them behind, R. and myself jogging ahead with Mulai Omar and Saïd, trusting that the heavy baggage would catch us up at lunch-time. One more delay—outside the Jewish cemetery was standing, waiting for us, the wife of Saïd: many tears were flowing, and sobs to be heard under the haik. Saïd produced some dollars, which were no doubt intended to last her during her husband's absence: he then rode on without attempting a farewell, and we were really off at last.

For the first five miles we hugged the coast in a northerly direction, keeping close to the sea: the tide was high; in one place, where we made a short cut, resulting in rather a nasty bit of riding, we were actually in the waves, slipping over black rock, with deep pools on each side. It was a grey day, not hot, and the hard flat sands, across which we rode for the most part, were excellent going.

The only wayfarers we met, tramped along behind camels. Untrustworthy brutes these animals are, especially the bubbling ones, out of whose way we most cautiously kept; for though a camel seldom bites, when he does it is serious. He never forgets an injury. A man in Mogador ill-treated one badly a few years ago: it went into the interior for a year, and came back to Mogador, and met and knew the man at once, taking him by the nape of the neck, as is its habit, and tearing the back of his skull off.

The sandy dunes on our right were covered with *r'tam* (white broom), slender, waving, silver-green stems, in seed just then. Only r'tam could grow in such poor soil. When we turned inland we found ourselves amongst dense undergrowth, a small forest, consisting chiefly of *tugga* (a sort of juniper), of myrtle, *sidra* bushes, and other shrubs, intersected by narrow paths, along one of which we paced in single file, the limestone which crops up all over the country making our pace a slow one. It was the middle of the day when we found ourselves in the thick of this jungle. Omar pointed out a little sandy clearing, and in amongst the bushes, out of earshot of the track, we halted for lunch. The mules had their packs taken off, and rolled themselves in the sand. A carpet was spread on a bank; and there, with the sea still to be seen behind us, the thickets echoing with familiar blackbirds, and every space glowing with thyme, iris, lavender, and other flowers, we spent the first of many lazy hours of the sort. Alas! our camel was still behind us, and never turned up: that was a wretched piece of *bundobust*. But long before we quitted Morocco we vowed never to have a camel for baggage again.

Only half-an-hour's halt we allowed ourselves; then saddled up, and were off again. Still through "jungle," and by a sandy path the trail led us, blocked often by stones and rocks, truly one of those

> . . . sad highways, left at large
> To ruts and stones and lovely Nature's skill,
> Who is no pavior.

The flowers became more interesting at every step; but

there was little time to get off and collect specimens, though the path was so narrow that, riding along, pink climbing convolvulus and tall lavender could easily be gathered off the bushes. For any unknown specimen some one dismounted, and it was stowed away in an empty tin kettle for safety.

By-and-by we dropped down into a narrow valley, green and cultivated: a lonely palm-tree or two stuck up—the "feather duster struck by lightning" of Mark Twain. A fine crop of beans was growing on our right, Indian corn and barley to the left: the land looked full of heart, rich, and unlike even the Tetuan country. We came across a man or two working in a dirty white tunic in the fields, and left behind some wretched huts down by a spring. About this time we lost Omar's dog, which was to have been our guard—a rather lame lurcher, which thought better of footing it all the way to Marrakesh.

The country was full of magpies—not nearly so smart as our Warwickshire mags, brownish about the tail, and with less white; yet they could scarcely have been in bad plumage at that time of year. In a narrow pathway we stood aside to let a camel pass: since we had left the coast wayfarers had grown rare for the most part. The place at which we had halted for lunch was El Faidar, within sight of one of Morocco's countless little white saint-houses—Sidi Bousuktor. Now, after a long climb over a ridge, we looked down from the top into a valley—Ain-el-Hadger; and Omar pointed out in the distance the spot he suggested we should camp at for the night. Descending the ridge was the roughest piece of riding on the road to Marrakesh: the shale gave way under the mules' feet; great rocks projected on the track. None of us dismounted, however: Tetuan had hardened our hearts and accustomed us to awkward corners, and the mules were clever. Slowly we slipped and slid down into the most luxuriant green vale, set in the scrub-covered hills, carpeted with fields of young corn, olive-trees, gardens, fruit-trees, and flowers abundantly.

To the north, upon our left, lay the Iron Mountains, no very great height, somewhere about two thousand feet, and famous for iron in the days of the Romans and Carthaginians, who both probably worked them. Now they are mined no more, and only known as the favourite quarters of wild boar, signs of whose existence we saw for ourselves, in patches of ground rooted and torn up.

We rode down through these fruitful acres as the sun was getting low : here and there lay a little white farmer's house; birds were everywhere—suddenly we heard a cuckoo, then a nightingale.

At a place where three little glens met we passed a tall look-out tower, standing sentry over each one, from the top of which the Ain-el-Hadger people could easily see an enemy coming. In England it would have been a ruin : in Morocco it was in active use,—it is still "the Middle Ages" in Morocco.

Leaving a garden on the left, surrounded by a high tapia wall, we crossed a little streamlet into the brook which waters the valley, and reached at last a corner surrounded with grey olives, deep in lush grass, and overlooked by the inevitable quaint white-domed saint-house on the top of a rocky hillock. It was an ideal spot. Omar and Saïd laid their two guns under a tree (they rode with them across their knees, ancient flint-locks, and carried bullets in bags at their sides, Omar possessing a French rifle as well); we off-saddled, unloaded the two men's mules, and unpacked what there was to unpack, the camel having practically everything. R. and I strolled about and photographed. A countryman brought us three fowls and some eggs. The sun set. Still the wretched camel had not come. Dew fell heavily, and Omar made a famous fire and supplied us with hot green tea. At last there were voices; a great form loomed in the darkness and swung towards us; the donkey followed. It was not long before the camel was unloaded, our big tent up, table and chairs and beds put together, and though dinner was late it was the more acceptable, The Saint proving a chef. A pannierful of bread was part of the camel's luggage, and intended to last us until we got to Marrakesh: vegetables we had in plenty for the first two or three days. And Omar worked wonders with the means at his disposal. Early we turned in: the stars were out; the frogs croaked in the streamlets. With the tent-flap tied back, and looking out into the quiet night, we slept as sound as tramps on the roadside at home.

I woke at 2 a.m. The guard had stopped talking, and were all asleep and snoring round the tents, except one old greybeard, who was sitting up by the fire. Four Ain-el-Hadger men had come to act as guard for the night, bringing their guns and long knives with them. It was oddly light—the "false dawn" of Omar Khayyām; but there were no stars.

Such a dawn woke us at five! Every bird for miles around was singing: blackbirds sounded like England, wood-pigeons cooed, cuckoos insisted, and among them all, strange and Indian, a hoopoe called. The sun climbed up behind the saint-house and solitary palm; the olives began to cast shadows; the grass was silver with dew. We breakfasted soon after six,

OUR CAMP AT AIN-EL-HADGER.

[*To face p.* 290.

A BLINDFOLDED CAMEL WORKING A WATER-WHEEL.

[*To face p.* 298

An Al-fresco Breakfast

our table out on the green lawn. Such air and scents of moist earth! It was chilly too. The mules fed busily in the long wet grass; behind the kitchen-tent the camel lay, chewing; an old sheikh turned up on a donkey, and joined the servants at breakfast round the fire, at one of those meals which were all green tea and tobacco.

Just as we were starting a party of fifteen sheikhs and countrymen rode up on their way to a distant "powder play" at the fête of some saint, two days' journey off. Passing our camp, they turned into a little three-cornered field of much poppies and little corn, and proceeded to bivouac for an hour or two. Tailing one after another through a gap in the hedge, on the finest barbs Southern Morocco can produce, heavy, but handsome in their way (particularly a white with flowing mane and tail, and two iron-greys), they pulled up underneath some dense green fig-trees, and dismounted in the shade, leaving their scarlet cloth saddles to match the poppies.

There was colour running riot indeed. Several of the stately figures, all in white, walked up to the saint-house to pray: one great man waddled down to the stream (to be great is to be fat, in Morocco), and a few began to groom their horses. The guns were piled: the sun glinted on them and on the silver-chased stirrups, and blazed on the snowy garments, on the poppies, and the saddles, one of which was blue, another yellow. We were in the land of Arabs: the Berbers were left behind at Mogador, and these tall lean horsemen, burnt coffee-coloured, were all descendants of the sons of the desert.

By this time the camp was scattered: the camel had risen from its knees and paced off under its medley load some time before, attended by Mulai Ombach, Mohammed, and the donkey.

The Ain-el-Hadger guard had each received a trifle for his night's services; Saïd had groomed and brought up our mules; we mounted, and, followed by himself and Omar, perched on the top of the two packs, their guns sticking out at one side, rode away. The first few miles were not marked by anything of particular interest: the collections of huts and bare walls which sometimes adorned the hillsides were far away; the curious piles of stones in the fields, almost like scarecrows, were only landmarks. But after a time we rode into the country of the argan-tree, that most interesting and unique specimen, which flourishes in this corner of Morocco, covering an area about two hundred miles long and forty wide, and growing nowhere else in the known world. Southern Morocco would be lost indeed without argan oil, which is used for cooking purposes as a substitute for butter, and of which we had with us a large supply. The oil is extracted from the fruit of the tree: at the end of March it should be fit to gather, looking much like a large olive, and possessed of a green fleshy husk, greedily eaten by camels, goats, sheep, and oxen. Thus, as well as gathering the nuts themselves off the ground, the country people allow their flocks to feed upon the fruit: having driven them home, the animals chew the cud, disgorging the argan nuts, which are collected, and eventually cracked by women and children in order to obtain oil.

The average height of the tree is twenty-five feet, but its rugged side branches will cover a space of seventy feet. Gnarled and twisted, the bark is a little like crocodile-skin, and forms in squares: the trunk has a way of folding upon itself, too, as it grows—slowly; for a large tree may be three hundred years old, and in consequence its wood is immensely hard. The argan is more or less tropical: though a tree has been known to live against a south wall in England, it was killed by the first severe winter.

Among the argans, little oxen were ploughing the red rich soil of the vale through which we rode; it was watered by a brook, and real hedges of pomegranate, out in brilliant flower, divided the fields. In one of these some Arabs were digging carrots; in another homely potatoes, the first we had seen, were doing remarkably well.

By this time the camel and attendants had been overtaken and left far behind, and since we had passed our heavy baggage no other forms of life seemed to be travelling along the same trail as our own: certainly a countryman joined himself to us, partly to point out our direction, partly for the sake of company; he held his stick behind his shoulders and stepped out well, but not for long. And after he had left we only saw a few women in the distance. These were often on donkeys, and some carried water-pots on their heads; but not one of them was "a beast of burden" in the sense of the women round Tetuan—not one crouched under an overpowering load of faggots or charcoal.

As we jogged on, the great barley-fields, all in ear, though still green, might have led us to believe we were in England, except that in the next sheltered spot a white saint-house would be found, with its dome and its palm-tree, perhaps a shady olive grove, allowed to flourish for the sake of the holy place. Yes, it was Africa.

Farther on, an Arab village lay close to the track, no windows in its yellowish flat walls, apparently no roofs: a stoned arched entrance was filled up with thorn-bushes, and the tops of the walls piled with the same to prevent outsiders from molesting the inmates. This warlike tendency was again shown in another watch-tower, built, like the last, at the conjunction of two valleys.

Meanwhile, the bare and uninteresting-looking Iron Mountains were disappearing from view: another ridge, which met them at right angles, spotted with argan-trees, looked in the distance like a tea or coffee plantation on Eastern hills—that too faded from sight; and we rode on—now through a blaze of flowers, for every hedge flamed pink and yellow, and even the dry thorns were blotted with colour—now past fields of mauve poppies and scarlet poppies and stretches of stainless blue. A white saint-house stood out against the colour, its dome like dazzling chalk, it shadows blue: we looked back at it from under an argan-tree, in the shade of which we rested for ten minutes, picking up a few nuts, and drinking long and deep out of Omar's stone water-jar.

Not far from this spot we came upon *Sok-el-Had* (the Sunday Market)—that is, a place where every Sunday a country market is held, and to which the whole country-side flocks to do its marketing. This was Tuesday, and therefore Sok-el-Had was forlorn and deserted, its rows of little mud huts and its meat-hangers empty, not a soul within miles. They are as old as Morocco, these places known by the name of the week-day on which the market is held—places so strangely deserted upon any other day.

Still we rode on for several hours, past Sheikh Boujiman Ben Hamed's white house, while the sun blazed on the bare path, and the argans stood too far apart to cast consecutive shade. It was with much satisfaction that we saw our next camping-ground in the distance about one o'clock: we had started early, and a long lazy afternoon was a good prospect. *Sok-el-Tleta* is named once more after its market—Tuesday Market. Even as Sok-el-Had was forlorn, so Sok-el-Tleta in proportion teemed with life. Held on the open hillside, upon a great bare space worn brown by cycles of Tuesday markets, the prevailing colour brown and white, hundreds of mules, hundreds of Arabs, the sight was one not to be forgotten.

We dismounted, and followed Omar into the thick of the fray, surrounded at once by a staring and interested crowd. It was an extraordinary scene. Streets were formed by rows upon rows of little mud cubicles, thatched over, inside which, on a mud shelf, the vendor sat, with his goods spread out for sale round him. Slippers were being mended; blacksmith's work was being done; cottons and stuffs were selling, sugar, groceries of all sorts, brand-new slippers and new clothes, vegetables and meat. Meat was the centre of the whirlpool, and round the carcases and shapeless joints the largest crowd: it hung on upright stakes and branches stuck in the ground, and the effect was that of a nightmare wood, in which the weird trees were bearing gory and dreadful fruit. It was all life and stir, that bare hillside; and by half-past one o'clock the whole thing had melted away, and there was no sign of a human being moving.

Mulai Omar was well known in Sok-el-Tleta, his wife's relatives living there: because he was a saint his clothes and slippers were kissed by every one who met us as we rode along to our camp beyond the Tuesday Market. We passed women and children digging for ayerna root: the corn not being yet ripe, they were short of food. The root of this weed, though eatable, is most unwholesome, and unless carefully prepared, people grow thinner and more yellow upon it daily.

But all our interest in a few moments was focussed upon a most imposing ruin, a real Windsor Castle of a rudimentary type, which commanded a hilltop on a table-land on the right, great walls rearing themselves up to the sky, towers defending every corner, a turreted gate-house the entrance, and the whole loop-holed, grim-looking enough. Obviously the kaid who built such a kasbah was a great man: his garden, a beautiful overgrown wilderness, gone like his castle to rack and ruin, lay below at Sok-el-Tleta, wisely situated, for vegetation would have been badly exposed upon the hilltop.

About twenty-seven years ago the kaid who built the kasbah—chiefly by forced labour on the part of all the country people for miles round, though skilled workmen came from Mogador and were paid—was attacked by the Arab tribes from end to end of his province of Shedma, and after a six-months' siege was forced to fly to Marrakesh, where he died in prison, the tribesmen demolishing the castle for hidden treasure, till every wall had yielded its secret. Probably he oppressed his province like every other kaid, and was well hated. We went inside, and it was a foregone conclusion that we should camp there upon the grass. The governor's own halls were in a block in the centre, room after room, most intricate. Our tents were pitched in the vast sunny courtyard. We wandered about, exploring the odd corners, all the afternoon: not a vestige of timber or decoration remained. Handsome little red-brown kestrels with grey heads hovered over us and sat on the old walls, uttering their querulous cry: a beautiful blue jay, with cinnamon back and black-tipped wings and tail, was nesting in a hole among the bricks, and let us come close to him. A *sib-sib* scampered along an old window-ledge, a little animal like a squirrel, grey with striped back, the stripes running from head to tail: it ruffled out its tail at will.

The camel turned up at five, having been nine hours on the road. Later on a *mona* (a present) was brought us, consisting of butter, in a lordly dish set round with pink roses. So in the deserted walls of the kasbah we passed the night. Ghosts ought to have haunted those horrible death-traps, the *matamors*, of which there are said to be a hundred. The ground seemed riddled with these "wells," intended for the storage of grain, but used by sheikhs and kaids as their private prisons, whence at their will they draft on luckless captives to the public gaols: an old enemy is quite harmless in a matamor, with a square stone over the top, for the rest of his life.

The wonderful cisterns were another feature of the kasbah, immense tanks underground, concreted and still water-tight—at the end of every dry season cleaned out and whitewashed, now half full of stinking rain-water and decay.

We got off at seven the next morning, struck the main road from Mogador, left it, and found ourselves in quite an agricultural country, green barley-fields, planted all over at intervals with figs and pomegranates, even hedges of a sort. Then again we were in the argan forest— the last of it, and the best: beautiful trees, with their knarled, twisted branches. I thought of yews on the Surrey hills. Here coarse grass grew between, something like a park at home: goats clambered up into the forks, feasting on the green fruit. But all too soon the argans came to an end, and we saw this phenomenon of Morocco no more.

Nor was the exchange of the argan forest for the everlasting *rtam* (white broom) and a sun-baked, arid wilderness, a welcome one. It always meant stones and sand and a general grilling, the r'tam, as it waved like pampas-grass to the far horizon. By-and-by palmetto cropped up, the fan-shaped dwarf palm, which makes ropes and twine, baskets, mats, dish-covers, leggings, hats, and girths. Here it grew in the middle of wretched little attempts at corn-fields—a drawback to farming, though from want of water farming might well have been let alone. Topping a rise, the whole undulating country was r'tam and palmetto: occasionally a flock of goats moved on its face, tended by thin mahogany-coloured Arab boys in dirty woollen tunics.

When a single olive-tree appeared, we hailed its shade for lunch. The mules, hobbled together, grazed: Omar and Saïd lay at a short distance, drinking green tea and smoking near the little fire they had lit. Botanical specimens had to be dried.

That night we camped outside the kasbah belonging to the most powerful kaid in the whole district: an immense reddish-yellow pile it was, built of *tapia*—that is, of mud, gravel, and water principally, poured into bottomless cases on the wall itself, and left to set. The kasbah had lived through a siege or two, and looked as if it would "ruin" quickly. From the arched gateway a crowd of squalid retainers emerged to stare at sun-helmets and Englishwomen: living like mediæval times within the castle's protecting walls, the "feudal system" practically obtains in Morocco in the present day.

Alas! the governor, Kaid Mohammed, was at Fez: his *khaylifa* (lieutenant) received us inside the filthy and squalid kasbah, seated on a doorstep—a better-dressed man than his retainers, curtailed perhaps in intellectual allowance, who gave us leave to camp outside.

That evening we watched a blindfolded camel turning

A BLINDFOLDED CAMEL WORKING A WATER-WHEEL.

a water-wheel, and some wretched prisoners, with irons on their feet, who shuffled out of the gate and drew water. A black slave brought Kaid Mohammed's horses to water one by one; then made each roll on a sandy patch of ground, off which he first carefully picked every stone.

The sun streamed in at our tent door next morning, but we were at breakfast before it had more than left the horizon, and soon on our way through a rough country of scrub and olives—a capital country for pig (which are shot in numbers), and practicable for spearing them, one would think. Jogging along little paths, with a cool breeze in our faces, which invariably went round with the sun, we came by-and-by to a valley, green and wooded with olives, where barley was growing, looking as if it had been kept under glass, it was such an even crop, and rooted in the richest soil. Crack—crack—ping! and a stone whistled over our heads: this meant Arab boys scaring birds with slings, made of dried grass, and probably after David's pattern.

From out of an Arab village a little black child ran with a bowl of very sour milk, which, however, Omar and Saïd appreciated: the child wore one filthy whitish garment and a bead necklace, a little inky-black pigtail completing it.

This was a day of all days, in that we had our first view of the Atlas Mountains—those mountains which we had come so far to see. There they were, first seen from a certain ridge, mighty peaks, snow-covered, filling one with an intense desire to travel into their fastnesses: a haze, however, hid the greater part of the range.

A countryman joined us for a short distance, to whom Omar gave a cigarette-paper and a pinch of tobacco. Again all cultivation was exchanged for uncompromising plain, stones, stones, and a soil like iron, on which nothing grew except the thorny zizyphus lotus, with the double row of thorns, one pointing forward, the other back, out of which the Soudanese make their zarebas. A colony of bottle-shaped nests, made of dried grass, in these thorn-bushes, tempted me to try for some eggs. The attempt proved what a barrier the thorny lotus can be. I was extricated with difficulty by means of Omar's gun-barrels and Saïd's hands; but not without one nest and eggs—they apparently belonged to a variety of sparrow.

A well with one tree, a spot of shade in the arid plain, intervened farther on. The mules drank. An Arab rode up, lean, walnut-coloured; slipped off his high-peaked red saddle, hobbled his mule, and lay down under the tree. Hot as it was, we pushed on. This plain is said to remind travellers of the stony part of the Sahara. In the air was a scent of burnt grass and flowers—a *honey* smell: every time a breeze came we were duly grateful. The mules clattered on over the stones until Sidi Moktar came in sight—a saint-house of the deepest sanctity, near which a country market is held one day a week. Up to this cluster of what Omar dignified by the name of *shops* we rode, and, dismounting, stooped our heads, and took possession of one of the minute mud-booths, the servants going into another next door. We could sit upright, though not stand, and there was shade in the shape of a thatched covering, while after the glare and flare of the sun outside it was as cool as a cellar.

From one to three we rested there, drank green tea after lunch, studied maps, took notes. But the sun was as hot as ever when we took to the open road again, plain before us, the Atlas dimly to be seen. Some oddly formed hills, from four to five hundred feet high, flat-topped, presently appeared: one, from its contour, is called

An Arab "Douar," or Village

Hank-el-Jemmel (Camel's Back). We rode past them. A layer of coarse chalcedony covers the flat summits, which would offer resistance when, ages ago, the Atlas wall was scooped into ridge and ravine, and the plain below washed bare, except for isolated remnants, such as these table-hills. We picked up fragments of chalcedony and small blocks of volcanic rock, or basalt.

About five o'clock we reached an Arab *douar*, or village, and decided to camp near it for the night. Twenty or thirty conical huts, made of branches and grass and anything which keeps out the sun, black camel's hair or a worn-out garment; the whole surrounded by a great hedge, or *zareba*, of the thorny lotus, not growing, but piled up, one hole left in the fence for exit, and closed at night by simply piling extra thorns in the space; a company of howling dogs,—such is an Arab douar, and it is probably unequalled for filth, though when the parasites become too many, even the thick-skinned Bedouin moves out, and a new douar is put up somewhere else. There was no choice as regards camping near such a spot: it may have been unsafe in the open— at any rate no servants could ever be induced to sleep except under the protection of a village or a kasbah.

It was five o'clock. An old sheikh or headman came out from between the thorn-barrier, welcomed us, and led the way inside to a perfectly impossible open space, a dunghill, amongst the huts, where we might camp; it was overrun with fowls, and covered with filth of every description. Therefore, though assured that we should be much safer within the zareba, and deeply against the wishes of the servants, we insisted upon leading the way outside, and choosing a spot as far removed from the fence as possible, though only too near for our own comfort. As soon as the tents were pitched and the sun had set, such a noise of goats (which had just been driven inside the douar) bleating, and donkeys braying, and dogs barking, and children crying, arose, as we prayed it might not be our lot often to hear at the end of a hard day.

An admiring throng had gathered round us while the tent was in course of erection, and we were sitting on the grass. One old woman squatted before us, cross-legged, not a yard from our feet, and *gazed*; she wore nothing but one woollen garment, apparently a square held together on the shoulders by steel pins: her skinny arms, legs, and feet were bare, of course. We did not encourage " the masses," but kept them at arm's-length with sticks.

That was a noisy night: half the douar was apparently being entertained in the servants' tent, which for safety was pitched all too close to our own, and they talked far on into the small hours in mumbling undertones, to the sound of which we finally slept, nor waked till a glorious dawn in a cloudless sky roused us at five o'clock. The herds were then wending their way out of the douar, filing across the plain, the mysterious delicate light of sunrise on the backs of the sheep and goats. By seven o'clock the sun was too hot to sit in for choice. We had already breakfasted in the conical shadow cast by the tent, a group of children watching every operation, some of them wearing the quaintest necklaces, of argan nuts strung together, and lumps of yellow sulphur sewn into perforated squares of leather: these were eagerly untied and handed over to us for a *bellune* (2½*d*.).

At eight o'clock we had left the douar behind, and were heading for Sheshaoua, south of the Camel's Back, along a trail more stony and desert-like than any before: even the few thorn-bushes did not flourish; perhaps the white snails, with which they were so thickly covered that the branches looked all in blossom, did not agree with them—snails which are beloved of partridges. We met no man nor animal, till at last a *rekass* passed us, a runner carrying the mail to Mogador, jogging along the two hundred and seventy miles' journey, for which he would be paid, there and back again, thirteen shillings. His stick was tucked under his clothes, down his back, for the sake of ventilation; his waistband was tightened; his palm-leaf wallet was on his back, with letters, possibly some bread, a match or two, and some hemp, inside. He was a long-limbed fellow, bronzed and bearded, with the vacant, glassy eyes of a kif-smoker; for kif kept him going often instead of food, and helped him to swing along day after day, untiring, like a camel, sleeping little, praying occasionally at a saint's tomb, fording the streams, trotting over the plains, his eyes fixed on the horizon—" eating the miles," as Arabs say. This particular rekass left Marrakesh on Monday morning at ten, and reached Mogador on Wednesday afternoon at three, doing his two hundred and seventy miles in forty-nine hours.

When Sir William Kirby Green died suddenly on an embassy in Marrakesh, a rekass carried the news to Mazagan, a hundred and sixty miles, in thirty-two hours; but the Vice-Consul told me that upon reaching his office the man fell down—he could not stand to tell the news.

We rode on, praying for a breeze which never came: the sun literally sizzled on the baked desert, the rocks gave out an oven-like heat, and the rarefied air oscillated over the wastes. It was too hazy for more than glimpses of the Atlas and their snows: as far as we could see stretched only illimitable drab-coloured plain, broken by the flat-topped hills. At last we stumbled along to the top of a ridge; and there, strange and delightful sight, away in the distance lay a green basin, trees, no mirage, but the valley of Sheshaoua.

Sheshaoua is a district ruled by a powerful governor, whose great kasbah lies somewhere about the centre, dominating a large village. The district is watered by a stream from the Atlas Mountains, which accounts for its fertility; for, except where irrigation is possible, there can be no cultivation in this sahara: wide ditches conduct the stream across the length and breadth of the province, resulting in a green ribbon upon the face of the plain, the fields being edged with little hard mud-banks, keeping the water evenly distributed over the surface when the crops need flooding.

To have lived upon sun-burn is to appreciate the colour green: the march lost its monotony and some of its heat, when green lay in front and came nearer with every stride. Two hours and a half were short: the end of that time found us riding between corn-fields, crossing streamlet after streamlet watering the vegetation, and at last jogging over real turf, instead of clattering on stones, which had made talking difficult for the last day or two; now the path was actually soft and earthy. A long string of camels kept pace with us for a time on a parallel trail; then a douar came into sight, afterwards two saint-houses and a ruined kasbah. That half of these castles are ruined is not to be wondered at, considering that they are mud-built, and that tribal disputes and invasions are interminable. Some of those same crumbling tapia walls which we passed supported immense earthen jars, standing out against the sky—jars which are stored with corn or butter, and sealed up: nine months' old butter has the reputation of an old wine.

Shady trees, standing for the most part by the stream, hung over our path, but would have made damp camping-grounds, and we rode on through a marsh, up one ridge, down the opposite side, and at last into the principal village of Sheshaoua, not far from which, on a hillside to the north-east, lay one of the familiar country market-places, with its collection of little shelters for the sellers, its upright branches on which to hang meat—Thursday's market this. A ruined, red-walled kasbah faced it, apparently inhabited by storks alone, busy building their great rough nests: some were in the village.

Sheshaoua was no douar, but a high-walled collection of houses, overlooked by the modern kasbah on the hill. Thither we rode, up the steep slope, to call on the kaid, Sekassam Belcady, and ask permission to pitch the tents in one of the gardens which fringed the stream below. This the khaylifa granted at once (the kaid himself being at Fez with the Sultan), pressing on us the alternative of putting up inside the kasbah itself; but the open air had stronger attractions, and we wound our way downhill to the stream, on the other side of which the kaid's own garden lay. There being no bridge, the stream deep, and the banks steep, the mules were driven over by themselves, and R. and I followed one by one on Omar's back—on and into a natural garden fit for the gods, one of Nature's own parterres, and a paradise at that.

On dry ground, underneath orange-trees covered with blossom, we lunched and lay down: of flowers, except wild ones, there were none, nor any attempt at cultivation; the terraces were dense in greenery and shade, interlaced with branches, intersected by streamlets, perfumed with orange flowers; water murmured; nightingales answered each other from every corner; wood-pigeons cooed content; most musical of all, the bulbul's throbbing, passionate note—not loud—was heard for the first time. Yes; we might have said: "If there is a heaven upon earth, it is this, it is this, it is this."

The snake creeps into most paradises: suddenly a thunderstorm invaded ours; heavy rain began even to penetrate the thick lace of leaves and branches over our heads, and, walking to the opening at the edge of the wood, it was clear that heavy storms were working up from the northeast; nor did the day improve. Having sat through two downpours, with every sign of more to follow, when another pressing invitation came from the khaylifa to spend the night in the kasbah, it seemed foolish to do other than accept; for bad weather under tents, which like ours did not claim to be waterproof, has no attractions. Further, the khaylifa had stated that the guest-house was new, and had never been occupied.

Thither we hurried through the rain. The inside of the "castle" was blocked by a collection of filthy-looking sheds or rooms, which seemed to be full of Arabs and negroes and women—wives of the khaylifa—all of them squalid and mannerless: the paths between were littered with refuse. A country kaid, judging from the state of his kasbah, is possessed of no refinement, and has less sense of decency and comfort, as European ideas go, than many members of the labouring class at home.

The appearance of the guest-house was, however, reassuring: the long lofty room into which we were shown had been newly whitewashed, the ceiling painted red and green; its double doors and two windows opened into a little courtyard, and rooms beyond housed the servants.

A sheep was being skinned in an adjoining shed: we were to be feasted.

Meantime, few, if any, of the kaid's retainers could have abstained from visiting us, to judge by the levée which we held for more than an hour: perhaps the black slaves were most interesting, but they were also hardest to remove, from the scene of such a phenomenon, as two Englishwomen within their own walls. Probably no such thing had happened within the memory of man; for Sheshaoua is off the beaten track to Marrakesh, nor do travellers as a rule sleep out of their tents.

While we had tea, under a battery of eyes, and further annoyed by the chatter at the open door and windows, a *mona* (a present from the governor) arrived, and was set down at our feet. It was not the time—just after tea—to eat an immense dish of *coos-coosoo*, or a steaming pile of hot mutton and raisins, cooked in oil, which lay on the round trenchers, when the great beehive-like straw covers were raised: some of the hot cakes accompanying them might be managed, but the rest was handed over to the expectant servants, to whom coos-coosoo is as roast beef to the British labourer, though less stimulating, for it only consists of wheat or millet or maize flour, granulated, steamed, and eaten hot, sometimes crowned with chicken.

Following hard on the mona came a message from the khaylifa asking for medicine. Graphically answering my question as to what was the matter with him, the messenger stroked his waist: we found a pill, which was carried off with much gratitude.

A short time elapsed, and then, to our horror, four slaves arrived, carrying great preparations for tea—brass trays, urn, and the whole paraphernalia—mint and sweetness filling the room. Again the servants benefited; and even a third time, after we were actually in bed; for the door was bombarded, and three women came in, and laid a great almond pudding, of much delicacy, covered with stripes of grated cinnamon, at our feet.

That night was the one bad experience of our time in Morocco. Though the guest-room was new and apparently clean, some matting had been laid on the floor, which we had not removed, and with the darkness its occupants came out in such numbers that, in spite of "Keating" round the legs of each bed, the long hours were taken up in warfare, and we never slept. Next day the room was scoured out, and the lively matting ejected, while we were strolling round Sheshaoua between heavy showers of rain, which reduced the clay country to a state of quagmire. However, Sunday, after a peaceful night both inside and out of doors, broke fresh and clear: all the great loose thunder-clouds had packed themselves into long cloudlets with ruled horizontal bases; and in clear, rarefied air, standing up almost unearthly in their beauty, the Atlas range from end to end, was to be seen at last. Chiselled peak after peak, upon which no traveller has ever set foot, glistened in the sun, apparently about ten miles off, in reality more like thirty or forty. It was one of those mornings which have been thoroughly washed, and the swirling pea-soup river bore witness to the operation as surely as the air of purity which the whole country wore. All was radiant: down below, the orange grove of our arrival rang with nightingales and bulbuls; there was a scent of heaven, an undertone of racing waters.

Just as we were packed up to start, the khaylifa sent and expressed thanks for our medicine, and asked that as a favour we would see his wives, one of whom was ill. They were found in mud rooms, dark and dirty, most uninteresting in themselves. One stout "lady"

SHIPS OF THE DESERT WE PASS ON THE MARCH.

[*To face p.* 308.

had a swelled neck, the other had cataract: both wished to be prescribed for. I recommended, through Omar, bathing the swelled neck: it was necessary from a cleanliness point of view. From the same point of view I shook hands hurriedly and departed, climbed into the saddle, and was soon far away from the kasbah at Sheshaoua.

CHAPTER XI

A PARTING MONA—FORDING SHESHAOUA RIVER—JARS OF FOOD—FIRST SIGHT OF MARRAKESH—A PERILOUS CROSSING—RIDE INTO MARRAKESH—THE SLAVE MARKET.

CHAPTER XI

> We who are old, old and gay,
>   O so old!
> Thousands of years, thousands of years,
>   If all were told:
>
> Give to these children, new from the world,
>   Rest far from men.
> Is anything better, anything better?
>   Tell us it then:
>
> Us who are old, old and gay,
>   O so old!
> Thousands of years, thousands of years,
>   If all were told."
>
> W. B. YEATS.

WE were once more upon the march; and yet all links with the kasbah were not broken, for we had gone but a short way when a servant ran after us, carrying a familiar dish, known from afar—a parting mona. Laid at our feet, we tasted, as courtesy demanded, a coos-coosoo made of grated almonds, powdered sugar, and cream—a sweet which cloys at an early hour in the day, though to Moorish servants, at any and every moment of their lives, it is as caviare to the few. A circle was formed round the dish: in two minutes, all that was left, was "an aching china blank."

Quantity rather than quality distinguishes Moorish cookery. The rich man's dishes are more or less like the poor man's, only that he has six times as many;

indeed, there are said to be dishes of coos-coosoo which seven men can barely carry. The Sultan's own cuisine is quite simple, better served, and more of it perhaps, than his subjects', but otherwise exactly the same.

Having disposed of the mona, our cavalcade started, and we rode down to the Sheshaoua River, still in heavy flood, but fordable since the fine night. The waters roared past between the crumbling banks: we saw in one place waggon-loads of red soil suddenly subside with a vast noise into the cataract which had undermined it. Upon the brink the men stripped themselves; then, wading into the torrent, hauled across mules, camel, and donkey one by one: we took our feet out of the stirrups, and managed to keep dry; the camel behaved admirably.

It was an uneventful day, across a bleak and stony country. Towards evening we passed a ruined kasbah, rose-red in the sunset. Riding due east, our long sharp shadows pointed ahead: there was a peace over all things. The shadowed heights on the right, scooped into blue gullies and mighty crests, carried a veil of cloud on their tops: the good little red path we were on, was without a stone. As the sun dropped we swung along into a dim grey beyond, to the muffled tramp, tramp of the mules' hoofs, *shuffle-shuffle through the night*, while a cool breeze got up, and a flight of birds high above us called aloud as they passed over. Ah! but how good it was!—no telegrams, no conventionalities, no possessions worth worry or consideration. Strange, the influence which such a simple life has upon the mind: letters, and newspapers, and the topics of the day, and the world in general, have little interest for the time being, and get buried in the wastepaper-basket of trivialities, while the weather, and the state of the track, and little things

TRANSPORTING OUR BAGGAGE.

[*To face p.* 314.

in Nature, assume gigantic proportions and fill the mind.

We camped that night near another red ruined kasbah, whose long line of crumbling tapia walls against the Atlas Mountains stretched itself out like a watch-dog beside the forbidden hills. In the morning Arabs were more importunate than ever, one woman thrusting her head between the flaps of the canvas while we were dressing. A deal, meantime, went on in the kitchen-tent over a lamb, Omar feeling its neck and tail, and subsequently buying it for five shillings, after which it was silently dispatched on the far side, skinned, cut up; and the donkey bore a pannierful of meat that day.

Our blue jay of the ruined kasbah at Sok-el-Tleta turned up again on the march, beautiful as ever, and no less tame; but all the birds shared that distinction, and were of a confiding nature delightful to see.

Before Frouga, one of our next camping-grounds, was reached, we passed a kasbah which six years ago was in the possession of a kaid, who may or may not be still alive, in prison. His province, at any rate, rose against him to a man at the late Sultan's death, and wrecked his castle, the Government disposing of him after he had escaped to Marrakesh. The orchards of almond-trees, with thriving beans planted underneath them, and the fat fields of barley, spoke volumes for the prosperity of his days. It takes much provocation to induce country people to rise and rebel against their kaid; for rebellion, if unsuccessful, brings down such awful vengeance on the heads of the tribesmen: therefore his hard case was probably just punishment.

Another river, the Asif-el-Mel, had to be forded on the same day. It was a bad crossing, we were warned by one sheikh not to attempt it, and neither of our men knew the ford; but some Arabs turned up, and they helped to get the mules safely across. R. and I had each four men with us: we tied our boots, stockings, camera and glasses round our necks, and rode over, careful not to look down at the race of the torrent, which has turned horsemen giddy often enough,—a raging river rather more than breast-high is not a thing to be trifled with. On the banks beyond lay a large and flourishing village, chiefly remarkable on account of its *Mellah* (Jews' Quarter),—a strange thing to find so far from civilization; and yet it was not, for the interior of Morocco is full of wandering Israelites, who, living and dying in remote Arab and Berber settlements, become naturalized to a certain extent, yet ever "keep themselves to themselves," housed only in their own "quarter," under lock and key after sundown, and subjected to a few irksome regulations. Some of them become rich on the profits of the "middle man," buying skins and produce of all sorts from the country people, and passing them through to the coast towns: such men may be worth from £3,000 to £5,000.

It is hard to conceive a race settling from choice amongst the squalor and filth of the lowest type of Arab, but as a matter of fact, the Jewish Quarter violated, over and above all the rest of the village put together, every tradition of cleanliness. The Berber villages of the north, dirty enough in all conscience, absolutely shone in comparison with the Arab douars in the south, or with their larger settlements, those semi-villages, whose flat-roofed huts were stacked with earthen or basket-work jars. These bottle-shaped jars, full of what Mohammed calls "the liquor of the bee," cream-cheese, barley, etc., were plastered with mud, and waterproof: when they occurred in twos and threes on every roof, the effect was striking.

It would have been a monotonous ride to Frouga except

for the Atlas Mountains on our right, which we had been steadily nearing for days: now comparatively close, their gleaming snow-peaks were never without interest, and Omar told tales of travellers' experiences up in one or two of the passes. The principal roads across the chain to Taroudant, Ras-el-Ouad, and the Sus, pass through Frouga, and make it an important place. It possesses an *inzella*, or sort of fondâk, where men and transport are safe for the night under the protection of the kaid of the district.

We pitched our tents among little fields of beans and barley, planted with olive-trees, close to a mosque, and awoke when *es-sbar* (sunrise) was called in sonorous tones from the top of the dome: a cuckoo answered the mueddzin, and a pair of little doves began to coo persistently.

The gardens of Frouga are celebrated—full of vines planted like hop-gardens, of prickly pear, figs, pears, apricots, and corn, in between the fruit-trees. And yet the owners are not rich: the governors of the district see to that; for supposing a man becomes richer than the governor, X., he goes to the Government and says, "If you make me governor instead of X., I will bring you more money than he does, and here is a present at the same time." The Government accepts the bribe, and gives the man a letter stating that he is made governor instead of X. The man collects his friends and ousts X., perhaps imprisoning him for life. A governor, therefore, never allows a man under him to possess capital. He may be rich in cattle and gardens, but he will have to pay the governor out of his profits from thirty to ninety shillings at stated times all the year round, and never have any "spare cash." If he refuses to pay, he is turned out of his own home and acres, which fall into the governor's hands. Naturally he prefers to cling to his gardens.

Beyond Frouga lay some of the most fertile land in Morocco. We passed wonderful crops of barley and wheat, which in an average year, for every bushel sown, yield forty bushels. Moors say that corn in Morocco is known to yield, not forty, but a hundred-fold. In England fifteen-fold is considered an average crop. Morocco grows two crops each year: there is a spring harvest and an autumn harvest. It would seem, therefore, that if agriculture were encouraged, and light railways laid down to the coast, money would pour into the country—especially supposing that, instead of wheat, such a crop as linseed was grown. Russian and American competition would probably diminish the profits to be made out of wheat, but a soil and a climate like Morocco might grow anything and everything. At present fraud and dishonesty seem the soul of trade: the Jew brokers cheat the Moors; the Moors sand their sheep's wool to make it heavy, mix paraffin candles with their beeswax, put all manner of things into oil, and so on. But a single example shows the spirit of the country. A friend of ours found his horses becoming poor, yet he saw their corn taken out to them every evening: he examined it; it was quite good. After a time it occurred to him to look inside the horses' mouths, and he found the gums cut and lacerated in order to prevent their eating their barley, which, after it had lain a certain time on the ground untouched, was confiscated by the servants.

Meanwhile, each day as we marched on, brought us nearer to our bourn, and at last we found ourselves on a wide flat plain, unbroken, except by the trail which we followed, consisting of six or eight narrow paths, winding on side by side like railway rails—a splendid

MARRAKESH.

[*To face p.* 318.

Marrakesh is Seen at Last

"high road" for Morocco. Truly it is a spare-room country. The snaking track might take up acres and acres of rich land. What matter! There is room.

It was still very hot: smoked spectacles kept off a certain amount of glare, and I wore two hats, a straw on top of a felt, having neglected to bring a solar topi; but even so the sun was unnecessarily generous, glowing on the splendid polish which some of the Arabs carried on their sepia-coloured skulls, and making it impossible to follow the crested larks, singing their heads off, up in the brilliant sky.

At last we felt a breeze, topped a low rise: an old greybeard all in white jogged up towards us on a donkey, a man running behind; a village lay below; but our eyes only went to one spot in the wide blue plain, which was spread out like a praying-carpet before us. That spot lay twenty-five miles off—a single tower, the Kutobea in Morocco City.

"Marrakesh!" cried Omar and Saïd simultaneously.

We rode on, across dry plain, over old river-beds, through patches of olive-trees, pink oleander, and castor-oil plant; leaving Arab douars behind; meeting with white cow-birds which recalled Tetuan; passing men with merchandise on camels and donkeys, strings of country people, and wanderers of all sorts; stopping to rest near wells where swallows were building in the brickwork and donkeys stood asleep in the shade; watching Arabs beating out corn with sticks, men ploughing, until we were once more amongst "greenery" and in a fertile stretch of country. Surely there was a river near. We passed fine crops of maize; onions were doing famously; fields of bearded wheat rustled in a life-giving breeze. And then the Wad-el-Nyfs, the largest river we had to cross, came into sight. Saïd at the outset precipitated himself into a great hole, and was well ducked: eventually we all landed safely on the other side, though the start was far from reassuring, some Arabs on the bank telling us it was "not good" to cross, and wading down into the torrent, for us to see that the water took them up to their necks almost at once, sweeping them down-stream. Before we rode into the water every man divested himself of each particle of clothing which he wore; and R. got across with two dark-skinned individuals clinging on to her legs, one on each side of the mule, a third hanging on to its bridle, and a fourth at its tail; while I followed also with four attendants. Not long ago, a party of missionaries was fording one of these very rivers, and neglected to have men at the mules' heads, one of which stumbled and threw its rider into the rapid stream: she was drowned. It was not deep at the time, or more precaution would have been taken: on the other hand, the stream is always like a mill-race, an accident can happen in a moment, and therefore a rule should be made, and never under any circumstances broken, to the effect that every rider have a man at the mule's head, and more than one, according to the state of the river.

We had a long hot ride to Tamsloect: the breeze, which was westerly, was useless to us; the track led over stony yellow hills; now and again we caught glimpses of the Kutobea standing up very far away; and all the time the great snow-fields, on the vast mountains, close upon our right, looked tantalizingly near and cold. Occasionally we watered the mules at a stream: tortoises were swimming about in one of these. But on the whole it was a singularly uneventful and a very sultry ride, until at last long lines of red mud walls, many gardens, three mosque towers, and some tall, dark, green cypress-trees

Hadj Cadour's Tea-party

proclaimed Tamsloect—an important village, possessing a Friday market, an unequalled view of the Atlas, and a saint, Mulai Abdullah Ben Hassi.

An Arab, Hadj Cadour, is one of the great men in Tamsloect; and to him, having an introduction, we went. The best hours spent in Morocco were those lived with certain of the Moors themselves, sharing for a short time their simple and yet fantastic life, learning something of their innate courtesy and generous hospitality. Hadj Cadour was a host of the old aristocratic school. He was out at his garden-house when we reached the village, entertaining friends at a tea party; and upon our message reaching him, he sent back a man on a white horse to point out another of his gardens close at hand, where he suggested that the tents should be pitched, while R. and I rode out and joined his tea party.

Leaving Omar to superintend the camp, we started off after the rider on the white horse : he led the way through the village, finally into a labyrinth of gardens, where we brushed through bearded wheat such as I have never seen before nor since, which luxuriated with olives, fruit-trees of all sorts, and pale pink monthly roses. Presently in the midst of the semi-wilderness a little white house intervened, half buried in trees, and close to it, in the shade, under an olive, was gathered Hadj Cadour's tea party, six or eight dignified Arabs, in those perfectly washed and blanched garments which so fit their solemn, dignified manners, their sad and intellectual type of faces : not that Moors are necessarily either of the two last ; but they look it—that is all.

A great tea-kettle, as usual, loomed in the background ; carpets and thick red Morocco leather cushions made seats for the members of the charmed circle : we reclined there with the rest, talking, as far as a few Arabic words would carry us, of our starting-point, our destination, the road, the rivers, the weather, Hadj Cadour helping us out, one and all interested and anxious to be understood and to understand. Our host dispensed *sherrub de minat*, the wine of the country, made from grapes; the little dome-shaped pewter teapot was there, with its fond associations of Morocco, together with the copper tray and circle of diminutive painted glasses; a gorgeous indolent sun poured down beyond the patch of shade; the hum and hover of insects vibrated in the air; and presently musicians were summoned—girls wearing pale green jellabs and silver ornaments, with yellow handkerchiefs twisted round their heads, men in bright colours. Sitting down between us, each was given a glass of sherrub de minat, and by-and-by they began to play. Weird and wild music it was, that of the *tareegea*, the *gimbi*, and the *tahr*, quaint native instruments of the roughest construction, and yet, as music, possessing fascination not a little.

The long kif-pipes were lighted, green tea and wine were sipped, the white figures stretched themselves on the cushions, and a great and dreamy content came over the faces under the white turbans. There was nowhere a trace of boredom such as mars so many European entertainments—rather the thing was loved for itself, and every man felt it and entered into its spirit. Now and then the musicians broke into a strange song, and the guests beat their hands and murmured in chorus; then again they would seem half intoxicated, in a harmless fashion, with kif and wine and music, and would appear to be absent in a world of their own. The music had a lilt in it, and often a suggestion of something half tamed, desperate, swung along with the cadences; and thin wreaths of smoke from the long pipes blew up through the olive branches, and an Arabic sentence dropped now and again on the ear: the hot, slow, sleepy afternoon waned. . . .

Poetry bulks so largely in the Arabic nature. Emotional and yet simple, that nature is, to a certain extent, appealed to by the refined. The sordid and vulgar have no attractions for it. There is no language more poetical than the Arabic language, where "snow" is called "hair of the mountain" and "rainbow" is "bride of the rain." "Red mullet" is "the sultan of fishes": "maiden-hair fern" is translated by "little cane of the well." Ordinary Arabic words show an extraordinary gift of description: the word for "secretly" means literally "under the matting," and "never" is expressed thus, "when the charcoal takes root and the salt buds."

Uncontrolled ascendency of imagination marks the Arab, and endows his nature with a fascination all its own: an outdoor life is his heritage, and the things of Nature are a part of himself. "Spring" he calls "grass"; "summer" is "gleaning"; "autumn" is "fruit"; "winter" is "rainy."

If only he could keep pure his race, Morocco had never stood among the nations where she stands now. The steady infusion of African blood is becoming her ruin: the sensual negro type, spreading rapidly, is eating its way into the heart of the people. When it is remembered that thousands upon thousands of slaves are imported into Morocco from the interior of Africa every year, that they become eventually "free," their children inheriting equal rights with other children, it is no longer a matter of wonder that the Moorish race shows signs of deterioration, that its people are effete. It is after meeting with men such as Hadj Cadour and many others, who hark back to the old type of chief and horseman and the desert life, touched with the old vein of poetry and chivalry, that one regrets the things which are. But we had spent an afternoon which was one worth recollecting; and when we had parted from that little circle under the shady olive, and were jogging back to our tents, it was to remember that there are still good things in Morocco.

The tents we found ready for us in a delightful spot enclosed by a wall: a tank lay in the centre of the garden, around it a few paths, and a great deal of mint. But a terrible ordeal awaited us—green tea and a great spread, provided by the brother of Hadj Cadour, who had also arranged carpets as seats around the tank. Again next morning, just after we had finished breakfast, this hospitable individual sent into our tent two steaming hot chickens fried brown in argan oil, with half a dozen round cakes of fine floor; and when, immediately afterwards, we rode to his house to say farewell and tender our thanks, he proffered green tea once more.

Heavy drops of rain awoke us in the middle of the night; but just as an ominous patter was coming through the old canvas and sounding on the bed-clothes, the shower stopped. Again later it came on, with thunder. Omar changed the smart clothes which he had put on in view of a triumphal entry into Marrakesh; we packed and got off as quickly as we could, expecting more rain; many good-byes were said; Hadj Cadour sent a servant with us to the gates; and we rode out of Tamsloect.

Outside, towards the east, its gardens were numerous: great black poplars and palms grew freely. For an hour we rode alongside a district which belonged entirely to Mulai el Hadj, the great man of Tamsloect, and a holy Sharīf to boot. This man is rich, and because he is a holy Sharīf he can never be dispossessed of his wealth.

THE OPEN GATE.

[*To face p.* 324.

His white house and cypress-trees stand out prominently in the village we had just left; throughout his gardens he has built a succession of water-towers, which irrigate his land; he is British-protected, and as important a man in the south as the French-protected Wazeer of Wazan is in the north.

All this time we were riding steadily towards Marrakesh, interest increasing with every step as we neared the city, to visit which we had left Mogador about ten days before.

That last day's march was not an interesting one: the great Atlas, upon which we had now turned our backs, were no longer to be seen, on account of clouds which the last night's storm had brought upon them; the plain over which we rode possessed a deadly monotony, for we were not entering Marrakesh upon its best side, where gardens upon gardens of palm-trees stretch beyond the city gates for miles and miles, but our road from Tamsloect was prosaic and dull. Certainly we crossed some of the wonderful underground canals, which carry water five and ten miles, from springs in the country, into the city—about whose origin nothing whatever is known, tradition remaining silent as to any builder. These great works are merely water-ways tunnelled through the solid earth, not at any great distance from the surface: along their courses the streams are conducted for great distances. There are openings at intervals which ventilate the tunnels: these are kept clean and easily examined by means of the same. The whole arrangement is very rough, very primitive, but perfectly answers the purpose for which it was made.

The crops which we left behind us at every mile looked well, and it was to be hoped would soon make good the failure of the preceding crop: that failure had accounted for the skinny children and lean women whom we had met, and was the reason of the country people's continuous digging for ayerna root, and washing the same by the roadside and in so many villages.

Meanwhile, Marrakesh and its adobe walls, of a sad yellow-pink tone, grew nearer and nearer, till at last the long line of crumbling tapia was but a short distance off, and the Báb-el-Roub, a massive gateway, plainly to be seen. Just outside the walls, Mr. Miller, one of the missionaries, met us: he had one piece of news, which carried with it regret wherever it was heard across the length and breadth of the British Empire—the death of Cecil Rhodes. Under the Báb-el-Roub we rode into the city of crumbling walls and silent sandy roadways: somewhat of a deserted city, the great southern capital appeared to be at first; but then we were nowhere near its heart, and the half of it is gardens and quiet houses, while a small part only, is wholly full of vitality: the whole is crumbling to pieces, and strange of all strangest cities ever seen.

We rode straight to Kaid Maclean's house, lent us by Lady Maclean—the best house in Morocco City, overlooking one of the many market-places, and that open space in which story-tellers and snake-charmers, surrounded by a dense circle of admirers, cater to an attentive throng. The house was empty, and we "camped" in several of the rooms, lunching in a long gallery which looked straight out on to the Atlas Mountains: the mules went into a capacious stable; the servants made themselves comfortable in the kitchens. It is hard to find houseroom in Marrakesh: of course a hotel is unheard of, nor is camping-ground to be met with easily. There are no foreign consuls in this far-off city, and no English element beyond the two or three missionaries who live there. Travellers have generally to depend upon the loan of some house for the time being, from a holy Sharīf or Moor of some standing; but the house may be anywhere, and comfortable or otherwise. Since the Sultan was at Fez, his army and his commander-in-chief, Kaid Maclean, were at Fez too: hence the reason of the Macleans' house standing empty, within which we were so fortunate as to find ourselves.

Marrakesh cannot be described: it must be seen. It is more suggestive, more intangible, more elusive— that is to say, its Eastern medley of a population is so, and its crumbling tapia-walled houses are so—than any other Moorish city. More ghosts should stalk the half-deserted yellow roadways of Marrakesh, more mysteries be shrouded within the windowless walls, than a man of Western civilization could conceive.

It is a vast city—other writers have chronicled the number of square miles which it accounts for—and yet, in spite of its size, the sum-total of souls it contains is not overwhelming. There are gardens everywhere, stretch after stretch of palm-trees, acre after acre of fruit-trees, and wedged among them all, lie the flat roofs, swarm the endless throng which spells humanity; and the oddest, most varied humanity—Arabs and negroes, men from the Sus, from the Sahara, from Draa, Berber hillmen, tribesmen from the Atlas, a tumultuous multitude, a hive of bees of whom no census has ever been made. We were among them all, the first time we rode through the city. No one walks in Marrakesh: as a matter of fact I did later on, often enough, sometimes alone, getting somewhat jostled in the narrow ways— beyond that in no way inconvenienced. But every one who can, is on a mule or a long-tailed countrybred, pushing along at a foot's pace, crying out now and then, and avoiding this pair of black toes, that coffee-coloured bare heel.

Beyond the wall, covered with nails, whereon heads are fastened after rebellions have been quenched and the time of punishment and warning has come, we rode into the land of little shops. Here, in another instance, Marrakesh is unique: the narrow streets were in great part entirely roofed in overhead either by vines or by bamboos; the brilliant sunlight streamed through the spaces between the vines and canes, and chequered the seething white throng which eternally passed underneath it. From an open street we plunged into the cool shade of one of these arcades. And how it moved! Nothing ever stood still in the Marrakesh soks. Life "travels" for ever and for ever there. Between the shops, themselves teeming with bustle and incident, moved up and down, the throng of white, draped, dignified figures, calling, heaving, struggling, jostling sometimes, chattering always, blotched with shifting yellow sunlight and black shadow cast by the lattice roof overhead. It was a transformation scene; it was a weird dream— weird to the point of seeming unreal, unlike men and the haunts of men, though all the time rampant with *humans*.

When the Sultan went to Fez, a party of soldiers and goldsmiths and craftsmen of all sorts went with him from the city of Marrakesh, in number over forty thousand souls. But the exodus made no appreciable difference in the soks. Not only the numbers, but the types of the stream of faces between which we rode were all striking, and each one so far removed from anything at all European. Humanity can indeed be separated from humanity by gulfs impassable, or gulfs which may alone be bridged over by a violation of

Photo by A. Cavilla, Tangier.]
THE KUTOBEA, MARRAKESH.
[*To face p.* 328.

Marrakesh

nature, on the part of the man upon the east bank or upon the west bank.

The palm-trees wave above Marrakesh, turtle-backed mosques and tall towers rise among the gardens and gleam in the sun, but above and beyond every other feature of the far-away fantastic southern capital one watch-tower rises over everything and rears itself into the sky—the Kutobea, built, according to tradition, by Fabir for the Sultan El Mansur. It stands in a vast empty space close to the Great Mosque: few people pass that way—their footfalls are almost unheard in the soft sand; and the lonely tower cuts the clear quiet sky. The Kutobea is built of dark red stone. There is a pattern, alternately raised and sunk, on the faces of the minaret, the sunk part cut deep, the raised part carved and standing out. A broad band of wonderful black and green iridescent tiles, snakes round the top like some opulent spotted serpent. Part of it has dropped away: the gilded brass balls, the cupola, are here and there tarnished; but the sun sets, and his indulgent rays swamp every defect, burnish and polish and gild corner-stone and fretted marble and emerald-green tile alike, until the "to-day" of the Kutobea is as triumphant as its "yesterday" of many hundred years. The design of the tower itself—the minaret—is said to have come from Constantinople, as did the Giralda at Seville, which it so resembles.

Of the mosque, beside the Kutobea, nothing was to be seen except its walls, and through an open door avenues of pillars. The huge building has an Arabic name meaning "The Mosque of the Books"; for what reason—who can tell?—tradition is silent.

Marrakesh itself is supposed to have been built upon the site of an immensely old structure, the ancient Martok. As it is now, Yusuf-ibn-Tachfin founded it in 1072, a city which covers almost as much ground as Paris—a purely African city. Fez, Tetuan, Tangier, have Spanish blood in them: Marrakesh is African to the core. Arabs here are in a minority: the spare Saharowi type, the shaved lip and cheeks and pointed chin-tuft of the Berber race, men from the mysterious sandy steppes below Cape Bojador, Soudanese blacks, men from Wadnoon—one and all congregate in this city. Even the music and songs are, naturally enough, all African, with the strange interval, the rhythm which halts and races where no European music ever halted or raced; and the tom-tom, the gimbri, the ear-piercing Moorish flute, all fall upon the English ear as things intensely strange and strongly fascinating.

Marrakesh boasts no aristocracy: it is a city of the people. It has few Sharīfs: it is a land of "traders," speculating, toiling, intriguing; between its yellow adobe walls, and its whitewashed dazzling walls, amidst its dense metallic semi-tropical vegetation, up and down its sandy silent ways, they live and die. Its fountains are beautiful: *Shrab-u-Schuf* (Drink and admire) is inscribed on one of them. But it is not by its architecture that Marrakesh stands and falls; rather by a personality all its own—by its many ruined walls, by its deserted streets, by the hot pulse of life throbbing imperiously through its arteries crowded to suffocation with humanity, by its flaring African sunlight, by the figures which can never be other than picturesque, by a thousand impressions which can never die. And by reason of all this Marrakesh is great.

Once upon a time it was impossible for an Englishman to see the Slave Market. Owing partly to the radical hatred of Europeans, partly to the suspicious and seclusive nature of the Moor, the presence of foreigners in the sacred Slave Market was tabooed. Not that the Nazarene was "taken up" or turned back if he showed his face inside the courtyard: on the contrary, he was allowed to walk in, and apparently no eye was aware of his presence. And yet in a few moments he would find himself alone. The Slave Market had vanished, had melted away: a line of disappearing backs was all which was to be seen. Supposing a Moor had connived at this attempt on the part of a Nazarene to see slaves being sold, that Moor disappeared, by order of the Sultan, and there was a funeral later on in the day.

However, while we were in Marrakesh, less rigorous orders were in vogue. Having come prepared to see the market disguised in native dress if necessary, we found that we were able to go there without much difficulty, and only escorted by one of the missionaries and a servant. Though slaves are bought and sold through the length and breadth of Morocco, it is not possible in any other city than Marrakesh for the European to see or know much about it. In the coast towns the sales are conducted privately. In Fez it is probable that they might be attended by others than Moors; but at the time of writing I take it that no wise European, if such should be there at all in these unquiet times, would venture to put himself into a position likely to attract all the bullets and knives in Fez in his direction.

Just at sunset—6.30, I think—the Slave Market in Marrakesh opens, and we went in. To some ears it would no doubt have sounded the strangest anomaly, that prayer to the Most High God, with which the sale was prefaced; but a Mussulman hallows every action, right or wrong, with a petition; besides which slavery is lawful and good in his eyes, is approved of and permitted by Mohammed in the written book of the Korān; is, in short, a part of the scheme of Nature which it were a serious mistake not to use and enjoy. So the line of auctioneers formed up, held out their hands, prayed, invoked a blessing over the proceedings, mumbling in sonorous tones for a few moments. Then silence. It was over: the sale began. There is nothing more easy than to be theatrical and emotional in describing scenes of this sort—one has read of them scores of times: words such as "degrading" and "harrowing" rise up in the mind's eye, coupled with violent epithets and stinging clauses. And yet, finding oneself in the centre of another just such a scene, one realized how impossible the thing was, to understand, or to feel, beforehand, and how curiously it played upon the emotions. Walking into the market with a sobriety, with a cold, critical interest such as a Nero may have felt towards his victims, one divined early in the proceedings that the scene tended unduly to intensify emotion. Truly no men think alike: a vast chasm yawns between the natures of the slave-trader and the European: that chasm is a universal education. To realize all which separates a native of Africa from a Frenchman or an Englishman, and the difficulties which lie in the way of promoting an understanding between the two, visit such a place as the Slave Market in Marrakesh.

Groups of slaves, more or less gorgeously dressed, some in rags where nothing better could be afforded, were sitting far back in little covered-in recesses which lined the square. All round the square stood, or sat upon their heels, intending purchasers, for the most part middle-aged elderly men, sleek and fat, in turbans and soft linen, white beyond reproach. Each auctioneer, the prayer over, advanced to the groups of slaves, and led out one or perhaps two or three, and paraded them round and round the square under the eyes of the buyers. At last a bid was made : the auctioneer walked on, pushing the slaves in front of him, and calling out the amount of the bid. A higher bid was made : he shouted out that bid, and still walked on. Then a purchaser signed to him that he wished to look at the slaves. The auctioneer at once marshalled the women or woman slave (there were many more women than men) up to the Moor who wished to examine her. She squatted in front of him, while he looked at her teeth, felt her arms, neck, and legs, and in a low voice asked her a string of private questions. After a time the woman was allowed to get up, the auctioneer called out the latest bid for her, and walked her on. Probably some one else would examine her "points," and another and another ; and her price would go up till the auctioneer should have got what he wanted, and the woman would be handed over to her new master.

Some of the slaves walked round with a profoundly indifferent air—none of them looked in wild spirits ; but, on the other hand, it was "Kismet" rather than misery which was written on their faces. It is a rare thing for any slave to object violently or to make any scene : as a rule they knelt down obediently enough in front of the fat Mohammedans, who thrust their fingers into their mouths, took them by the chin, and treated them with great familiarity. But, oddly enough, on one of the nights we attended the market a scene did occur. A middle-aged woman, absolutely refused to walk round—we were told probably because she had been parted from her child, and could not bear to be sold. The poor creature wept wildly, and hid her face in the red cloth round her head. She was, however, in the end forced along like a recalcitrant mule, her cloth torn off, herself made to kneel down at the bidding of a group of traders, and undergo the usual examination. Some of the young girls looked shame-faced, shuffling along behind or in front of the auctioneers with bent heads. The sad middle-aged woman fetched in the end seven pounds ten shillings. A little child was going for three pounds ten. A girl of thirteen—that is, at her very best—was selling for fifteen pounds: she was of course unusually attractive.

The slave trade of Africa receives an apparent stamp of legality from the fact that religious warfare and the taking of prisoners in war and making them slaves are looked upon as Divine institutions. There is no obligation on the Mussulman to release slaves, and as long as wars and raids last, the mass of slaves in Mohammedan countries tends rather to increase than otherwise, their progeny ever adding to the original number. There is no restriction as to the number of slaves or concubines which a Moor may have: it entirely depends upon his purse. His women are his luxury, and an expensive one. A concubine may be sold at any moment, and the position is thus precarious and varied: it has one saving clause, which I have already explained—the woman who bears a son to her master is free, and at his death his property will be divided between the sons of concubines equally with the sons of his wife and wives. Mussulman raids still continue against the negroes of Central Africa, against tribes in Persia, in Afghanistan, and other parts of the world; indeed, as long as Mohammedanism lasts, there is very little chance of the abolition of slavery.

One afternoon we went over the garden belonging to the late basha of Marrakesh—Ben Dowd—almost the only garden I have ever seen in Morocco which had in it

Photo by A. Cavilla, Tangier.]
THE WAD-EL-AZELL.

flowers; and these were roses from Spain, valuable and beautiful, the pride of the basha. There was a charming summer-house half built, and a conservatory nearly finished, in different parts of the garden. In the midst of his prosperity, only eight months before, Ben Dowd had been arrested and put into prison. It was the old tale of jealousy. The Grand Wazeer was afraid of the basha, and in order to secure himself from harm succeeded in having Ben Dowd deposed and put entirely out of harm's way. Though an explanation is always forthcoming for violent proceedings such as the above, it would be unwise to assume in Morocco that the explanation had a grain of truth in it. Wheels within wheels; intrigue after intrigue; lie, topped by lie, make up the sum of Moorish diplomacy, and render the coil of politics in that country an absolutely fascinating study, not because it is so surreptitious, but because it is clever as well as cunning, and all the time involves bigger interests than ever appear on the tapis—interests which concern France, Austria, England, Germany, and other Powers, all of whom struggle for a finger in the seething pie.

To return to Ben Dowd. He was "detained" in a house—not ignominiously committed to the common gaol, an unusual respite—allowed twelve shillings a day, and his wife's company. He was in Fez with these restrictions at the time we were looking over his gardens; and half of his wives were left behind at his own house, costing him a pound a day, we were told, in the face of which his allowance seemed inadequate.

When the Government seized him, no money was found in his house; but three hundred thousand dollars' worth of goods in the shape of carpets, mirrors, gilt bedsteads, etc., were confiscated. His post, however, is still vacant: he is a good man, and possibly the Government will repent of its hasty step, and in due time restore such a valuable servant to favour. On the other hand, Ben Dowd may be ruined for life.

The bashas and kaids of Morocco were all gnashing their teeth, while we were at Marrakesh, over the new system of taxation, which the Sultan and a certain progressive member of his Government, are endeavouring to introduce into the country. The main idea in these new regulations is, that governors will be paid specified salaries by the Government—that they will collect taxes as usual, but send the amount of money collected intact to Court, not, as has been the custom hitherto, docking off the half, it may be, and pocketing it as their own pay. Again, each province has been lately inspected by a certain number of trustworthy men, who have fixed its rate of taxation. The countryman is to pay so much upon his possessions—for example, ninepence for a cow, three shillings for a horse, twopence-halfpenny for an olive-tree, three shillings for a camel, no more and no less—instead of having the utmost squeezed out of him, which has been the practice of the governors up till now.

The scheme sounds excellent. A letter has been read aloud in every city and country market-place, apprising the people of the new law, and they are delighted in proportion, but scarcely believe that the Government will be strong enough to enforce it. Indeed, it is hardly probable that the new taxation system can succeed unless two important steps are first taken—the tribes must be disarmed, and a new set of governors be appointed to take the place of the old. As long as the tribesmen are armed, there can never be law and order, any more than there can be settled peace upon the Indian frontier under the same conditions. At one moment the tribes will side

New System of Taxation 337

with the Government, at another they will take the part of a governor, at another they will attack a neighbouring tribe. It is all very well to tax such men justly and to treat them like civilized beings, instead of trampling them underfoot, preventing their becoming rich, and holding them to be ignorant devils; but they are not civilized, unfortunately—they have not sufficient education to know when they are well off and to profit by it. Every man of them has a gun, and bloodshed and plunder are life itself to him. Treat him well, he bides his time, grows rich with the rest of his tribe; together they descend upon their neighbours, avenge an old wrong, loot to their hearts' content, perhaps attack the Sultan himself. But disarm one and all such men, and in the far future a peaceable agricultural folk may reign in their stead. It would be a work of time, but it has been effected before in the annals of history.

The second condition, which would go far towards the working of the new system of taxation, is the appointment of new governors. The salary which the governors are to receive, is a comparatively small one, compared with the vast sums which they have been in the habit of accumulating, by means of extortion and by defrauding the Government. It is hardly fair to expect a man to cut down his expenses, give up half his wives, sell his slaves, and fall in the estimation of those under him. The thing must assuredly lead to dispute, born of peculation, and fighting must be the inevitable result. But if, on the other hand, new men are appointed, who from the first suit their expenditure to their means, a more peaceful working basis will be established.

The old Oriental policy of the "balance of jealousies" will doubtless play its useful part: that is to say, each governor will watch his next-door neighbour like a cat watching a mouse; and if he detect any underhand dealings, or evasions, or infringements of the new law, he will report at once to the Sultan, and thereby gain *kudos*, perhaps a substantial reward, for himself. In this way the Government may receive support at the hands of the men whom it is keeping in order.

CHAPTER XII

THE THURSDAY MARKET—WE MIGHT HAVE GONE TO GLAOUIA—LEAVE MARRAKESH AND SET OUT ON OUR LAST MARCH FOR THE COAST—FLOWERS IN MOROCCO—ON THE WRONG TRAIL—ARAB TENTS—GOOD-BYE TO EL MOGHREB.

CHAPTER XII

The best that we find in our travels is an honest friend. He is a fortunate voyager who finds many. We travel, indeed, to find them. They are the end and the reward of life. They keep us worthy of ourselves; and when we are alone, we are only nearer to the absent.

THE great Thursday Market is one of those things in Marrakesh which, once seen, is stamped deeper than a hundred other memories upon the mind. It is held in a sun-baked open space outside the Gate of the Thursday Market, just beyond the city walls, within view of the plains and a distant low range of mountains. Thousands and thousands of tall palms, groves of them, wave in the wind all over the surrounding country: a few great watercourses, worn and eaten out of the red soil, burrow between the forests on their way down to the great river.

To reach the market we rode out along a road thronged with people selling all sorts of goods, from splendid old flintlock guns from the Sus chased with silver and gold and going at three pounds, to striped carpets strong and violent in colouring at seven-and-sixpence each, and second-hand clothes of the most varied description. At last, topping a little hill, we rode down into the market: it is, more correctly speaking, a horse fair,—mules were also for sale. The horses down in the south are without doubt very different from the poor little ponies bred up in the north; but even these, in comparison, for instance, with a thoroughbred hunter at home, fell far short of what my defective imagination had led me to expect of Arab stallions in Morocco. For the most part there was nothing for sale except great heavy brutes with small heads and proud arched necks. Every one of them fell away in the hindquarters.

As usual the sale was prefaced by a prayer: hard bargaining, sharp practice, and much or little swindling, inseparable from horse-dealing, must all of it, first of all, be watered by prayer. Therefore the horsemen formed into a line; the central figure chanted some verses from the Korān; the rest held out their hands palms upwards, then joined in a sort of Amen, the instant afterwards sticking their spurs into their horses and dashing forward, charging in a line over the plain between two rows of spectators, and pulling the horses up on to their haunches at the end, red with spur-marks and white with foam. This was repeated two or three times, the short space in which the riders pulled up out of a full gallop being sometimes almost incredible; then a great circle was formed of would-be purchasers and onlookers, and the horses were ridden into the circle and then round and round to display themselves, each rider at the same time *auctioning his own horse*, yelling out the bids for it, as they rose, at the top of his voice. When the last bid was made, and he could get no more, the rider, after shouting the price, added that he "would not consult the absent one," meaning thereby that the owner of the horse, whether himself or not, would raise no objection to the animal's being sold for that price. Unless this sentence had been pronounced, the purchaser could not have been certain that the owner would not say afterwards he did not intend to sell for that sum. Most of the horses fetched from three pounds twelve to four pounds ten.

Mules were sold in the same way—the prayer, the parade round the circle, each rider seated almost on his mule's tail, urging him on, with hands and heels, to pace his best, the mule's nose up in the heavens. Some of them were splendid animals, which I would have given anything to have possessed—perfectly made, looking more intelligent than many humans, and full of pluck and staying power: these fetched rather more than double, what the best horse in the whole market sold for. But in criticising the horses, I speak of what I saw on this occasion: there may be, and no doubt are, fine arabs to be had in Southern Morocco—at least so I am told—but I came across only what may be called "a cart-horse stamp."

And yet they look very fine, these same sensible-looking beasts, with their great eyes, and flowing manes and tails, and proud carriage. There is something, too, eternally fascinating in the beautiful seat of an Arab on his horse—not of a fat sheikh or a rich basha or a thriving merchant, but that of the lean and wiry Arab horseman born and bred, who, as he thunders past at full gallop, puts himself into a dozen positions, is at home in them all, shoots behind him, above him, below him, without drawing rein, turning in any direction, while he makes the whole air ring with his wild cries. The Moorish saddle of course helps his grip; but beyond that, there is something cat-like in the lithe swing of his body, and it is that body's right and natural function to be upon a horse. The white turban, the flowing white garments, the gorgeously coloured saddle, the great silvered stirrups, are all part of the whole—and an attractive whole—born of the limitless desert, the great far-reaching sky, the pure wind: it is Arabian, that is all—*and so much.*

Meanwhile, camels were selling in another corner of the market, being made to lie down and rise and generally show themselves off: they were fetching from three pounds ten upwards. Cows, goats, and sheep were less interesting; but the throng of men which filled up the fair was, as ever, more than a study. Above and beyond all, stood out the wild inhabitants of the Atlas, and men from the Sus, wearing black camel's-hair jellabs with a great russet-red or saffron-yellow patch let into the backs of them. The origin of this striking "badge" is not known, but the jellabs themselves looked absolutely in keeping with the lawless ruffians, on whose shoulders they hung, and the wild blotch of bizarre colour was "just themselves."

Bay, is the colour which in a horse the Moor chooses first—the pearl of colours, sober and most hardy; while a light chestnut brings ill luck, though a dark chestnut is the colour of the wind, can "travel," and was Mohammed's favourite. A horse must have the colour of its saddle in harmony with itself—an apple-green saddle for a black horse, scarlet for a white, the whole beautifully worked and embossed in silk, and when on the horse's back, should be set, perhaps, upon as many as *nine* different coloured saddle-cloths, one on top of each other.

Of all filthy quarters in the filthiest of cities, I think the Jewish Quarter in Marrakesh has a fair chance of ranking first,—outside it, rubbish, a manure-heap eighty feet high, which no one troubles to remove; inside the walls, black mud, feet deep, streets which are sewers, collections of dead dogs, rotting vegetables, refuse of all sorts; amongst it all, a dirty people, callous beyond belief as regards sanitation, with sore heads, sore eyes, matted rags.

Photo by A. Cavilla, Tangier.]

THE SULTAN'S GARDEN.

[*To face p.* 344.

Not a butcher's shop which is not black with flies and "high" with rotten meat: flies lie upon every article of food.

And in the very votex of this muck-heap—astounding to the traveller—are content to live wealthy Jews, happy to flourish all their lives shoulder to shoulder with unutterable squalor.

We went over a house belonging to a Jew millionaire, well built, lavishly decorated, as luxurious as money and Morocco would permit, evidently the pride of the whole family. Probably few of them went far outside the city walls: they were born to the Mellah. His success as a trader might have given the head of the house a country place in England, shady lawns, a carriage and pair to drive in: he preferred his own muck-heap. But I cannot conceive upon what he spent his money, other than the glorification of the inside of his house.

The Sultan's palace looked deserted: it is long, however, since he left it, and high time he was in Fez again; for Fez is more in touch with Europe—Fez means a shade more progression and civilization than life in Morocco City. Round the palace lay bales of goods which had been ordered by him and sent out from England—things such as waggons, motor-cars possibly, which are supposed so much to shock his narrow-minded subjects. They imagine that his Sharīfian Majesty wastes vast sums of money; whereas for a great monarch, the ruler of an empire, his private bills are probably absurdly small. He may have fireworks let off every night for ten minutes, horrifying Marrakesh; but the cost of his amusements, considering his position, must be curiously reasonable: so one considered, as one looked at the "parcels" awaiting his return to the capital, which lay in the immense courtyard outside his palace, where "powder play" is held, and where he receives foreign ambassadors, marching through the great gateway which leads to his own private rooms, over which is inscribed in Arabic an odd sentence; it reads literally, "What God wills: there is no power but God."

The days passed, and our time in Marrakesh drew to an end. In spite of all that had been told us in Tangier, of the difficulties and dangers which would attend an expedition into the Atlas Mountains, in spite of the verdict that we should not be given a permit, should be "stopped and not allowed to continue the journey," we found that, once upon the scene of action, there would have been little difficulty in getting at least as far as Glaouia, and in pushing up through one or two other passes.

The ride to Glaouia might take five or six days: there were several other places and a district or two which would have been worth visiting ten times over. The missionaries in Marrakesh were willing to make all arrangements: one of them would have gone with us, and under that escort it would have been possible to travel into the Atlas without risk. We should have gone "privately," without troubling any one, without formality; and in all probability no one would have troubled about us: that, after all, is the only way to travel satisfactorily in Morocco, not with half a dozen soldiers and a vast noise.

But for this year at any rate our travels in Morocco had reached their limit. R. was not strong enough to face more marching: the hot sun, long rides, and general "roughing it" had told upon her, and the responsibility of taking her on farther afield, into remote regions of uncertain climate, was too great.

Early one morning we set forth upon our last march, back again to the coast, by the track which leads eventually to Mazagan, a seaport some distance farther north than Mogador. Here we hoped to pick up a steamer, and proceed, *viâ* Tangier, across to Gibraltar,

Photo by A. Cavua, Tangier.

THE RIVER TENSIF OUTSIDE MARRAKESH.

[*To face p.* 346.

where it would be possible to get a P. & O. boat and head for home.

The march to Mazagan was easy, and contained little incident. After leaving the plains of Marrakesh and its waving palm-trees, and seeing the tall Kutobea disappear at last, we found ourselves in the "Little Mountains," and along the rough road began to fall in continually with parties of tribesmen, Arab country people, all mounted, who had been commandeered to accompany the Sultan as far as Fez, and who were now coming back to their homes. Splendid bronzed fellows they were, dark brick-dust colour, wrapped in long white cloaks, with the hood of an under garment pulled down over their faces: sometimes a white cloth swathed their heads; their chins were hidden in soft folds which reached up to their hawk-eyes, veiling the face, like true sons of the desert, as a protection against sun and wind. Guns were slung across their shoulders: they wore long yellow riding-boots and spurs, with half a dozen saddle-cloths; and all rode horses, strong little beasts, well groomed, some hog-maned, but usually with great locks of hair sweeping over their necks, and their tails almost touching the ground behind. On grey or white countrybreds as a rule, they wound along the mountain path in single file, these tall white-cloaked horsemen, in nowise differing from their ancestors of a thousand years ago—Arabs of unbroken descent: as they emerged from between the wild hills it would have been hard to find a more picturesque sight.

One of the few peaceful camping-grounds between Marrakesh and Mazagan was at a little distance outside an Arab village of about thirty little pointed thatched huts, enclosed within a zareba of thorn-bushes: it was called Smeera.

We camped near some trees and water: the fig-trees were full of crows, which came in to roost in thousands, and The Little Owl (*Athene noctua*) haunted the place. In the early half-light of the morning this wise-looking little bird was found, when we awoke, to be sitting upon the edge of the flap of the tent in the doorway, gazing in upon us with round yellow eyes; nor was it the least nervous.

I recollect how, the evening before, there sat outside Smeera, as so often may be seen outside the like villages, away beyond the huts and the zareba, where it was very quiet, upon some flat grey stones, eight or twelve village men—Arabs. Sitting there in the sunset, wrapped in their white hooded mantles, this conclave of wise white owls, easily to be mistaken for grey stones, so rigid are their backs—of what do they talk as the hours go by? There is no joke nor song nor a drop of liquor going, as in a "public," where our labourers at home would naturally congregate. But this charmed circle sits on, staring into the west: the tall bearded wheat rustles in the wind close to them; the illimitable plain stretches away to the horizon, flat as their own uneventful lives; the sun drops behind the soft straight line of Earth; they do not move,—wondrous picturesque figures, long white folds, peaked hoods, sitting, their knees drawn up to their chins, for how long? What is time to an Arab?

One evening our camel never turned up, and we fully expected to have had to sleep without beds or any other of the night's usual adjuncts. We had started that morning at seven, had ridden till twelve, had halted for an hour and a half, starting again at half-past one, and riding till half-past five; and all the way, after a mile out of Sok-el-Tleta, where we watered the mules at a pond and the trail forked, we were on the wrong road.

We Lose the Trail

Only the man with the camel knew the Mazagan line of march thoroughly well : he had explained it beforehand to Omar. Omar made a mistake, and the camel and attendants were behind ourselves. However, news travels oddly fast in uncivilized countries, and the camel-driver heard after a time that the "advance squadron" was on the wrong trail. He set out after us, and ran and walked, and caught us at three o'clock in the afternoon. The wretched camel followed his steps all the way, with Mulai Ombach in charge of our baggage, three donkeys, and a boy, who were afraid of being cut off from us, and dared not risk a night by themselves. The camel-driver put us right, Omar and Saïd were well cursed, and we began a toilsome journey across rough country, hoping to hit the right trail in time.

We found ourselves in the wildest and dirtiest of Arab encampments now and again, where infuriated dogs, unaccustomed to visitors, rushed out and almost bit us upon our mules, amidst a hail of stones from Omar and Saïd. A valley luxuriating knee-deep in flowers—the Flower Valley we called it—was the one redeeming feature of that march. There are certain times for seeing the wild flowers in Morocco—perhaps April in the south is the best month : so far we had not been as much struck by them as report would lead one to expect. And yet they were most beautiful. Picture corn-fields full of love-in-a-mist; orchards of fig-trees, with the grass ablaze with golden pyrethrums; red mallow standing up in the barley; the ground carpeted with blue-and-white convolvulus; masses of carmine-coloured convolvulus densely festooned over the thorn-hedges; on the barest, stoniest of soil stretches of cistus, pale pink to faded mauve; asphodels everywhere; sometimes the wild spring form of the cultivated artichoke, the small variety of the ice-plant, the larkspur, the lupin, and several varieties of lavender. All these we met with, over and over again: rarer plants were to be found for the looking. R. collected specimens of them all, to be classified by the authorities at Kew Gardens on our return.

The Flower Valley yielded one or two which we had not seen before, and we would have lingered there, but that time was precious and we had no notion of our exact whereabouts. It was a case of going on and on and meeting no one: evening began to draw near, and still we were off the right track, while our baggage might be anywhere. There was nothing for it but to push forward and trust to luck: in time we cut into innumerable little paths, which snaked side by side in the same direction across the plain, pointing towards the coast, and these we surmised to be the trail to Mazagan, which proved to be correct. But at that moment, though we were anything but certain, it had become absolutely necessary to halt for the night. It was dark, and the mules were done. An Arab village lay on a hillside not far off, and we made for it.

Omar and Saïd had with them on their mules our tent and two or three necessaries for cooking: we had therefore a roof over our heads, and in time a fire was made, odds and ends were scraped up, and we ate a meal of sorts sitting on the ground beside a candle stuck on a stone. The night grew very cold: there was, however, a bit of thin carpet, which we proposed to wrap ourselves in to sleep. Now and then one of us looked out between the flaps of the tent into the darkness and watched—a case of "Sister Ann! Sister Ann! do you see any one coming?"

We had, however, grown tired of looking out, and were just arranging ourselves on the ground, when familiar

ONE OF OUR LAST CAMPS. LOADING THE CAMEL.

[*To face p.* 350.

noises sounded outside, and Omar's voice crying joyfully, "Le chameau arrive!"

Perhaps, above all else which was interesting on the road to Mazagan, the little Arab settlements, composed entirely of tents, interested us most. In them, was lived the truly nomad, gipsy life of the wandering Arab, who is a herdsman by heritage, and in following that vocation *a roamer par excellence.* They live, these Arabs, in tents: the sides are made of straw and wattle hurdles; over the top is stretched an immense piece of brown or black camel's-hair cloth. The tents are barely five feet high in the middle, less at the edges: squat brown mushrooms they look, or something like the keels of boats turned bottom upwards. All of them were open in front, "very public" the world would say; which primitive and open-air mode of living was indeed their great feature. Some of them were divided off down the middle by a hurdle, thus forming two "rooms": the hurdles were occasionally faggots, without straw. Around the tents lay the flocks, chewing the cud or browsing on the scanty grass-land: children ran out to us with bowls of milk: when the grass gave out within reach all round, the tents were taken down, the hillsides deserted, and the families wandered in search of pastures new, carrying a few chickens, some pots and pans, two or three bundles of rags, and leaving behind a good many parasites and a bare patch.

Thus Arab life in Southern Morocco—a thriftless, desultory existence, yet with the charm of continual change and of living with the earth. "To take no thought for the morrow" is the practice of all Moors, whether Arabs or Berbers: no Moor spends money on anything which will not bring him in immediate profit; and this accounts for the fact that trees and forests are never planted, or schemes started for working mines, or roads made, or bridges built; even if the capital were forthcoming, what would be the use of spending money only to be repaid little by little, year by year?—a man may die before he profits for all his trouble!

After all, argues the Moor, who could wish to alter Morocco? Is it not perfect as it is?—veritably, "*the tail of the peacock*," the sun of the universe!

Its very imperfections are among those things which in this fanatical Mohammedan land so fascinate the traveller. Its sad colours, its air steeped in mystery, its courtly unknowable people, its wild tribes, its white shut houses, its concealed women, its mad fanaticism, its magnificent stoicism—one and all are sufficient to hold the European, and to call him back again long after El Moghreb has forgotten his face. Another of those chains has been forged which bind certain places and certain countries to a soul, each henceforth belonging the one to the other, and each gaining a little something thereby; nor can the links of these chains be broken, since unseen possessions, such as they, are among those things which no power on earth can touch, which can neither be given nor taken away.

> It's North you may run to the rime-ringed sun,
>   Or South to the blind Horn's hate;
> Or East all the way into Mississippi Bay,
>   Or West to the Golden Gate,
> Where the blindest bluffs hold good, dear lass,
>   And the wildest tales are true,
> And the men bulk big on the old trail, our own trail, the out trail;
> And life runs large on the Long Trail—the trail that is always new.

Printed by Hazell, Watson & Viney, Ld., London and Aylesbury.

www.ingramcontent.com/pod-product-compliance
Lightning Source LLC
LaVergne TN
LVHW091243080426
835510LV00007B/135